OPERATION BOWLER

Also by Jonathan Glancey

Spitfire: The Biography

Harrier

Concorde: The Rise and Fall of the Supersonic Airliner

The Story of Architecture

London: Bread and Circuses

Architecture: A Visual History

Lost Buildings

Nagaland: A Journey to India's Forgotten Frontier

The Journey Matters

Giants of Steam

PEGASUS BOOKS
NEW YORK LONDON

OPERATION BOWLER

THE AUDACIOUS ALLIED BOMBING
OF VENICE DURING WORLD WAR II

JONATHAN GLANCEY

OPERATION BOWLER

Pegasus Books, Ltd.
148 West 37th Street, 13th Floor
New York, NY 10018

First Pegasus Books cloth edition July 2025

Frontispiece: Calm before the storm. A Venetian steamer is berthed in front of the Danieli hotel. To its left, the old Prison, the Doge's Palace with the domes of the Basilica of St Mark's behind it, Piazzetta San Marco, the Marciana Library and the campanile of St Mark's, Grand Canal, Venice, c.1930.

ISBN: 978-1-63936-919-5

10 9 8 7 6 5 4 3 2 1

Printed in the United States of America
Distributed by Simon & Schuster
www.pegasusbooks.com

In memory of Tudy Sammartini

CONTENTS

Italy and the Gothic Line, 1944–5. Encyclopædia Britannica.

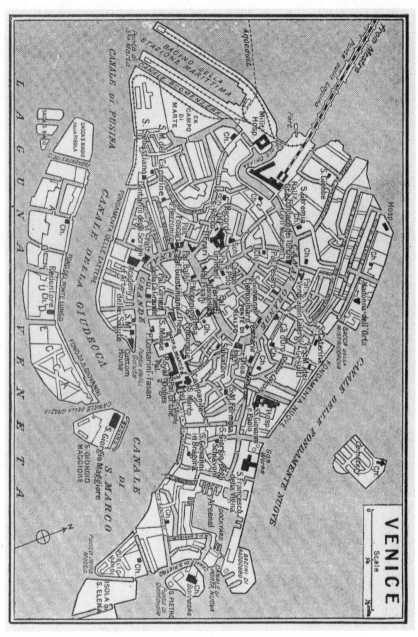

Map of Venice, 1923. Alamy.

USAAF P–47D Thunderbolt unleashing rockets in a ground attack.

VENICE

21 March 1945

1530hrs

Bursting from a hazy sky, a swarm of Allied fighters swept northwest from the Adriatic over German-occupied Venice. Rockets streaking, machine guns blazing, puissant North American Mustangs and burly Republican Thunderbolts from RAF, USAAF and Commonwealth squadrons strafed forty-five anti-aircraft and other gun emplacements protecting the lagoon city and its principal port, Stazione Marittima.

The fighters climbed away as twenty-six-year-old Wing Commander George Westlake DFC, the operation's leader, rolled his Curtiss Kittyhawk into a sixty-degree dive. Straightening out now, Westlake spearheaded forty-eight dive bombers down through smoke and vicious flak to 1,500 feet, where the first in a cascade of 500lb and 1,000lb bombs was unleashed on the port, its warehouses and armaments depots, and the mercantile and military ships berthed there.

1

From balconies and rooftop loggias dangerously close to the docks, Venetians, taken aback by this sudden onslaught on their city, caught sight and sound of this blistering show of intensely focused aerial force. What on earth was happening? Were there other aircraft about to attack? Where else in Venice might be next? Who had dared to press such a ferocious attack on the city of St Mark's Square, of leaning Gothic campaniles, of churches by Andrea Palladio, secret gardens and mysterious canals, of Titian and Tintoretto, of Danieli's and the Gritti Palace, of Harry's Bar and the Lido beaches, a city described by Ruskin as 'set like a golden clasp on the girdle of the earth', her history written 'on the white scrolls of the sea-surges', this gathering of 'the glory of the West and of the East'?

This was Operation Bowler, the unprecedented and audacious Allied air attack on Venice, the fabled art-historic city that friend and foe alike had promised to leave well alone during the Second World War. By common consent, Venice had been all but sacrosanct.

By early 1945, however, with the end of the war in sight, the city had become what Allied commanders would call a 'legitimate' target. Despite promises to the contrary, Rome and Florence had been bombed and the abbey of Monte Cassino, one of Europe's great art-historical, religious and literary treasures, had been reduced to rubble. Safe, or so it seemed, behind *Generalfeldmarschall* (Field Marshal) Albert Kesselring's Gothic Line, a bristling wall of daunting coast-to-coast fortifications and gun emplacements built across the inhospitable reaches of the high Apennines, here this late in the war in Europe, battle-hardened German divisions were still dug in across northern Italy. They were supplied, now that Allied air forces had cut off virtually every last possible route into the region, with fuel, armaments and ammunition from ships sailing, as if innocuously, in and out of Venice. By March 1945, how could the city not be a military target?

Futurist artist Tullio Crali's *Nose Dive on the City* (1939) evoked Filippo Tommaso Marinetti's call of 1910 to 'repudiate the old Venice'.

PRELUDE

PIAZZA SAN MARCO

8 July 1910

A summer evening in Venice. Steamers have arrived back from the Lido. A chattering, day-tripping throng, warm from the beach, shaded beneath wide-brimmed hats wrapped in tulle, straw boaters and parasols, and garbed in linen, white cotton and canvas – sailor costumes for children – drifts between the Doge's Palace and Sansovino's Marciana Library. Suddenly, the sky above Piazza San Marco is aflutter, not with pigeons' wings as the Venetian day trippers would expect, but with what looks like thousands of paper birds or butterflies. Children rush to catch them mid-air.

The paper flyers, all 80,000 of them, stamped with the slogan *Contro Venezia passatista* (Against Past-Obsessed Venice), have been hurled from the roof terrace of the piazza's late fifteenth-century clocktower, facing the campanile of St Mark's Basilica. In florid, yet stentorian language, this

5

curious manifesto barks, 'We turn our backs on historic Venice, worn out and brought to ruin by centuries of pleasure seeking... we reject the Venice of foreigners, this market-place of fake antique dealers, this magnet for universal snob-bery and imbecility, this bed worn out by caravans of lovers, this jewel-encrusted hip bath for cosmopolitan whores, this immense sewer of traditionalism.

'Let us fill the stinking canals with the rubble of the crum-bling, leprous old palaces. Let us burn the gondolas, rocking chairs for cretins, and raise to the sky the majestic geometry of metal bridges and smoke-crowned factories, abolishing the sagging curves of the old architecture.'

The perpetrators are a group of young artists and poets, the self-proclaimed Futurists led by Filippo Tommaso Marinetti, author of the *Passatista* rant, a pugnacious and slyly witty thirty-four-year-old self-publicist who revels in contrariness. The previous year, he had declared that 'Art... can be nothing but violence, cruelty and injustice.' In the founding *Futurist Manifesto* published in February 1909 on the front page of the leading French newspaper *Le Figaro*, Marinetti opined, 'We want to sing of the love of danger, the habit of energy and rashness... we will glorify war, the world's only hygiene... Heap up the fire to the shelves of libraries! Divert canals to flood the cellars of museums! Let the glorious canvases swim ashore! Take the picks and hammers! Undermine the foundation of venerable towns!'

Here in Venice and not content with showering what must have seemed like madcap leaflets on the heads of Venetian families, Marinetti and his chums – among them the artists Umberto Boccioni, Carlo Carrà, Aroldo Bonzagni and Luigi Russolo, as well as the poet Armando Mazza, as free with his fists as he was with his pen – went on to take to the stage that evening for a Futurist event at Teatro La Fenice. With its Neoclassical façade of 1792 and lavish gilt 1830s Rococo auditorium, long resounding to Verdi's *Rigoletto* and *La traviata* and the operettas of Bellini, Donizetti and Rossini, the city's opera house was a glorious artistic retort to Marinetti's industrial-era iconoclasm.

'Venetians! Venetians!', needled Marinetti, 'Why do you still desire to be ever the faithful slaves of the past, the filthy gatekeepers of history's biggest brothel, nurses of the most wretched hospital in the world in which souls are languishing, mortally corrupted by the syphilis of sentimentalism?

'Yet you were once invincible warriors and brilliant artists, daring navigators, ingenious industrialists and tireless traders…and you have become hotel waiters, guides, pimps, antique dealers, fraudsters, makers of old paintings, plagiaristic painters and copyists. Have you forgotten that you are first and foremost Italians, and that this word, in the language of history means builders of the future?'

Allora. This was telling languorous Venetian audiences what the Futurists thought of them and their cherished city. 'We want electric lamps to brutally cut and strip away with their thousand points of light your mysterious, sickening, alluring shadows.' A fight broke out in the opera house between those in the seats and those on stage. The house lights went up. The police were called on to intervene. The Futurists were in their element. Marinetti's aim, after all, was to reawaken a new creative and martial spirit throughout Italy, a country he believed to be trapped by its art-historical

7

past, and consequently weak and looked down on to its detriment by vigorous modern-minded foreign nations.

Between 1880 and 1915, thirteen million Italians abandoned their country in search of a better life, most of them crossing the Atlantic to seek work in Argentina, Brazil and especially the United States, where Sicilians and others from the south were not just looked down on, but poorly treated. Marinetti would have been aware that in March 1891, eleven Italian Americans were lynched together in New Orleans. The leader of the lynch mob, John M. Parker, a prominent New Orleans businessman, said that Italians were 'just a little worse than the Negro, being if anything filthier in their habits, lawless and treacherous'. Parker went on to become Democrat governor of Louisiana. He had the *New York Times* on his side. An editorial of 16 March 1891 foamed, 'These sneaking and cowardly Sicilians, the descendants of bandits and assassins, who have transported to this country the lawless passions, the cut-throat practices, and the oath-bound societies of their native country, are to us a pest without mitigation. Our own rattlesnakes are as good citizens as they... Lynch law was the only course open to the people of New Orleans.'

It was clearly time for Italians to shape a new world, a new image of themselves, that would be admired worldwide, and Venice was a spectacular place to start. Foreigners, of course, and no matter how noble minded, seemed interested only in its past glories, revived in so many influential minds by the alluring writings of the nineteenth-century English critic John Ruskin, whose passion for Venetian Gothic architecture went mind-in-hand with his pioneering campaigns for conservation. For Marinetti, Ruskin was responsible for turning Venice into a museum. To a British audience, he demanded, 'When, oh when, will you rid yourself of the sluggish ideology of that deplorable man, Ruskin, who – I should like to convince you once and for all – is utterly ridiculous.'

And how scathing Ruskin had been of Venice's few moves into the future. Not just the railway bridge and the gas lamps, but the Lido's transformation into a fashionable bathing resort reached not by gondolas but by steamboats. On his 1872 trip to the city, Ruskin said he was unable to write one morning 'because of the accursed whistling of the dirty steam-engine of the omnibus for Lido, waiting at the quay of the Ducal Palace for the dirty population of Venice, which is now neither fish nor flesh, neither noble nor fisherman; cannot afford to be rowed, nor has the strength nor sense enough to row itself; but smokes and spits up and down the piazzetta all day, and gets itself dragged by a screaming kettle to Lido next morning to sea-bathe itself into capacity for more tobacco.'

Whatever Ruskin might have argued, old Venice must now go, railed Marinetti. It must be demolished in large part with a road and tramway replacing the fetid Grand Canal and its cretinous gondolas. Aircraft would buzz overhead. 'We will sing,' Marinetti had railed in his *Futurist Manifesto*, 'of…the flight of aeroplanes whose propellers sound like the flapping of a flag and the applause of enthusiastic crowds.'

The day after the Piazza San Marco clock tower incident, and over four thousand miles away in Atlantic City, New Jersey, Walter Brookins, about to celebrate his twenty-first birthday, flew a Wright biplane to an altitude of 6,175ft – the first person to fly more than a mile high. Trained and employed by the Wright brothers, Brookins went on to perform stunt flights for audiences across the United States that year, culminating in a display on 20 December, when, after a dazzling sequence of downward spirals, he made a series of heart-stopping dives towards the ground, pulling up each time at what appeared to be the very last moment. If only Marinetti could have been a witness. It was as if the dive bomber, future nemesis of historic towns and cities, had been invented there and then.

Shortly before the outbreak of the Second World War, the Fascist-leaning artist Tullio Crali painted one of the most arresting of all Futurist images, the dizzying *Nose Dive on the City*, a celebration of the vertiginous manner in which aircraft would assault and destroy existing cities in preparation for some new, forward-looking and, ideally, militarised social order. His friend, Marinetti, who, in 1919 co-wrote the *Fascist Manifesto*, could only applaud. Venice, this 'jewelled hip bath for cosmopolitans', this 'great sewer of traditionalism', deserved to be tipped over and flushed by war from the modern world. Artists, of all people, with a little help from the dive bomber, would surely see to that.

The first aerial bombardment in history – in July 1849, Austrian forces launched a balloon attack on the besieged Venice, in the Republic of San Marco.

ONE

BALLOONS, BOMBS
AND BRAVURA

12 July 1849

Sixty years before Marinetti called for the destruction of old
Venice, the Austrians had bombarded the city while seeking
to reoccupy it during the agonising months of the short-
lived Republic of San Marco. From the fall of Napoleon
after Waterloo in 1815 until the revolt led by Daniele Manin
in March 1848, Venice had been in Habsburg hands. By the
summer of 1849, the rebellious Venetian republicans, chased
from the mainland by encroaching Habsburg armies led by
the veteran Field Marshal Graf Radetzky – for whom
Johann Strauss senior wrote the ebullient 'Radetzky March'
after his defeat of Italian forces at Custoza, near Verona, the
previous June – had been holed up in the sanctity of their
lagoon for an entire year. What destruction might the
Austrians visit on the city? There was everything to be
concerned about.

Memories of the last time Venice had been invaded and touched with a very heavy hand indeed, its serenity dispelled, were rife. That singularly heavy hand belonged to Napoleon Bonaparte, who seized the city on 12 May 1797. Fearful of what the impetuous young French general might do to it, the chronically weakened thirteen-hundred-year-old republic abolished itself that same fateful day. The French proceeded to loot the city, torch the Arsenale and destroy the Venetian navy. They smashed and burned the *Bucintoro*, the elaborate, gold-encrusted ceremonial barge used by doges in the ritual annual marriage of Venice and the sea.

Churches, monasteries and other religious buildings – seventy-two of them in all – along with eighty *palazzi*, were damaged, looted, turned into barracks, abandoned and even razed to the ground. Nothing was sacred to the French and their cocksure twenty-seven-year-old general, certainly not the church of San Geminiano in Piazza San Marco. Completed in 1557 by Jacopo Sansovino – architect of the peerless Biblioteca Marciana facing the Doge's Palace across Piazzetta San Marco – with funding from Tommaso Rangone, a physician and patron of the arts who got rich from a cure for syphilis, endemic in Venice, the domed church on the west side of the square was used as a barracks before being torn down. It was replaced with a matching extension of the Procuratie Nouve, a palatial new residence for the Viceroy of the Kingdom of Italy – Napoleon's stepson, Eugène de Beauharnais – and should he ever return to Venice, which he never did, for the future French emperor himself.

The four ancient Byzantine, or possibly Ancient Greek, copper horses that had pranced so elegantly from the west front of St Mark's since the sacking of Constantinople in 1204 were carted off to Paris, while more than 25,000 paintings (including master works by Bellini, Carpaccio, Tiepolo and Tintoretto) vanished. The destruction visited on Venice by the seemingly implacable Napoleon was incalculable. No enemy has wreaked such havoc on the city since.

In the summer of 1849, the Austrians held rebellious Venice in a pincer movement. What hope was there for the city? How could it possibly hold out? On the plus side, Venetian coastal defences were formidable, the lagoon notoriously difficult to navigate and St Mark's and the Arsenale shipyard long shots for Austrian guns. On the downside, Venetians were trapped. While the 25,000 or so artillery shells aimed at the city that August caused proportionately little damage, they did much to erode the confidence of the 200,000 civilians living between Cannaregio and Chioggia, especially now, with food and drinking water in perilously short supply and cholera rife.

For a moment, though, it had seemed as if the Austrians might have ended the siege by a new form of warfare. How astonishing it seems, in retrospect, that of all the cities in the world, Venice was to be the first target of aerial bombing. The idea was the brainchild of the Austrian inventor and artillery officer Franz von Uchatius. Time-fused paper balloons heated by charcoal and greasy cotton, carrying bombs weighing between twenty and thirty pounds, would be launched from the mainland at Mestre or from the Lido and the deck of SMS *Vulcano*, a paddle steamer built in 1843 for the Austro-Hungarian Navy at the Venice Arsenale, and dropped on the alleys, canals, piazzas, landing stages and workshops of the city.

The attack – there may have been a second – was made on 7 July. Reports of this historic event are patchy and hard to follow with any certainty. The number of balloons launched varies in different records from as few as two to as many as two hundred. According to a contemporary report in the *Morning Chronicle*, 'The captain of the English brig *Frolic* [a sixteen-gun sloop launched in 1842] and other persons then at Venice, testify to the extreme terror and the morale effect produced on the inhabitants.'

Not so, according to the American diplomat Edmund Flagg, whose book *Venice, the City of the Sea: From the Invasion by Napoleon in 1797 to the Capitulation to Radetzky in 1849* was published in 1853. Flagg recalled how 'small cloudlets', about twenty of them, 'came swaying slowly and majestically on from the Lido… The balloons appeared to rise to about 4,500 ft. Then they exploded in mid-air or fell into the water, or, blown by a sudden southeast wind, sped over the city and dropped on the besiegers.

'Venetians, abandoning their homes, crowded into the streets and squares to enjoy the strange spectacle… When a cloud of smoke appeared in the air to make an explosion, all clapped and shouted. Applause was greatest when the balloons blew over the Austrian forces and exploded, and in such cases the Venetians added cries of "Bravo!" and "Good appetite!"'

Whatever the truth, the balloon attack was a failure. While Venice gave up the struggle soon afterwards, concentrated artillery fire, disease, hunger and thirst had been the main incentives to surrender. Franz von Uchatius, however, had embedded a line of military thought that would lead to the next Austrian air raid on Venice, this time by powered aircraft, on 24 May 1915.

Between Radetzky's triumphal entry into Venice and the Great War of 1914–18, a rather different conflict raged on and off in waves in the lagoon city, the results of which would help determine its fate in the Second World War. The Austrians were keen to industrialise. They brought the railway here in 1846, building a bridge – designed by Italian engineers Luigi Doudo and Tommaso Meduna – more than two miles long on 80,000 wooden piles and 222 masonry arches across the water from Mestre on the mainland. The railway's arrival prompted far greater destruction than Austrian artillery cannonballs or weaponised balloons were to in the summer of 1849. Although no fan of Palladian architecture, John Ruskin was shocked by the demolition of the convent and church of Santa Lucia, along with historic houses, and its replacement by the new railway terminus.

In a letter to his father sent from Venice in 1845, Ruskin had noted the damaging changes the Austrians had made even before the arrival of the railway. Of a gondola ride along the Grand Canal, he wrote, 'it began to look a little better as we got up to the Rialto, but, it being just solemn twilight, as we turned under the arch, behold, all up to the Foscari palace – gas lamps! on each side, in grand new iron posts of the last Birmingham fashion, and sure enough, they have them all up the narrow canals, and there is a grand one, with more flourishes than usual, just under the bridge of sighs.' Piazza San Marco, Ruskin might have added, had been gaslit since 1843, which meant – horror of horrors – that Venice now had an unsightly 'Birmingham-fashion' gasworks, too.

Ruskin's passion for Venice had, he said, been ignited first and foremost by the Romantic poet Lord Byron (George Gordon Byron). It was to Byron living in the Palazzo Mocenigo on the Grand Canal with his servants, monkeys, fox and mastiffs we owe the English name 'Bridge of Sighs' for the covered white limestone passage leading over the Rio di Palazza from the Doge's Palace to the prison from which Giacomo Casanova, the Venetian adventurer, escaped in 1756. And it it is Byron who was remembered for his epic swims from the Palazzo Mocenigo to the old Jewish Cemetery on the Lido, a serene setting beloved by Shelley and Goethe, too.

In *A Time of Gifts* (1977), Patrick Leigh Fermor wrote, 'All dwellers in the Teutonic north, looking out at the winter sky, are subject to spasms of a nearly irresistible pull, when the entire Italian peninsula from Trieste to Agrigento begins to function like a lodestone. The magnetism is backed by an unseen choir, there are roulades of mandoline strings in the air; ghostly whiffs of lemon blossom beckon the victims south and across the Alpine passes. It is Goethe's Law and is ineluctable as Newton's or Boyle's.'

Subject to Byron's Law, although he knew Goethe, too, the young Ruskin had fallen head over heels in love with Venice. His first sight of the city was from Mestre – he had come, aged sixteen, by horse-drawn carriage with his parents from London – 'when everything, muddy Brenta, vulgar villas [he was possibly thinking of Palladio's serene classical villas lining the Brenta Canal], dusty causeway, sandy beach, was equally rich in rapture…and the black knot of gondolas in the canal of Mestre more beautiful than a sunrise full of clouds all scarlet and gold.'

This Romantic sensibility was new and very different from that of eighteenth-century English travellers like Elizabeth, Lady Craven, who, writing in 1789 (quoted by Ruskin), 'expected to see a gay clean-looking town, with quays on each side of the canals, but was extremely disappointed; the houses are in the water, and look dirty and uncomfortable on the outside; the innumerable quantity of gondolas too, that look like swimming coffins, added to the dismal scene, and, I confess, Venice on my arrival struck me with horror rather than pleasure'. Curiously, and despite Ruskin's romantic projection of Venice, Lady Craven's sense of horror lurked on. In his novella *Death in Venice* (1912), Thomas Mann asks, 'Who has not battled a fleeting shudder, a secret dread and anxiety upon boarding a Venetian gondola for the first time or after a prolonged absence? That strange conveyance, coming down to us unaltered from the days of the ballads and so distinctively black, black as only coffins can be – it conjures up hush-hush criminal adventures in the rippling night and, even more, death itself: the bier, the obscure obsequies, the final, silent journey.'

'The beginning of everything,' Ruskin wrote in his poetic autobiography, *Praeterita*, 'was in seeing the gondola-beak come actually inside the door of Danieli's, when the tide was up, and the water two feet deep at the foot of the stairs; and then, along the canal side, marble walls rising out of the salt sea, with hosts of little brown crabs on them, and Titians inside.'

During his stay in the city over the winter of 1849, Ruskin – who had no time for the Republican cause – measured and drew St Mark's and other Venetian monuments, recording them for posterity in minute detail. His fear was that Venice was under the threat of cultural vandalism, not least, of course, from the invasive Austrians. From the time of his writing *The Stones of Venice*, published in three volumes between 1851 and 1853, Ruskin became an ardent and highly persuasive conservationist. The stones of Venice must be preserved or, as progressives jeered, pickled in Ruskinian aspic. The Venice we experience today is to a remarkable degree the city Ruskin did so much to help preserve in both reality and as an idea and ideal. This, of course, is the city Marinetti was to rail so vehemently, and amusingly, against in 1910.

In Venice Ruskin was seen, if not as a joke, then as an eccentric, clambering across the exterior of St Mark's, tape measure in hand, pockets crammed with pencils and notebook, while his coquettish young wife, Effie, dined, danced and flirted with well-turned-out Austrian officers. She spoke good German. Effie was particularly taken with 1st Lieutenant Charles Paulizza, the very Austrian officer who had directed the intense artillery fire against the city her husband was working so strenuously hard to protect. She believed her 'greatest triumph' was meeting Field Marshal Radetzky and being invited to the first of his balls celebrating the Austrian victory.

The tussle between modernisation and conservation continued throughout Venice's Habsburg years and far beyond. A row, sparked in 1879 in England by William

Morris and Edward Burne-Jones over what they saw as the over-restoration of St Mark's, prompted an editorial in the *Times*. 'St Mark's,' it mooted, 'is, in a way, the pride and possession of the whole world.' This was an important statement. Venice was seen increasingly by those beyond its boundaries, and besotted by it, as an art-historical object, a precious jewel of sorts, that belonged not just to Venetians, Austrians or Italians but to the world, and needed its care. Left to their devices, what might the industrious Austrians and even the indolent Venetians themselves do to this precious city? Soon enough, and as if to prove the point, there emerged in 1884 a vast flour mill (the Molino Stucky) on the Giudecca – the nearest island to Venice. The mill was given a forceful Neo-Gothic makeover in 1895 by Ernst Wullekopf – a Hanoverian architect who ran an office for *industrial* architecture – and in 1899 the nearby Junghans clock and watch-making factory. Canals, meanwhile, were filled in, as Napoleon had ordered, to shape new, gas-lit pedestrian streets.

In 1881, the first *vaporetto*, a paddle-steamer water bus, began plying the No. 1 route along the Grand Canal. For tourists – whose numbers rose from around 160,000 in 1883 to 3.5 million in 1907, by which time the beaches and grand new hotels of the Lido had become ultra-fashionable – Venice and the modern industrial world were incompatible. Visitors to the city wanted to see old, untouched Venice, as they still do more than a century on in their tens of millions. If this view was frustrating to progressive Venetians, it was also one that was to help save the city from destruction in the mid-twentieth century.

When, though, on 23 May 1915, Italy, of which Venice had been a part since 1866, declared war on Austria-Hungary, the city was attacked from the air before sunrise the following day. Aerial warfare – *pace* Franz von Uchatius – was in its infancy, and bombing wildly inaccurate. What seems clear, though, is that the Austrian-Hungarian air force was aiming for what it perceived to be 'legitimate' targets – the railway station, nearby munition stores and the Arsenale – rather than civilians and art-historical monuments.

It was Italy, in fact, that had pioneered the dropping of bombs from aircraft. On All Saints Day 1911, *Sottotenente* Giulio Gavotti primed and hurled 4½lb grenades from his pretty Austrian-built Taube monoplane on Ottoman positions in Libya during the year-long Italo-Turkish War. No one had done this before.

As for Venice, the idea that its historical status and sheer beauty could protect it from destructive assault cut some ice with the enemy, yet for all its charms the city was nevertheless the hub of a powerful military machine. By now, for example, the Arsenale was building its nimble motorised MAS (*motoscafo armato silurante*) torpedo boats. Among their successes were the sinking of the coastal defence ship SMS *Wien* in Trieste harbour in December 1917 and, six months later, the capsizing of the 20,000-ton battleship SMS *Szent István* at sea off the Croatian island of Premuda. Given its legendary ability to build complete warships in a single week, the Arsenale was inevitably a prime target for Austro-Hungarian bombers.

It should perhaps be remembered that Venice had been, a long time before Napoleon barged his way into the city, a powerful and aggressive military power. It was the Venetian navy, by most accounts, that first mounted gunpowder weapons on its ships. These were employed in June 1380 during the decisive Battle of Chioggia, when the Venetians destroyed the rival Genoese navy. These early guns were used to bombard enemy fortifications from the sea. Pietro Doria, commander of the Genoese, was killed when a wall he was standing against, hit by the projectiles fired from the Venetian fleet, collapsed. The Genoese were never again to threaten Venice.

Nor should it be forgotten that in 1204 Venice played a key role in the savage sack of Constantinople. The occasion was the perversion of the Fourth Crusade decreed by Pope Innocent III. The crusading army, comprising knights and soldiers drawn mostly from France and the Holy Roman Empire, was to have set sail from Venice in a fleet of fifty brand-new war galleys and 450 troopships, built at efficient speed at the Venice Arsenale and crewed by Venetians, with doge Enrico Dandolo in command. The plan was to first conquer Ayyubid-controlled Egypt before pushing on to the Holy Land, where the Ayyubids held Jerusalem.

However, many actually sailed from other ports, including Genoa, Venice's longstanding enemy, and in lesser numbers than planned originally, so the crusaders left Venice with a glut of costly and redundant new ships. The Republic insisted the crusaders still pay the contracted cost. This could be recouped in part by a crusader attack on the lucrative, rebellious (and Catholic) city of Zadar on the east Dalmatian coast, bringing it under Venetian control. The crusaders, caught in a web of political intrigue, diverted to Constantinople. Here they sacked a city of 500,000 people boasting huge financial and artistic wealth and which retained the air of Ancient Rome, complete with theatres, arenas, forums, aqueducts, libraries, public baths and chariot races. The Hippodrome, around which *quadriga* chariots raced, boasted a monument crowned with four magnificent Greek copper horses.

The siege involved horrendous cruelty, slaughter, defilement and rampant looting. The horses, of course, were shipped to Venice. In the packed streets of Constantinople, Christian soldiers killed, raped and tortured fellow Christians. Churches, convents and monasteries were defiled, as were the tombs of Roman emperors including Constantine himself who, in 330, had given his name to this 'New Rome', known till then as Byzantium. One of the greatest losses, among other monumental works of art smashed or melted down by the crusaders, was a statue of Hercules commissioned by Alexander the Great from Lysippos, his court artist. In sacking Constantinople, the crusaders presaged its decline and, ultimately, in 1453, its conquest by the Muslim Ottomans.

Over three years during the First World War, Venice was bombed on forty-two occasions. Fifty-two people were killed and eighty-four injured. The biggest single raid was made on 26 February 1918, when big, long-range Mercedes-powered Gotha bombers flew over the city for a total of eight hours, dropping 32,000 pounds of bombs. One bomb blasted a Corinthian column from the portico of the church of San Simeone Piccolo opposite Santa Lucia station into the Grand Canal. It sunk eleven gondolas. One person was killed.

By the end of the war, two churches – Santa Maria degli Scalzi, by the railway terminus, and Santa Maria Formosa, perilously close to St Mark's – had been badly damaged. Incendiaries had flamed through the roof of the former, a great Baroque set piece designed by Baldassare Longhena, architect of the sublime Salute church, destroying an ambitious ceiling fresco, *Il trasporto della Santa Casa di Loreto*, by Giambattista Tiepolo depicting the Virgin Mary's house being flown, according to legend, by angels from Nazareth to Loreto. Were the Austrian aviators somehow forgiven five years on from the incident, when in March 1920 Pope Benedict XV proclaimed Our Lady of Loreto patron saint of all who travel by air?

San Giovanni e Paolo ('Zanipolo') and San Franceso della Vigna, near the Arsenale, were slightly damaged. The sandbagged façade of St Mark's was scuffed several times. Miraculously, or so it seemed, a bomb falling through the vault of Santa Maria Gloriosa dei Frari and landing in front of Titian's *Assumption of the Virgin* altarpiece failed to explode.

To our twenty-first-century eyes, accustomed to spectacles of mass destruction, these bombing raids seem mere scratches across the body of the city. It is difficult to know quite what Venetians made of them. Contemporary reports speak of children playfully collecting bits of shrapnel and of adults strolling with *sangfroid* by the sides of canals as bombs fell, as if there were nothing to be concerned with. Yet the Venetians had been under siege not just from the air, but from the land, too. By late November 1917, the Habsburg and German armies had advanced as far towards the city as Piave, twenty-five miles north. At this distance, the rumble of enemy artillery could be heard in St Mark's Square. At the Battle of Caporetto, German stormtroopers had attacked

Italian lines with flamethrowers. The Germans also employed huge numbers of canisters spreading poison gas through Italian trenches, fortifications and dugouts. The enemy was increasingly frightening and reaching ever closer to Venice.

In the city, works of art were removed – the San Marco horses packed off to Rome for safekeeping – or if unmovable, wrapped and otherwise protected by sandbags. Buildings, too. Anti-aircraft gun posts were set up on the city's wooden rooftop terraces (*altana*). Equipped with rifles, these were more a way of keeping spirits up than actually shooting down enemy aircraft. Tourism ground to a halt. Venice, railed Ezio Maria Gray, the journalist who would go on to serve Mussolini, could no longer be 'a museum, a hang-out for idlers or convention centre for eccentric art'.

And yet, one of the great acts of Venetian defiance, made in August 1918, was, in essence, a work of art. This was the improbable long-distance flight over the Alps that month from Venice to Vienna, where, in an echo of Marinetti's 1910 manifesto, thousands of red, green and white leaflets calling on Austria to surrender were dropped on the very centre of the Habsburg capital. This curious, daredevil mission was led by the poet, playwright, decadent novelist, politician, philanderer, egotist and war hero, Gabriele D'Annunzio. Although not a Venetian – he was born in 1863 in Pescara in the Abruzzo – his 1900 novel *Il fuoco* (*The Flame*), a love story set in Venice, had won him many admirers in the city. In 1916, a marble plaque set into a wall of Palazzo Albrizzi in San Polo framing the remnant of an Austrian bomb bore the dramatic inscription, 'This splinter of Barbary/Mounted in noble stone/Accuses the eternal enemy/Who added shame to his shame/And glory to our glory'.

The words were by D'Annunzio, who lived in Venice for much of the war, and in some style, at either the Hotel Danieli – where John and Effie Ruskin had stayed in 1849 – or Casetta Rossa, a house built facing the Grand Canal at the end of the nineteenth century for the Austrian prince, antiques dealer and German spy chief, von Fritz Hohenlohe-Waldenburg-Schillingsfürst. D'Annunzio was fifty-two when he began flying reconnaissance, strafing and bombing missions as an observer pilot with the Corpo Aeronautica Militare. He had been thrilled with the idea of flight and first took to the air in September 1909 in a Wright brothers biplane, piloted by *Sottotenente* Mario Calderara, who had been taught to fly by Wilbur Wright, on a promotional tour of France and Italy, the previous year at the inauguration of Italy's first airfield at Montichiari near Brescia. D'Annunzio never lost his passion for flight even after losing his right eye when, in January 1916, his Macchi L1 seaplane was forced to ditch during a reconnaissance mission near Grado on the Adriatic coast west of Trieste. He rose after the war to the rank of brigadier general in the reserve of the new *Regia Aeronautica* (Royal Air Force), and chose to be buried, in 1938, in his air force uniform.

D'Annunzio saw flight as a poetic adventure, yet he was also a lively propagandist for torpedo attacks by seaplanes and the precise, targeted bombing of enemy factories, airfields and city centres. He flew a fine aerial line between romance and reality, as did the French pilots based, from 1915, at the new San Nicolo airfield on the Venice Lido. Charged with protecting

Venice with their Nieuport 10 and Spad S.VII biplane fighters, the pilots were quartered in the Albergo Paradiso. They ate and drank exceptionally well, having brought four top-notch French chefs with them, while socialising with Italian and English royalty – the Prince of Wales paid a visit – along with the Venetian aristocracy accompanied by artists, writers and intellectuals. They were joined by Italian pilots who flew seaplanes from the neighbouring island of Sant'Andrea de Varriale. D'Annunzio was a frequent guest.

While out of action for nine months after losing his eye, and writing his extraordinary prose-poem *Notturno* (Night) one line at a time on strips of paper while wrapped in bandages and recuperating, D'Annunzio dreamed of an air raid on Vienna. Over the following two years, the purpose of this ambitious flight changed from a bombing raid – bringing the war to the heart of the Habsburg Empire – to one of pure propaganda. Bluster, bravado, bravery and unprecedented aeronautical skill. It became possible only as the right aircraft became available.

The aircraft in question was the Ansaldo SVA, an exceptionally fast (135mph), stable and largely reliable all-Italian biplane produced in large numbers from the beginning of 1918. The SVA.5 single-seat model equipped Venice's very own 87th Squadriglia *La Serenissima*, based at the four-teenth-century castle of San Pelagio near Padua; the flanks of the aircraft were emblazoned with large, colourful images of the winged Lion of St Mark accompanied by the stirring Latin motto *Iterum rudit leo* (The lion roars again).

After two attempts, dogged by fog and heavy wind, had failed, *Maggiore* Gabriele D'Annunzio's raid on Vienna took to the air at 5.50 a.m. on 9 August 1918. D'Annunzio flew as observer pilot in a specially modified two-seater SVA.10 piloted by *Capitano* Natale Palli. Three of the eleven Ansaldos suffered technical problems, two returning to base, one forced to land *en route*. The remaining eight reached Vienna, a flight made for the most part over enemy territory.

'When we left at 6 o'clock in the morning,' D'Annunzio wrote, 'the weather was splendid, but we were soon enveloped in a thick mist. We kept at a height varying from 8,000 to 11,000 feet. In crossing our former frontier, I was deeply affected at looking down upon [the town of] Cividale and the wide stretches of our country that have been held for the last nine months by the enemy.

'We reached Vienna about 8 o'clock in the morning [9.20 a.m. in fact] and descended to within 1,500 feet. The people in the streets were at first terrified and fled in panic until they saw that we were throwing out only manifestoes. Then crowds assembled and watched in intense curiosity. I particularly wished to approach close to the museum that contains the authentic image of St. Catherine of Alexandria and made a detour which permitted observation of this point.'

Shortly after the German surrender in May 1945, Flying Officer Keith Miller, better known as the legendary Australian Test cricket all-rounder, diverted his de Havilland Mosquito fighter-bomber over Bonn in the course of a flight showing a senior officer the state of German cities carpet bombed by the RAF. On his return, late, back at RAF Great Massingham, Norfolk, Miller told his CO, Squadron Leader Nevil Reeves, that he had wanted to see Beethoven's birthplace. Miller had loved Beethoven's music from an early age. D'Annunzio would have approved. Art was long, bombing raids brief.

There you have it. Only manifestoes. From their aircraft, D'Annunzio's pilots hurled two sets of leaflets on the city centre. Fifty thousand, printed on green, white and red cards, bore a message written by D'Annunzio. The Italian still is quite tricky to read. There was no translation. What on earth did the Viennese on their way to work that morning make of these bizarre leaflets? Here is a literal translation.

On this August morning, while the fourth year of your desperate convulsion comes to an end and luminously begins the year of our full power, suddenly there appears the three-colour wing as an indication of the destiny that is turning.

Destiny turns. It turns towards us with an iron certainty. The hour of that Germany that thrashes you, and humiliates you, and infects you is now forever passed.

Your hour is passed. As our faith was the strongest, behold how our will prevails and will prevail until the end. The victorious combatants of Piave, the victorious combatants of Marne feel it, they know it, with an ecstasy that multiplies the impetus. But if the impetus were not enough, the number would be; and this is said for those that try fighting ten against one. The Atlantic is a path already closing, and it's a heroic path, as demonstrated by the new chasers who coloured the [River] Ourcq with German blood.

On the wind of victory that rises from freedom's rivers, we didn't come except for the joy of the daring, we didn't come except to prove what we could venture and do whenever we want, in an hour of our choice.

The rumble of the young Italian wing does not sound like the one of the funereal bronze, in the morning sky. Nevertheless, the joyful boldness suspends between Saint Stephen and the Graben an irrevocable sentence, O Viennese.

Long live Italy!

Fortunately, an accompanying batch of leaflets, written in Italian and German, was also dropped within Vienna's Ring. The text was by D'Annunzio's friend Ugo Ojetti, journalist, author and art critic, who, since 1915, had been involved with the protection of Venetian works of art. In March 1918, he had been appointed Royal Commissioner for Propaganda over the Enemy. D'Annunzio's raid allowed him to live up to his title.

Learn to know the Italians.

We are flying over Vienna; we could drop tons of bombs. All we are dropping on you is a greeting of three colours: the three colours of liberty.

We Italians do not make war on children, on old people, on women.

We are making war on your government, the enemy of national liberty, on your blind, stubborn, cruel government that can give you neither peace nor bread and feeds you hatred and illusions.

VIENNESE!

You are famous for being intelligent. But why have you put on the Prussian uniform? By now, you see, the whole world has turned against you.

You want to continue the war? Continue it; it's your suicide. What do you hope for? The decisive victory promised to you by the Prussian generals? Their decisive victory is like the bread of Ukraine: You die waiting for it.

PEOPLE OF VIENNA, think of your own fates. Wake up!

LONG LIVE LIBERTY!

LONG LIVE ITALY!

LONG LIVE THE ENTENTE!

The aircraft carried cameras, so we can witness the leaflets fluttering over Vienna as the Ansaldos circled for around twenty minutes. The luck of the Venetian pilots had held until now. It was high time to turn around, recross the Alps and head back to Padua.

'The weather became bad on our return trip,' D'Annunzio recalled, 'and we experienced dangerous air currents while crossing the Alps. We also were attacked by hostile artillery fire and a fleet of hydroplanes but came through safely by noon of the same day.' One of the pilots, *Tenente* Giuseppe Sarti, did not make it through. Before reaching Vienna, an engine fault forced Sarti to make an emergency landing near Schwarzau am Steinfeld. He set his overturned Ansaldo alight before being captured. The next day, an equally dashing Austro-Hungarian pilot dropped a message over San Pelagio. *Tenente* Sarti was alive and well.

The Italian planes had been in the air for more than six and a half hours, a remarkable achievement. Perhaps at the time, and certainly in retrospect, the mission may have seemed odd, even slightly mad. It was, though, proof that if they had wanted they could have dropped bombs on the very centre of Vienna, something the Austrians would have thought highly improbable before 9 August 1918. D'Annunzio's flight, though, was something else. Yes, a propaganda effort – an extra edition of *Die Zeit* published on the afternoon of the raid was headlined quite simply and presumably disturbingly for its readers *Die Italienischen Flieger über Wien* (Italian Aviators over Vienna) – but also a work of Futurist art. Just as Marinetti had no real intention of damaging Venice when he dropped those thousands of manifestoes from the clock tower of St Mark's Square, D'Annunzio had not wanted to bomb Vienna. His flight had been a glorious, outlandish and aesthetic adventure.

One of the single-seat Ansaldo SVA.5s that took part in the Vienna mission is on display at the Italian Air Force Museum overlooking Lake Bracciano at Vigna di Valle, not far from Rome. A painterly thing, it stands beside a portrait on an artist's easel of D'Annunzio. D'Annunzio's two-seater SVA.10, nicely restored in recent years, hangs from the dome of the Auditorium, one of the playful buildings of the curious Fondazione Vittoriale degli Italiani at Gardon Riviera on Lake Garda. This was D'Annunzio's home and personal museum from 1922 until his death in 1938. It seems appropriate that these two veteran aircraft are art objects. They belong very much to the story of Venice, a city that from 1918 hoped to be safe, through its art and artistry, from future attack. Surely now, when even her military aircraft were works of art and in their most celebrated mission had dropped leaflets written by a poet and an art critic rather than bombs, Venice deserved immunity from military assault.

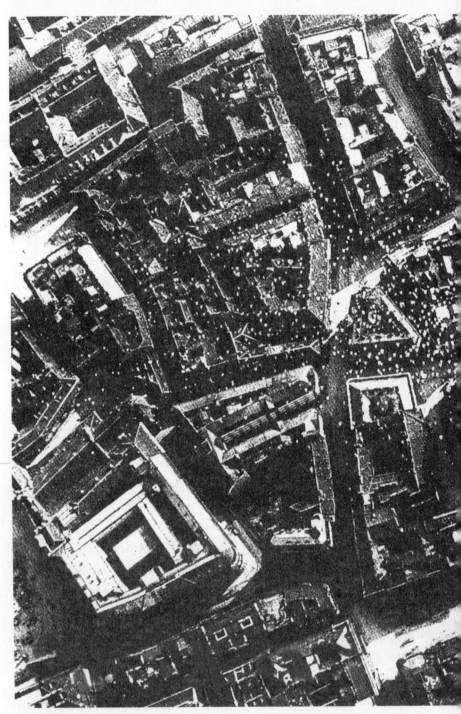

D'Annunzio's leaflet-drop over Vienna. St Stephen's Cathedral, top right.

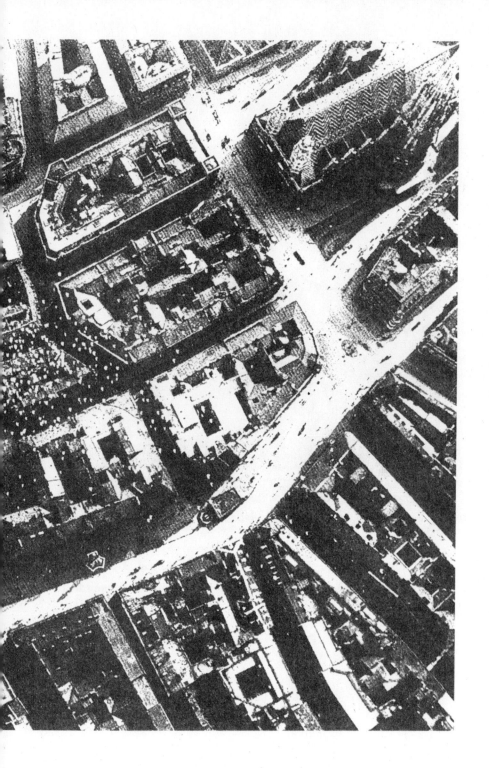

George Westlake 213 Sqn

Pilot Officer George Westlake, second from left, and 213 'Hornet' Squadron colleagues sitting on the wing of a Hawker Hurricane Mk 1, RAF Tangmere, 1940.

TWO

THE PILOT OFFICER

Isle of Wight, 15 November 1940

Electric light bulbs appeared to flash by the canopy of his Hawker Hurricane. Instinctively, Pilot Officer George Westlake half-rolled the lithe fighter, diving and twisting towards the sea. Just as well. The flashing lights had been explosive 20mm cannon shells shot through the noses of pursuing Messerschmitt Bf 109s. Hunting in pairs, eight of the Luftwaffe fighters had swept down on the tails of the Hurricanes of 213 and 145 Squadrons, on their second patrol that day from RAF Tangmere over Portsmouth and along the rain-swept Channel coast.

A Hurricane might be slower than a Bf109, but, a nimble machine, it could out-turn its German opponent. Now, in a hard, full-throttle climbing turn, Westlake popped up behind one of the Messerschmitts. Right thumb on the gun button. A staccato rattle from the wings of the Hurricane as a

three-second burst of eight Browning .303 machine guns –
450 rounds – found its mark. Witnessed by Squadron Leader
Adrian Boyd of 145 Squadron, the Messerschmitt fell into
the sea off Selsey Bill. Westlake's first 'kill'. In his logbook,
Westlake wrote: 'Patrol I.O.W. Attacked by 109's. Chased.
Scrap out to sea. Got 1 109.'

News had come over the wireless at Tangmere that
morning of the 'blitz' on Coventry. Charged with destroying its munitions, aircraft and engine factories, more than
515 German bombers had blasted – accidentally or not,
the verdict was out – the centre of the Midlands city. Its
medieval cathedral was the greatest physical loss. Its narrow,
cobbled streets and half-timbered buildings vanished in
flames and acrid clouds of smoke and dust. Officially, the
death toll was 554. Gas, water and electricity supplies,
together with the city's tram and telephone networks,
were badly disrupted or destroyed. More than 4,300 houses
were wrecked. The Luftwaffe lost just one aircraft – a
twin-engine Dornier Do 17 light bomber struck by
anti-aircraft fire – in the eleven-hour raid that had
continued throughout the night of 14–15 November. In
exceptionally bright moonlight, Coventry had been a
sitting duck. The Heinkel IIIs, Junkers Ju-88s and Dornier
Do-17s of Field Marshal Albert Kesselring's *Luftflotte* 2
and Field Marshal Hugo Sperrle's *Luftflotte* 3 dropped
more than 30,000 incendiaries, 500 tons of high-explosive
bombs, fifty landmines and twenty incendiary oil mines
on the city. While three-quarters of Coventry's factories
were damaged, the greater wreckage in terms of morale
was the devastation of the city's historic core.

For George Westlake, his 'kill' that day made up not so much for Coventry as for his slightly shaky start with 213 Squadron. A 'red line' entry to his logbook for 22 October made by his 'CO', Squadron Leader Duncan Macdonald, noted 'Crashed. Failure to change from "Gravity" to "Main" tank after take-off. Gross carelessness.' With the fuel-starved Hurricane written off and only his pride injured, the ebullient Westlake was not to make such a mistake again. In the heat of battle, when everything happened so very quickly, the most experienced pilot could make costly errors. After one dogfight over the Channel, Squadron Leader Macdonald had turned to land. When very low he spotted traffic driving on the 'wrong' side of the road. This, George's CO intuited, was not Sussex. Climbing at full throttle and pulling his Hurricane around, Macdonald recrossed the Channel flat out, making it back safely to Tangmere.

By October 1940, Westlake was, in fact, an experienced pilot. A student at the de Havilland Aeronautical Technical School at Hatfield set alongside the company's aerodrome and new headquarters, with its Art Deco admin building, flying school, club house and bright streams of DH aircraft taking to the Hertfordshire sky, in 1937 George had joined the RAFVR (Royal Air Force Voluntary Reserve). He had learned to fly two years earlier on the Miles Hawk, a lightweight low-wing wooden monoplane.

From Hatfield he reached for the sky in de Havilland Tiger Moths and Hawker Harts, the former a delightful RAF biplane trainer that could flutter safely down through the air like a falling autumn leaf or a Futurist pamphlet dropped from a Venetian clock tower, the latter a supremely aerobatic light bomber biplane powered by the V12 Rolls-Royce Kestrel. Ten of these engines had been sold pre-1939 to Junkers of Dessau for the German firm's prototype Ju-87 Stuka dive bomber.

George's ambition was to be taken on by the de Havilland sales team. For this to happen, he needed to up his flying hours. Following the advice of Peter de Havilland, one of Geoffrey de Havilland's three test-pilot sons, he took a flying instructor course, joined the London Aeroplane Club at Hatfield and taught proud new owners of de Havilland Tiger Moths, Hornets, Puss Moths, Leopard Moths and Moth Minors how to fly. As an instructor he got to fly for free. There had been one condition. The de Havilland family thought George looked far too young to be a credible instructor. He needed to go away for a spell and grow a moustache, which he did. George would sport a moustache for the rest of his life.

It was a wonderful life for a dashing young pilot. According to its brochure, the aerodrome club at Hatfield possessed 'the atmosphere and attractions of a country club of the highest class'. It was the centre of a lively sporting and social scene. Squash courts. Tennis courts. Open-air, all-year swimming pool 'maintained at a pleasant temperature by steam injection'. Riding. Dancing. A cocktail bar and restaurant. 'No expense or effort has been spared at Hatfield to make it the finest private aerodrome in the country.' Inevitably, it attracted a glamorous and well-connected clientele.

Such attractions aside, George was well paid, too, his earnings in 1938 promising to top £700 (c.£60,000 in 2024). Not bad for a twenty-year-old. His best-paid assignments were for Reg Salmon of Fox Photos. For £4 an hour, George flew the enterprising photographer from Hatfield in Salmon's three-seat, high-wing Leopard Moth monoplane while he shot events for the syndicated press. The Boat Race. Cowes Regatta. Train crashes. The raising of HMS *Thetis*, the Royal Navy submarine that had sunk during sea trials in Liverpool Bay. With little or no red tape, few forms to fill, no clearance required, flying, much of it low-level, was free-spirited dare-devil stuff and marvellous fun. Such flying demanded the acutely honed skills that would stand George in good stead throughout the war. To get the shots he needed, Rex Salmon directed his uninhibited young pilot towards tightly focused targets, often very close to the ground and sea.

For George, a job with de Havilland sales also spelt the possibility of returning, for a while at least, to Rangoon, the Burmese river port where he had been born in April 1918. His father, Herbert Westlake, was Rangoon Harbour Master and Master of the Irrawaddy, a high-ranking position in the colonial service. The Irrawaddy River, also known as the 'Road to Mandalay', was the main channel of communication through Burma.

George and his younger brother Ronnie, born in 1919, had loved Rangoon. They lived by the harbour, watching the 'chunkin' paddle steamers of the Irrawaddy Flotilla Company with their exotic cargos and complements puff in and out of port, in the golden shadow of the ancient and exquisite 2,500-year-old Botahtaung Pagoda facing the Rangoon River. For George and Ronnie, Rangoon was a fairy-tale city by the river and close to the sea. The house was large and generously staffed, the boys fond of the servants. They were enchanted by the wild gibbons that dropped by at mealtimes to help themselves to food.

Shoreham Grammar School, Sussex, where both boys were dispatched in 1928 – with glum holidays spent with reserved spinster aunts in the Lake District – did its English best to dispel the sorcery of the Far East. The boys saw nothing of their family, including the two young additions, a sister Isobel and a brother John, until their parents returned to England in the mid-1930s.

Called up on 1 March 1939, George was posted as flying instructor to 9 ETFS (Elementary Flying Training School) Ansty, east of Coventry, moving on to South Cerney, near Cirencester, training pilots on Hawker Harts and twin-engine Airspeed Oxfords. Commissioned at the end of August 1940, Pilot Officer Westlake converted to the Hurricane at 6 OTU (Operational Training Unit) Sutton Bridge, Lincolnshire, before moving on to RAF Usworth, Sunderland, to join 43 Squadron, which had been pulled from the frontline days earlier to recuperate and regroup. George flew five sorties a day with 43 Squadron. If you weren't dripping with sweat by the end of each 'trip', the battle-hardened veterans said, you weren't trying.

Three hours after passing through the gate at RAF Tangmere, West Sussex – he had now been posted to 213 Squadron – George was flying a 320mph, Rolls-Royce Merlin-powered Hurricane into a 300-plus formation of Dornier Do-17 and Heinkel-111 bombers escorted by nimble Bf109s. George tried to stick with his wing leader as he endured a sky full of seemingly random aircraft thrown chaotically in each and every direction, and then suddenly empty as they fizzed high above them. One moment he was working flat out to avoid being shot at while trying to get on the enemy's tail, the next was this surreally vacant sky. This was more frightening, he thought, than being in the thick of the action. Surely there must be someone, something there, a 109 perhaps, closing in from a position George hadn't considered or couldn't spot.

George and his colleagues were, says his son Richard Westlake, a former RAF Harrier pilot, 'obviously very conscious of the chances of not coming out alive. I am named after one of his best friends of the time, Richard Kestin, who I think flew with him in the Battle of Britain but was killed shortly after. They agreed that if either made it and the other didn't, they would name their first son after the other.

'No surprise, then, that they played hard when they weren't in the air. He often used to mention that the best hangover cure he knew was to select 100 percent oxygen for breathing right from take-off. Your head would be clear by the time you got to patrol height!'

For the most part, the daytime skies over the English Channel cleared in autumn 1940. Unable to defeat RAF Fighter Command, the Luftwaffe's *Luftflotte* 2, commanded by Field Marshal Kesselring, switched tactics. Instead of raiding airfields close to the coast, like Tangmere, and dicing for air superiority with an ever-emboldened Fighter Command, Heinkels, Dorniers and Junkers bombed cities – port cities in particular, London especially, and mostly by night.

The East Anglian ports of Ipswich, Harwich and Felixstowe were targets of the short-lived *Corpo Aereo Italiano*, an expeditionary offshoot of the *Regia Aeronautica*. Opportunistically,

Italy had declared war on France and Britain on 10 June 1940, when German victory over France was assured. Unwanted by Kesselring and his fellow German commanders, the Italians proffered open-cockpit biplane Fiat G.50 monoplane and CR.42 biplane fighters. Most were without radios and incapable of spending more than ten minutes over England before having to return to base to refuel. Furthermore, the Corpo's twin-engine Fiat BR.20M bombers, advanced when new in 1934, were outdated by 1940. These inappropriate single- and twin-engine aircraft were flown, with accidental losses on the way over the Alps, from Italy to airbases in Belgium, to take up the fight against Britain. For diplomacy's sake, the Luftwaffe had to accept this tentative Italian involvement in the final stages of the Battle of Britain.

Abandoned in January 1941, after little more than three months, the Italian adventure had not proved a success. The *Corpo Aereo* had failed to shoot down a single British aircraft, while its bombing raids caused little significant damage. Following a forced landing on the shingle beach at Orfordness, Suffolk, on 11 November 1940, twenty-three-year-old *Sergente* Pietro Salvadori of 95a Squadriglia, who was uninjured, told his British interrogators that his Fiat CR.42 – its tail emblazoned with the Venetian dialect slogan *Ocio che te copo* (Watch out, I'll kill you) – had suffered a broken oil pipe soon after take-off from Eechlou, northeast Belgium, on a bomber escort mission to Harwich.

Unable to keep pace with his twenty-one CR.42 comrades, two of whom were shot down by Hurricanes of 46 and 257 Squadrons and Spitfires of 41 Squadron, Salvadori was happy to have left the war. A reservist, he said he was dissatisfied with Italian commanders, with Belgian weather – he flew in an open cockpit – and with the Germans and their horrid food. Better to be a prisoner of war in Britain. His story made the papers. His Fiat biplane labelled 'museum material' by the Royal Aircraft Establishment, Farnborough, in 1943, when it was just three years old, is on display today at the RAF Museum, Hendon. (After the war ended, Pietro Salvadori continued in service with the Italian Air Force. He died in April 1953 after an accident flying an F-84G Thunderjet fighter.)

Neither Italian nor German pilots and air crews knew anything like the extent to which those fighting them in the skies over Britain in 1940 were from countries other than Britain itself. To those like George Westlake, a child of the British Empire, it was perfectly natural to mix day to day with people from different lands and cultures. One in five British pilots, in fact, came from somewhere other than Britain. To name just some of the countries concerned, they came from Poland, Czechoslovakia, New Zealand, Canada, Ireland, Australia, Jamaica, Barbados, Belgium, India, South Africa, France, the United States, Southern Rhodesia, Denmark, Egypt and Austria. Flying Boulton Paul Defiant night-fighters from Prestwick as an air gunner with 141 Squadron and, later, as a navigator on Bristol Beaufighters with 409 (RFAC) Squadron in North Africa, Alfred Lammer DFC was from Linz, the Austrian town he had fled that happened to be the home of Adolf Hitler for much of his youth. Others, from elsewhere around the globe, were waiting in the wings to join the fight against the Axis powers.

George spent a perishing cold winter – the coldest since 1895 – with 213 Squadron protecting the principal Royal Navy base at Scapa Flow in the Orkneys, at first from Castletown in Caithness and then from Sumburgh on the southern tip of the Shetlands. From here, the Hurricane pilots chased snooping twin-engine Junkers 88 bombers and four-engine Focke-Wulf Condors, too fast in dives it was said – perhaps so in the case of the Ju-88 – for the RAF fighters to catch. The long-range Condor, known as the 'Scourge of the Atlantic', was an airliner-turned-long-range bomber and death sentence for all too many Allied ships plying the Atlantic that brutal winter.

Looking down at the fleet at Scapa Flow, George recalled his father refusing to allow him to go to sea. Although Herbert Westlake and just about every male antecedent George could think of had been a sailor, the Navy was considered too dangerous. Flying. Now that was the safer option. An odd thought for a Battle of Britain pilot. Ronnie, though, had joined the RNVR (Royal Navy Volunteer Reserve) in 1938, serving on the battleship HMS *Rodney* before transferring to destroyers the following year. On escort duty somewhere out there in the North Atlantic his ship was torpedoed. Ronnie had spent several days bobbing about on a life raft before being rescued.

Spring 1941 promised something very different for both Westlake brothers. In March, Sub-Lieutenant Ronnie Westlake, now serving with the destroyer HMS *Walker*, was part of a sequence of actions involved in protecting Atlantic convoys that took out three U-boats in quick succession. George, meanwhile, was posted to RAF Turnhouse, near Edinburgh, as

213 Squadron was prepared there for going overseas. The pilots guessed they might be on the way to relieve Crete, under threat of German invasion, or the island fortress of Malta, Britain's 'aircraft carrier' in the Med. Without Malta, it would be next to impossible to supply the British forces fighting the Italians and Germans in North Africa.

From their base in Egypt, the British had been in action in North Africa since the previous June. Over the winter, the 250,000-strong Italian 10th Army commanded by the brutal Governor-General of Libya, Marshal Rodolfo Graziani, 'Pacifier of Libya', 'Butcher of Ethiopia', was crushed by a British force fielding 36,000 soldiers led by Lieutenant General Richard O'Connor. Proclaiming, for 'strategic, political, and psychological reasons, Germany must assist Italy in Africa', in response to the Italian fiasco, Hitler had General Erwin Rommel flown to Tripoli in January to take command of the newly formed Afrika Korps.

'Without Malta,' Rommel warned, 'the Axis will end by losing control of North Africa.' Malta was key to the British supply line to North Africa. Bombed relentlessly by the *Regia Aeronautica* from June 1940, at that time the island was defended from the air by RAF Gloster Gladiator biplane fighters, of which just three out of six were ready at any one time to take on the invaders. In November 1940, Malta was holding on. Just.

Whatever its destination and the challenges ahead, with sunshine and warmth on the cards, the Mediterranean adventure had to be a better option for 213 Squadron than frustrating ops over the foggy Atlantic and freezing North Sea.

Field Marshal Albert Kesselring, with baton, in the back seat of his Horch 830 staff car, visiting German front line positions, near Bologna, 1944.

THREE

THE
GENERALFELDMARSCHALL

A6, Bologna to Forli, 23 October 1944

It had already been a long day. Starting at 4 a.m., Field Marshal Albert Kesselring, supreme commander of German forces in Italy, had been driven from one division defending the north flanks of the Apennines to another. The mountains were his Gothic Line, the physical barrier barbed with newly constructed German fortifications, holding Allied armies back from the Po Valley to the north, and thus from the great industrial centres of Milan and Turin, and the ports of Genoa and Venice. If the US 5th and British 8th Armies crossed these formidable, gun-entrenched peaks, the next and last of Kesselring's defences was the Venetian Line, designed to close the forty-mile-wide corridor leading into northeast Italy between the Adriatic Sea and the Dolomites bordering the Alps. Beyond the Alps lay Austria and Bavaria, heartlands of Hitler's German empire. Best to hold the Gothic Line for as long as possible.

The long, straight Roman road from Piacenza (south of Milan) to Rimini (on the Adriatic coast) was lined intermittently that foggy autumn day with columns of troop carriers, tanks, armoured half-tracks and towed artillery pieces harassed relentlessly and without the slightest warning by the heavily armed ground-attack fighters and dive bombers of the Allies' Desert Air Force (DAF). Concentrating hard, Kesselring's driver put his foot down whenever there was a clear view ahead over the long bonnet of the Field Marshal's powerful eight-cylinder Horch 830, the elegant car's roof rolled back. Very much on view, Kesselring waved his Field Marshal's baton to roadside troops, flashing the famous grin that had prompted the Allies to call him 'Smiling Albert'.

Two more divisions to meet, greet, advise, encourage. Kesselring was in good spirits. He enjoyed the company of the soldiers he commanded. In turn, they liked and respected their competent and generally good-natured jack-of-all-trades 'Uncle Albert'. Good natured, that is, until crossed or following a questionable directive from Berlin.

Darkness now. Blackout regulations in force. Somewhere west of Forli, a heavy tractor unit towing an 88mm anti-aircraft gun pulled out from a side turning in front of the Horch. It was the last thing Kesselring's driver saw. He was killed outright as the car smashed into the gun-trailer. Unconscious, his skull fractured and face cut wide open, the Field Marshal was rushed to a nearby field hospital before being spirited to Ferrara for intensive medical treatment. He was not to return to his Italian HQ in the spa town of Recoaro, within easy reach of the Gothic Line until 15 January 1945. In his absence, his formidable barrier held.

Recuperating at home in Bavaria and in hospital at the Austrian spa town Bad Ischl, Kesselring recalled other near-death experiences. On 8 September 1943, the day the Italians – German allies – surrendered, his General Headquarters Mediterranean at Frascati, southeast of Rome, had been bombed by the Allies. He had stepped away from his office seconds before a bomb exploded right by its glazed balcony. One-hundred-and-fifty German soldiers and a thousand Italian civilians were killed in the raid. Damage to historic buildings was considerable. Kesselring was unscathed.

Back in 1940, he had, uncharacteristically, taken a few days' leave over Christmas. Touching down at a forward French airbase at the controls of his personal Fieseler Storch to pay a seasonal visit to fighter commander *Generalmajor* Theo Osterkamp, he had been fired on by a 20mm German anti-aircraft gun. The excuse from the trigger-happy gunners was that an 'English bomber' had been heard approaching. And then, shortly before the car crash near Forli, he had been shot down close to the Gothic Line flying his Fieseler Storch on a visit to his deputy, General Heinrich von Vietinghoff.

Whenever possible, Kesselring had chosen to lead from the front. During the Battle of Britain, he had watched through binoculars from the shores of northern France as *Luftflotte* 2 roared off over the English Channel. Constantly on the move in North Africa and Italy, he was very much a 'soldier's soldier'. War was his profession, and he had risen to the top. At home now in Bavaria, he thought of Marksteft, the small town beside the Main where he was born in November 1885 and where the Kesselring family owned the brewery, Brauerei Kesselring, they had founded in 1668. Marktsteft was truly a tight-knit world. Albert's father, Carl Adolf Kesselring, a teacher, and later Schools Director in Bayreuth, had married his second cousin, Rosina Kesselring. Albert was their sixth and youngest child.

At school in Bayreuth his teachers described him as 'good tempered and upright', 'composed and decent'. He was diligent in studying English and Italian, learning to speak both languages well. Joining the army in July 1904 as a *Fahnenjunker* (Corporal Cadet) in the 2nd Bavarian Foot Artillery Regiment, in March 1906 he was commissioned. Confirmed in his new status, he wed 'Liny' (Pauline) Keyssler, daughter of a wealthy Bayreuth apothecary, converting from the Lutheran to the Roman Catholic church for her, and her family's, sake. The Lieutenant and his wife honeymooned in Italy. Enchanted by Florence, Rome and Venice, Albert was happy, like many other fellow German officers, to call himself an Italophile.

German travellers, and honeymooners, had long been in thrall to Venice. By the early thirteenth century, German merchants were well established in the city. Business thrived and the city took its cut through lucrative commissions. The Senate of the Republic granted the Germans a bespoke rental palazzo, built in 1228, close by the Rialto bridge. By now, Venetian trade stretched east along the Silk Road to far-flung Cathay (China). Precious Chinese silks were traded in the Fondaco dei Tedeschi (the German Merchants' Hall), finding their lucrative way north across the Alps to Germany.

In the 1270s, the Venetian merchants, brothers Maffeo and Niccolò Polo and Niccolò's son Marco, ventured to China where they met and, for several years, worked for the powerful Mongolian emperor Kublai Khan. Marco, who dictated his memoirs on his return home while held as a prisoner of war during Venice's clash with the Republic of Genoa, served as an emissary for Kublai Khan in what would have been far-flung countries that we know today as Sri Lanka, Vietnam and Indonesia.

Destroyed by fire in January 1505, the original Fondaco was replaced as a matter of priority by a prominent and capacious four-storey courtyard building designed by Hieronymus Todescho (Girolamo Tedescho, or Jerome the German). A local architect, Antonio 'Scarpagnino' Abbondi, was placed in charge of construction. Completed three years later, it housed offices, a warehouse and rooms for between 100 and 200 visiting German merchants on its upper floors. To highlight the Fondaco's importance to Venice, its exterior was adorned with frescoes by Giorgione (on an astrological theme) and Titian, whose work included a female figure depicting justice raising her sword to protect a soldier representing Venice – and graced inside over the years with further frescoes by Titian, Veronese and Tintoretto.

Giorgione and Titian were young and supremely talented artists who lived at the time in the home of the hugely busy painter Giovanni Bellini, then in his mid-seventies. Picking up on Bellini's radical, sumptuous and glorious use of colour, Giorgione and Titian heralded a fanfare of lustrous Italian Renaissance painting. One of their wartime German admirers, as Kesselring well knew, was *Reichsmarschall* Hermann

Göring. Among the fifteen paintings Göring bought from the Florentine art dealer and Italian senator Alessandro Contini Bonacossi was a *Leda and the Swan* by Titian. It cost the Air Chief 1.35 million *lire*. (By this time the Fondaco had become Venice's principal post office.)

A rumour had spread to the effect that Göring's agent Josef 'Sepp' Angerer, a Berlin art dealer, had paid a visit to Bonacossi. He was accompanied by Gerhard Wolf, the German consul in Florence. Angerer liked to play brutally hard. 'What a pity you're not a Jew', he said to Bonacossi while making a throat slitting gesture. 'If you were a Jew, we could do just that!' And walk away with Venetian and other Italian masterpieces for free. Just as well that Angerer appeared not to know that the count's father was from a Jewish family.

Göring's lust for both paid-for and looted European works of art was so great that he had felt forced to add a substantial, museum-grade extension to Carinhall, his Swedish-style 'hunting lodge' in the Schorfheide Forest north of Berlin. Designed by Werner March, feted from 1936 as the architect of Berlin's Olympic Stadium, Carinhall was named in honour of Göring's Swedish first wife, Carin (née Fock), the former Countess von Kantzow of Irish, British and Swedish descent, who died of heart failure while visiting Stockholm for her mother's funeral. She was forty-two. Göring, who had been devoted to Carin, brought her body back to Germany, where her internment at Carinhall was attended by Adolf Hitler.

Werner March, as Kesselring knew, had later enlisted with the military and served as a staff officer in Italy under Admiral Canaris, head of Abwehr, the military intelligence service. Canaris, of course, had been involved in the 20 July 1944 bomb plot to assassinate Hitler and was now rotting in Flossenbürg concentration camp. According to some of Karl Wolff's SS colleagues, Canaris's treachery was made worse by the fact that he had issued passports to numerous Jews, helping them escape Nazi-held territories. March, perhaps playing the apolitical card as many successful architects tend or try to do, was alive and as free as any German soldier was in 1944. Perhaps he might return to Germany after the war to realise Göring's plan to transform Carinhall into the 'Norddeutsche Galerie', an ambitious museum with a completion date of 1953 to mark the *Reichsmarschall's* sixtieth birthday.

By the outbreak of the war, Carinhall was already a remarkable and decidedly curious place, as anyone who had visited, including King Edward VIII and his American wife, Wallis Simpson, could tell you. It boasted a burgeoning and voluptuous art collection, Titian and all, including *Danäe*, a portrait of the mythological princess ravaged by Zeus in a shower of gold. This had been painted for Cardinal Alessandro Farnese, grandson of Pope Paul III, whose mistress, Angela, was most probably the artist's model. Up in its spacious attics, Carinhall also possessed an ambitious model railway over which aircraft attached to wires could drop wooden bombs on circuiting trains.

Since the end of January 1943, when Stalingrad fell to the Red Army, Göring knew that the war wasn't going exactly to plan. So many successes until the fateful invasion of Russia in June 1941, and even that had seemed a triumph in the making with the fall of both Moscow and Leningrad seemingly on the cards before the snows fell, and Göring's pilots were forced to resort to lighting fires under the engines of their aircraft to melt the ice inside them. Göring moved a large part of his private art collection to a converted salt mine to the north of the Austrian spa town Altaussee. If German forests and salt mines seemed unlikely settings for works of art created by the sea and under the sun in Venice, the cultural bridge across the Alps had, in fact, been created centuries before Göring got his plump hands on a Titian.

That bridge, between late Gothic Germany and early Renaissance Italy, was established by the German artist Albrecht Dürer. Hugely talented, Dürer, then in his early thirties, arrived in Venice from mercantile Nuremberg in 1505 – he may or may not have been there before – while the new Fondaco was under construction. Here he met Giovanni Bellini, whose work he greatly admired, as did Bellini Dürer's, and the young artists making their mark on the city, in particular Giorgione and Titian. Dürer was delighted by the colours, costumes, dances, festivals and what was for him the sheer exoticism of the city. Delighted, too, that Venetian artists were held in such high regard. 'I am a gentleman [in Venice]', he wrote to his close friend, the Nuremberg lawyer Willibald Pirckheimer, 'at home, a parasite.' The Italian Renaissance had transformed what had been skilled and largely anonymous craftsmen into high-flown and famous named artists feted by princes and plutocrats alike. How self-conscious they had begun to be, painting self-portraits and often so groomed and dandi-fied. Pirckheimer had helped pay for Dürer's trip. In Venice, the artist, who revelled in fine clothes, and self-portraits, bought fine feathers for Pirckheimer's impressive collection of hats.

Here, Dürer created work that captured and celebrated the glowing use of colour made by the Venetian artists, notably the glorious *The Feast of the Rosary* (1506), an altarpiece for the German merchants' church of San Bartolomeo. Venetian artists were impressed by this sumptuous feast of reds and blue and gold. So, too, was Doge Leonardo Loredan, whose appearance and character generations have known from Giovanni Bellini's compelling and beautifully executed 1501 portrait. The Doge, from the Latin *dux* (leader), or *duce* in Italian, was the Venetian head of state, elected by chosen members of the Great Council of Venice. The job was for life as it had been since 697, when the first Doge, Paolo Anafesto, took office. Looted during Napoleon's rampage through Venice in 1807, Bellini's portrait of Loredan was bought soon afterwards by William Beckford, England's richest man, who sold it in 1844 to the National Gallery, London, where it has hung in splendour since.

Doge Loredan came to see Dürer at work on the altarpiece. Such was his admiration of Dürer's talent, Loredan offered him a retainer of 200 gold ducats to stay on as an official Venetian artist, a handsome sum and a high honour for an artist from north of the Alps. Although flattered, Dürer turned the Doge down, writing to Pirckheimer before he returned to Nuremberg, 'I have silenced all the painters who said that in print I'm good, but with painting I do not know how to handle the colours.'

A greater compliment, perhaps, was the influence Dürer had on Venetian painters, with Titian, for example, adopting the flora and fauna of the German artist's engravings in his own paintings. Dürer, however, was not amused when the print-maker Marcoantonio Raimondi made copies of his engravings, complete with his well-known 'AD' monogram. He tried, only partially successfully, to get Venetian law on his side. The city's courts ruled that the monogram was his alone, but that there was no other restriction on the copying of his work.

Dürer's one true disappointment was in trying to get to Mantua to meet Andrea Mantegna. He wanted to pay his respects to the great painter and to understand his extraordinary use of low and foreshortened perspectives witnessed, for example, in his masterly and deeply moving *Lamentation of Christ* (*c.*1480). Mantegna, who was married to Giovanni Bellini's sister Nicolosia, died shortly before Dürer set out on horseback from Venice. Failing to meet Mantegna, Dürer said, caused him 'more grief than any mischance that had befallen him during his life'.

The German–Italian link continues when the lauded German poet, playwright, lawyer, scientist, artist and novelist Johann Wolfgang von Goethe arrived in Venice in 1786 – returning in 1790 – the church of San Bartolomeo had been rebuilt to a significant degree, its bell tower capped since 1747 with a Bavarian-style onion dome, a little piece of Germany crammed into the narrow alleys of Rialto. Like any other German pupil, Kesselring would have read or been taught Goethe, together with Schiller and Shakespeare. 'We are all pilgrims who seek Italy,' wrote Goethe, encouraging fellow Germans, a people of the dank, dark North to drink deep of the warm, sunlit and seductive South. He was already working on *Faust*, his *magnum opus*, on his second trip to

Italy. Here, perhaps especially in Venice, he found a way of connecting the classical, rational values of the Enlightenment with those of the burgeoning Romantic movement. With his friends Friedrich Bury and Johann Heinrich Meyer, he explored every church and gallery he could find to witness and understand Venetian art. Like Dürer long before him, he was seduced by the colours, sensuality and sheer licentiousness of the city itself.

Goethe's *Venetian Epigrams*, written in 1790 back home in Frankfurt, were laced through with an earthy eroticism engendered by the enticing twilight world of the city's alleys he enjoyed exploring as much as he did its fine art and architecture. This is the author of *Faust* (as translated by the American poet James Rothenberg, 1931–2024):

> Doesn't surprise me that Christ our Lord
> Preferred to live with whores
> And sinners, seeing
> I go in for that myself.

Between 1858 and his death in 1883, Hitler's favourite composer, Richard Wagner, visited Venice six times. Over the winter of 1882–3, Wagner and his family rented the fifteen-room mezzanine floor of the late fifteenth-century Palazzo Vendramin, designed by the architect Mauro Codussi for the Loredan family and financed by Doge Leonardo Loredan, overlooking the Grand Canal. This is where the composer died.

In Venice, Wagner wrote the sublime second act of *Tristan und Isolde* and the haunting third act of *Parsifal*, his last work.

His first sight of Titian's *Assumption of the Virgin*, the altar-piece painted for the great Gothic church of Santa Maria Gloriosa dei Frari but relocated to the Accademia art gallery between 1817 and 1919, retriggered, according to Wagner himself, what became *Die Meistersinger von Nürnberg*, an opera he had been toying with since the mid-1840s. This was to be Hitler's especial favourite. It heralded the opening of Leni Riefenstahl's portentous Nazi propaganda film *Triumph of the Will* (1935) depicting the 1934 Nuremberg Rally. Snatches of the score were played through numerous wartime news-reels. It was the sole work performed at the 1943 Bayreuth Festival, with choruses performed by the *Hitlerjugend*. Thirty thousand soldiers and armaments workers attending one of sixteen performances sat through the four-and-a-half-hour opera as guests of the transfixed Führer.

Nuremberg, of course, was where the vast Nazi rallies were conducted in epic parade grounds designed by Albert Speer. The home of many of the merchants hostelled in the Fondaco dei Tedeschi and of Albrecht Dürer, it was to become the spiritual home of the Nazi movement and where the Laws for the Protection of German Blood denying citizenship to Jews and other non-Aryans had been announced in 1935.

From high-end medieval commerce and high Renaissance painting to lush nineteenth-century sensualism, whether in music or art, and on to 1930s cinema, Venice was a source of evergreen inspiration to generations of Germans. In a lighter mood than Wagner's, Venice had inspired the Viennese composer Johann Strauss's operetta *Eine Nacht in Venedig*, premiered in Berlin in October 1883. A comedy film of the same name, loosely based on Strauss's operetta and directed by Robert Wiene, best known for the weird and wonderfully Expressionist *Das Cabinet des Dr Caligari* (1920), entertained German audiences in 1934. Wiene, a Protestant by birth but with a Jewish background, left Berlin for Paris the same year. One of the film's stars, Ludwig Stössel, a Jew, emigrated to the US. Soon playing opposite the likes of Gary Cooper and Ronald Reagan, he also appeared in the wartime propaganda films *Hitler's Madman* and *The Strange Death of Adolf Hitler*, both released in 1943. The year before he had played Herr Leuchtag in *Casablanca*, a German Jew attempting to escape Europe with his wife for the US via North Africa and Rick's Café Américain.

Hollywood's 1935 *Top Hat*, a song and dance spectacle starring Fred Astaire and Ginger Rogers, was set in a fantasy Venice Lido. The film was directed by Mark Sandrich, a New York-born Jew, who made propaganda films during the war including *So Proud We Hail!* (1943) starring Claudette Colbert, Veronica Lake and Paulette Goddard as three Red Cross nurses posted to the Philippines. Paulette Goddard's fourth and final husband was Erich Maria Remarque, the German-born novelist well known for his anti-war *All Quiet on the Western Front* (1928). The book was banned by Goebbels.

On 16 December 1943, Remarque's sister, Elfriede Scholz, a wife and mother of two children, was beheaded in a German prison for 'undermining morale'. She had been heard saying that the war was lost. Many German generals had said as much in private. During her trial, Elfriede faced Roland Freisler, an extreme anti-Semite and the singularly vicious President of the People's Court. 'Your brother is unfortunately beyond our reach. You, however, will not escape… If Frau Scholz wants to blame her pessimism partly on the influence of her brother, the author of the notorious shoddy effort *All Quiet on the Western Front*, that cannot excuse her because, by her own admission, she has not seen her brother for thirteen years. Rather, she is a shameless traitor to her own and our German blood, to our life as a people, a propaganda agent who stirs up defeatist attitudes in favour of our enemies. There can be only one punishment for a woman who has so forgotten her honour and who will therefore be forever without honour: the death penalty.'

Well out of reach for the duration of the war in, at first, Beverly Hills and then New York, Remarque enjoyed affairs with the German-born actress Marlene Dietrich, who he had met on the Lido in September 1937 during the Venice Film Festival, with the Mexican actress Dolores del Río and with Hedy Lamarr, the Austrian actress, a Catholic convert whose parents were Jews. Early in the war, Lamarr helped invent a radio-guided system for Allied torpedoes employing a frequency-hopping technology to block radio jamming by the enemy.

Remarque found out about his sister's death only after the war ended. Freisler, he was pleased to learn, was killed during an air raid on Saturday, 3 February 1945. In court that morning and relishing the thought of a fresh round of death sentences, Freisler was pinned to the floor by a column that collapsed as a bomb dropped by an American B-17 Flying Fortress hit home. The bombing mission, comprising 1,000 aircraft, was led by Lieutenant Colonel Robert Rosenthal

DSO DFC, a Brooklyn-born Jewish lawyer who went on to serve as an assistant to the US prosecutor at the 1946 Nuremberg trials. Among those he interrogated was Hermann Göring.

Joseph Goebbels, a keen visitor to the Venice Film Festival, had tried to woo Marlene Dietrich back to Germany, where she had been hugely popular from the outset of the 1930s, but, seeking citizenship in the US, she refused. Goebbels, meanwhile, had a lengthy affair with the young Czech actress Lída Baarová, who had been offered work in Hollywood but, under pressure in Germany, turned it down. 'I could have been as famous as Marlene Dietrich,' she said. The same month that Kesselring's car crashed on the road to Rimini, *La Fornarina* (The Baker's Daughter), a historical drama starring Baarová as Raphael's model and lover, premiered in Rome.

Incidentally, if Kesselring had wanted, while recovering from his injuries he could have tuned in to the anti-war, anti-Hitler broadcasts made by Thomas Mann, the Nobel Prize-winning German author of *Death in Venice*, now living in Pacific Palisades on the Californian coast. Mann's *Deutsche Hörer!* (Listen, Germany!) programmes were recorded on vinyl discs and dispatched to NBC in New York. From here they were transmitted by telephone to the BBC in London. Pressed into vinyl again, they were broadcast to the world by long-wave radio. High-ranking German officials and officers aside, it was an offence to tune in to Allied airwaves.

With so many Germans captivated by aspects of Venice since the thirteenth century, surely none would ever wish to inflict damage on this bewitching city? To date only the

French and Austrians had done so. Hitler, of course, was Austrian and while an artist himself and an architect manqué, could an Austrian really be trusted with Venice, or any other historic Italian city for that matter? As for Kesselring, while he had a fondness and respect for Italian culture, soldiering was what he did best, from learning to shoot accurately to flying as an observer in hot-air balloons and mastering the latest developments in artillery. In the First World War, during which he was awarded the Iron Cross first class, he was soon picked out as general staff material and, despite doubts, chose to remain in the army after the German surrender. He was not, he liked to think, a political animal, but he recalled being shocked by the behaviour of communist-influenced soldiers at the end of the war and humiliated when a warrant was made for his arrest for an alleged *putsch* against the social-ist-influenced command of his III Bavarian Army Corps.

Instinctively conservative, Kesselring had never become a member of the radical National Socialist German Workers' Party. Even so, he rose rapidly to become the Administrative Chief of the Air Ministry, Berlin, and then Chief of the General Staff of the Luftwaffe. He worked flat out to ensure that investment in the revived German aviation industry and the new-born Luftwaffe was spent effectively. There had been the new aircraft types – notably the Bf 109 fighter and the Ju-87 Stuka dive bomber – a paratrooper corps, a new generation of 20mm, 37mm and 88mm anti-aircraft guns, and airbases designed by the best young architects, engineers and artists. Nothing was too good for the Luftwaffe.

At the age of forty-eight, Kesselring had learned to fly. After all, a man who is not an airman, he said, cannot build an air force any more than a man who is not a horseman can form and command a cavalry division. Before taking up flying, he had imagined no greater thrill than riding, ballooning and motoring. How dull life would have been, though, he said after he had gained his 'wings', had he never held a joystick and experienced the heights and depths of a pilot's life.

The Luftwaffe had been organised as a tactical air force, supporting the troops on the ground, focussing on military targets. When, in November 1937, Willy Messerschmitt had shown Hitler a mock-up of a four-engine long-distance bomber at his Augsburg factory, the Führer made it clear he was not interested. Again, the Luftwaffe was a tactical air force. Two engines were sufficient. But while the Luftwaffe was in its element in the early stages of the war – the invasions of Poland, Denmark, Norway, Belgium, France, the Netherlands, Luxembourg, France, Yugoslavia and Greece – as Kesselring had to admit, it had been hard pressed over Britain.

When Kesselring turned *Luftflotte* 2's attention from raids on RAF airfields to British cities, the bombing was less precise than that achieved by Stukas in Europe. Coventry was not meant to have been a terror raid, but what with smoke, weather conditions and other factors it had been difficult for crews to keep strictly 'economic' targets in their sights. The British, of course, had been targeting German cities with their heavy bombers. Indeed, from 1942, 'area bombing' became a British government-approved policy. Nothing under the flight paths of RAF bombers was sacred. Historic cities, their civilians and working-class housing districts were wilfully set on fire and blown to pieces.

The Luftwaffe's tactical role had, however, been proven over and again as Germany conquered great swathes of Europe west and east of Berlin. In command of *Luftflotte* 1 from 1 September 1939, Kesselring's howling Stukas had kept General Heinz Guderian's Panzers company as they blitzed their way through Poland, reaching Brest-Litovsk. Here they met the Red Army and in doing so neatly divided the harried country between Germany and the Soviet Union. The two countries had signed a non-aggression pact in 1939. If not exactly allies, they were working together in a relationship of mutual convenience to carve up Eastern Europe between them. In an audience with Hitler, following their success in the Polish campaign, Guderian and Kesselring were awarded the Knight's Cross of the Iron Cross.

The opening weeks of Operation Barbarossa, the German invasion of the Soviet Union, in June 1941 had also gone well for Kesselring. Beyond all expectations, in fact. By the third day of the attack – the biggest in history – the Luftwaffe had destroyed 3,100 Soviet aircraft. Even *Reichsmarschall* Göring was sceptical. That many? No. The actual figure was 3,922. This rose to 6,670 by the end of November 1941, when Kesselring was posted with *Luftflotte* 2 to Italy.

Although by this stage a master of most forms of modern warfare, Kesselring had never quite understood British radar, nor had he known that the British were able to decipher secret German military messages sent using the supposedly infallible electro-mechanical Enigma machine. The Enigma coding had, in fact, been cracked by the twenty-seven-year-old Polish mathematician Marian Rejewski as early as 1932, his discoveries shared, unbeknown to the Germans, with the

French and British weeks before the invasion of Poland. After secret sojourns in France and Spain, in 1943 Rejewski was spirited to England. He was not, though, to be a part of the top-secret deciphering team at Bletchley Park because this was operated as an exclusively British and American operation. Very few of those working at Bletchley Park knew anything of the founding Polish contribution to their project.

Recuperating in hospital in 1944, had Kesselring kept up with recent news from Poland? Following the crushing of the uprising in Warsaw in August, the SS commander Erich von dem Bach-Zelewski had deported more than half a million citizens and begun razing the historic city almost completely to the ground. Before Kesselring was back in action in January 1945, special units of German *brandkommandos* (in charge of setting fire to buildings) and *sprengkommandos* (demolition) systematically destroyed 923 historic buildings and 9,532 others. Schools and cultural buildings, especially museums and libraries, received special attention.

The idea was to reduce the core of the historic city to rubble and erase Polish culture. Factories, hospitals, roads and railways were also destroyed. This prompted much talk in some German circles about the development of a nuclear bomb. Bach-Zelewski was able to do to Warsaw, as photographs bore witness, what a nuclear bomb might have done a little more quickly, yet no less destructively.

Hitler had admired a plan he had seen in June 1939 for a new Warsaw prepared by the architect Friedrich Pabst. This envisioned the elimination of the existing city and its replacement with an ethnic German town of 130,000 people served by enslaved Slavs encamped on the other side of the River Vistula.

Warsaw was a Slavic city and so, as far as Hitler was concerned, worthy of erasure. As, of course, were Russian cities. 'It is the Führer's firm decision to level Moscow and Leningrad, and make them uninhabitable,' wrote General Franz Halder in his war journal, 'so as to relieve us of the necessity of having to feed the populations through the winter. The cities will be razed by [the] Air Force…a national catastrophe which will deprive not only Bolshevism, but also Muscovite nationalism of their centres.' From 1939 to 1942, Halder was the Chief of General Staff of Army High Command. He had directed and planned the detailed execution of Operation Barbarossa.

This was all malicious madness. Poland and Russia boasted glorious cities and refined and imaginative architecture. The finest Baroque, Rococo and Neoclassical buildings in and around Leningrad (formerly St Petersburg) had been designed by the likes of Francesco Bartolomeo Rastrelli, Parisian-born son of a Florentine architect and sculptor, and Naples-born Carlo Rossi. The Winter Palace, the Catherine Palace and the General Staff Headquarters building were hardly the works of the subhuman Slavs of Hitler's fevered imagination.

Could such wilful and perverse destruction happen in Western Europe? Well, yes. Kesselring himself had felt forced to strike a heavy blow against Rotterdam in May 1940 to bring a speedy and successful end to the Netherlands campaign. For his part in that massively destructive operation, he was invited by the Führer to a ceremony held in the

Berlin Opera House – a fine Palladian design commissioned by Frederick the Great exactly two hundred years before – where he received his Field Marshal's rank and baton, the one he liked to wave in salute to troops from his speeding Horch. As for the RAF, look at what they were to do to Hamburg in July 1943, creating a superheated firestorm that, blazing uncontrollably through the city centre and its working-class districts, swept pedestrians from pavements into vortexes of flaming air.

Promoted *Oberbefehlshaber Süd* (Commander-in-Chief South), Kesselring's new role in charge of all German armed forces in Italy and North Africa, was never less than complex and hugely demanding. He was to be both military commander and a diplomat. In Italy there had been Mussolini to deal with, as well as the king, Victor Emmanuel III, and in North Africa, the independent-minded Field Marshal Rommel.

Six years younger than Kesselring, Rommel was a legendary commander, hugely popular with his soldiers, and a favourite of Hitler's. Like Kesselring, he was a professional soldier with no reputation for unfairness or brutality. His wife Lucia was of Italian and Polish descent. A brave front-line officer in the First World War, as indeed he was in Europe and North Africa in the Second World War, he had been decorated with the coveted 'Blue Max' (*Pour le Mérite*, the highest order of bravery for German officers) for service in northern Italy. As a tank commander in the 1940 Battle of France, his lightning advances were remarkable. In Africa he was known on both sides as the Desert Fox. He was admired by friend and foe alike. Rommel complained about the inefficiency of the Italians and had a habit of leading attacks without them. Good soldiering, Kesselring thought. Poor diplomacy.

Kesselring himself held a poor view of the fighting quality of the Italians. Yes, there were many brave soldiers and acts of individual heroism, but the level of inefficiency, both at staff level and in the field, was exasperating. It seemed to Kesselring as if the Italian armed forces had been trained more for display than action – air force pilots, for example, appearing to put more effort into aerobatics than they did into attack. George Westlake was to observe the same behaviour.

According to Luigi Barzini in his book *The Italians* (1964):

Italian artillerymen in the Western Desert fired Austrian guns of first world war vintage, built by the Škoda works in 1908 or thereabout, against the very modern American and British models. Mussolini lacked raw materials, fuel and food to fight a long war, and he lacked merchant ships with which to supply the far-flung theatres he had chosen to fight in, since many Italian ships in foreign waters, not having been informed about their country's entry into the war, were immediately impounded. His tanks were small, weak, slow, tinny affairs, which could be pierced by machine-gun fire; he had chosen them because they were cheaper and, for the same price, he could have more of them. He said they were faster than the heavier models, more 'attuned to the quick reflexes of the Italian soldiers'. He had no aircraft carriers. His planes were good but too few to count; he could not replace them fast enough. They were clever toys, elegant models laboriously made by hand by ingenious mechanics for peacetime reviews, rather than industrial products which could be turned out fast enough to produce results. His navy, which had somehow managed to run itself for years, was relatively efficient, but certainly not big and advanced enough to stand up to the combined strength of the fleets he attacked. It lacked radar and, what is worse, it never suspected such an invention existed, which made Italian ships sitting ducks.

Italian officers were often quite divorced from the men they led. They certainly ate better food. And, as for leading from the front, Kesselring remembered how shocked the Italian Commander-in-Chief, *Maresciallo* Ugo Cavallero, had been when in January 1942 he flew the Marshal in his feather-weight Storch to a conference in Libya in January 1942. Surely German Field Marshals had pilots to fly them? The conference overran. Kesselring had to fly back to El Agheila in the dark, which the plane wasn't design to do. Kesselring managed to find his way home and touched down safely. When Marshal Cavallero insinuated his way from the aircraft, he was swept into the arms of his relieved generals. Kesselring found the *abbracci* and *baci* (hugs and kisses), if not wholly embarrassing, hard to understand. These were soldiers, surely, trained to face hardship and danger and not characters from some comic Italian opera.

Since he had withdrawn his forces to mainland Italy, life and war had taken different turns. In September 1943, a week or so after the air raid that nearly killed him, Kesselring had met with Marshal Cavallero at Frascati to discuss what the Italian C-in-C needed to do now that Italy had sought an armistice with the Allies and King Victor Emmanuel III had declared war on Germany. Orders from Berlin insisted that Marshal Cavallero lead the fight with Germany against the Allies. Cavallero said this would only incite civil war. He would not continue the fight. Quite what happened next had been something of a mystery. The following morning the Marshal, seated on a bench in the garden of the Hotel Belvedere, was found dead. Suicide most probably. Shot through the head with a revolver, although Cavallero was left-handed, and the gunshot was on the right side of his head.

The suspicion, of course, was that he had been killed on orders from Berlin given behind Kesselring's back. Berlin was confused as to quite how to advance the war in Italy now that the King had switched allegiances, declaring the country ready to fight on the Allied side against Germany. Where German power held sway, Italian troops were disarmed, made prisoners of war, forced into what was effectively slave labour or deported, some to concentration camps. It was, to say the least, a volatile situation.

More recently, Kesselring had SS-*Obergruppenführer* (General) Karl Wolff – the eyes and ears of *Reichsführer*-SS Heinrich Himmler – looking over his shoulder in Italy and up to anything and everything out of his sight, if not altogether from his mind. With Himmler as its head, the SS had grown all-powerful. From its beginnings as the Nazi Party's paramilitary wing, it had developed into a formidable organisation with its own Waffen-SS regiments, its guards, its concentration and extermination camp corps and its control of the secret police and intelligence services. By 1943, Himmler was not just the head of the SS, but Minister of the

Interior and chief of the Criminal Police. In fact, many regular Wehrmacht soldiers despised the SS; its reach, its ears and eyes, were everywhere.

While this was hard enough, Kesselring was fighting a defensive war and had been doing so since Rommel and the Afrika Korps were defeated by General Bernard Montgomery, and the British Eighth Army, in co-operation with the Western Desert Air Force, following the momentous Second Battle of El Alamein fought in October–November 1942, an outstanding British victory. Effectively, Kesselring's job was to retreat as slowly as possible towards the Alps to stop the Allied armies moving up through Italy from joining forces with their compatriots either on the Western or the Eastern Front.

Now, in 1944, Kesselring was fighting not just against the British, Americans and their allies, but Italian partisans, many of them avowed communists. And what a bloody affair it was with the partisans. It had been hard enough dealing with Italian deceit following the dismissal of Mussolini. The King had assured him that Italy would fight on against the Allies and he had believed him. Hitler had not been fooled. 'That fellow Kesselring,' he said, 'is too honest for those born traitors down there.' Kesselring was an Italophile, too soft on those who might yet betray him further. Hitler was also critical of Kesselring's decisions to declare Rome an 'Open City', withdrawing troops from there, and to allow disarmed Italian soldiers to return home. They should all be arrested and packed off to POW camps in Germany. Even Hitler, though, had agreed that Rome should not be bombed. The British did bomb it. They bombed Florence, too.

The Desert War had, by common consent, been a much cleaner affair. A fight between soldiers – on land, at sea and in the air – with very few towns or monuments in danger of being hit. Few civilians in danger of getting caught up in military operations. Kesselring respected the British, especially their fighter pilots. Their bravery and manoeuvring skill. The way they handled their aircraft perfectly as they dived through the middle of closed German bomber formations...

Shark-nosed RAF 112 Squadron P-40 Kittyhawk IIIs prepare to take off from a makeshift desert air strip, Medenine, Tunisia, March 1943.

FOUR

DESERT WAR

Mediterranean, south of Sardinia, 21 May 1941

This was something different. Full throttle, full boost. Flight Lieutenant George Westlake launched Hurricane Z4270 into the wind off the deck of HMS *Furious*. The converted First World War cruiser had ferried 213 Squadron – 'The Hornets' – from Liverpool to Gibraltar, shadowed by HMS *Ark Royal* with the accompanying Hurricanes of 229 and 249 Squadrons. Escorted by Fairey Fulmar naval fighters of 800 Squadron Fleet Air Arm, the fighters sped over the Mediterranean for three hours and forty-five minutes before landing at RAF Hal Far on the southern tip of Malta. The British airbase had been bombed that morning.

The young pilots had time for no more than a brief leg stretch and an improvised lunch before the refuelled Hurricanes were in the air again, flying a second three-hour-forty-five-minute leg to RAF Mersa Matruh, 150 miles west of Alexandria on the Egyptian coast. Heavily armed twin-engine Bristol Beaufighters joined the Hurricanes some way into the flight. It was a relief to see them. These were dangerous waters, threatening skies. Sailors called them the 'Sicilian Narrows', a bomb alley pinched between Sicily and Tunisia. Ships sailing here were threatened by mines and attack from the air. Less than a fortnight before, the brand-new Alexandria-bound 9,228-ton cargo steamer SS *Empire Song* had hit a mine and sunk, with the loss of eighteen of its Indian Merchant Navy crew, fifty-seven tanks, ten Hurricanes, lorries and ammunition. The Luftwaffe might strike at any moment. Westlake and his fellow pilots were thankful for the strong tail wind that hurried their Hurricanes over and along the Med.

Of the three routes chosen to send fighters from Britain to Egypt, George's was by far the shortest, but also, in terms of potential enemy attack, the most dangerous. The safest, and slowest, was the long route around Cape Horn and up the East African coast. The third route meant flying across the Sahara from West Africa. It had its own risks. Crated Hurricanes were shipped to RAF Takoradi on the Gold Coast, where the British had built a deepwater seaport in the late 1920s. It was home to the Wellington anti-submarine and convoy protection bombers of SAAF (South African Air Force) 26 Squadron.

Assembled fighters were flown from Takoradi across Nigeria, French West Africa, Sudan and then up the Nile to Cairo. But with rainstorms, sandstorms and ferocious winds like the khamsin that could lift sand up to 10,000 feet from the desert floor, causing pilots to see what appeared to be land below their wings while their altimeters said differently, flying across Saharan Africa was rarely a piece of cake. Especially when Hurricanes came to land, whether to refuel or with engine trouble, their young pilots were aware that these vast sun-blasted territories were truly another world. Dry riverbeds, nomadic tribespeople, intense heat, dust, incessant insects, dunes, camel trains and, at the end of their epic flights, the Pyramids, seen before by most of the pilots only in picture books and films.

From Alexandria, George Westlake's 213 'B' flight was given a temporary posting to 80 Squadron in Palestine. With 213's ground crews and equipment on the way to Egypt via the Cape of Good Hope, the Red Sea, the Gulf of Aden and the Suez Canal, it would be some months before the squadron was fully operational and ready for the fight across North Africa. It had been sent there in response to the arrival of Rommel's Afrika Korps and the Luftwaffe in March 1941 in the wake of the shortcoming of the Italians on the battlefield.

'B' flight's role with 80 Squadron was to engage in Operation Exporter, the invasion of Vichy French-held Syria and Lebanon. Its principal duties were to protect the Royal Navy's Mediterranean Fleet from Vichy French bombers operating from Syria and Luftwaffe Ju-88s on the prowl from Crete, to attack Lebanese ports, shipping and oil installations and to strafe Syrian airfields that the Luftwaffe was keen to use in future raids on British-controlled Egypt and Iraq.

George shared his first victory in the Syria–Lebanon campaign – a twin-engine French Potez 630 fighter-bomber shadowing the British Fleet between Haifa and Beirut – with 80 Squadron's Pilot Officer Roald Dahl. Dahl, George noted, was so tall it was a wonder he could fold into the cockpit of a Hurricane.

The brief Syria–Lebanon campaign of June–July 1941 was a lesson for young RAF pilots and crews, fresh from defending their home country, in how they were now fighting in what was developing into a world war, its barbed tentacles engulfing an increasingly wider spread of the atlas month by month. The Germans were interested in Syria because it offered them a base from which the Luftwaffe and the *Regia Aeronautica* might launch attacks on Egypt from the east, while Rommel's newly formed Afrika Korps struck swiftly across the desert from Libya with the aim of defeating the British in Egypt and seizing the Suez Canal.

With this strategic waterway in their hands and Syria an ideal air base for raids on Iraq, the Germans and Italians would have a good chance of capturing Iraqi oil wells while threatening India from the north and west as their Axis allies, the Japanese, sought to invade from the east. While Syria would have seemed a sideshow at best to most Europeans in May 1941, it was far more important than that.

Strategically positioned Syria was a political tightrope. Controlled by the Vichy French under General Henri Dentz, C-in-C of the Army of the Levant, whose allegiance was nominally to Nazi Germany, it was opposed by the Free French led by the imperious General Charles de Gaulle. Nothing, though, was as straightforward as it seemed. Until persuaded otherwise, General Dentz said that he would fire on any military aircraft of any nationality flying over Syria.

By mid–May, sixty–six German and Italian combat aircraft and forty transport planes had landed at Syrian airfields. The Vichy French fleet itself comprised a jumble of machines, exotic to young British eyes, including Bloch MB. 200, Farman 222, Dewoitine 337, Lioré et Olivier Le0 45 and Martin 167 Maryland light bombers, Potez 630 fighter-bombers, Loire 130 flying boats and Morane-Saulnier M.S 406 and D.520 fighters. The last of these, a lightweight liquid-cooled V12-powered machine, was intended as a rival to the Supermarine Spitfire and Messerschmitt Bf 109. Fortunately for the pilots of 80 Squadron, it was no such thing. According to Captain Eric Brown RN, commanding officer of the Royal Aircraft Establishment's Captured Enemy Aircraft Flight, 'It was a nasty little brute. Looked beautiful but didn't fly beautifully. Once you get it on the ground, I was told not to leave the controls until it was in the hangar and the engine stopped.'

Air Marshal Arthur Tedder's concern, meanwhile – he'd been promoted from Deputy to C-in-C RAF Middle East Command on 1 June – was that the Free French might act ahead of the British in Syria. Lieutenant General John Bagot Glubb was C-in-C of the Transjordan League, the British-Arab force patrolling the region, which knew him as 'Glubb Pasha'. He warned Tedder, as the Air Marshal recalled, that there were some 'who preferred any Frenchman in Syria to any Englishman and tried to arrange deals by which the Vichy French should hand over to the de Gaullistes so as to keep us out'. Tedder was equally concerned that if the Free French attempted to invade Syria without British and Commonwealth support, they might well be defeated.

Air Marshal Tedder had a low opinion of de Gaulle. He considered the Free French leader to be 'violently anti-British'. In a letter of 3 June to the Vice Chief of the Air Staff, Air Chief Marshal Sir Wilfrid Freeman – who had introduced the RAF to the Hurricane and Spitfire – he wrote, 'I do not think he is half as big a man as he thinks he is. He is being incredibly stupid and rigid over the Frenchmen who have joined us and whose last wish is to become Free French. He has the effrontery to issue an order proscribing those people (some officers and some men) in the RAFVR [RAF Volunteer Reserve] and saying that if they do not join him, they will be liable to arrest. I tried to get him to see reason, but it was hopeless...'

As for the Syrians themselves, Tedder thought they were hostile to the French whether Vichy or Free, and weren't that much happier with the British. Relationships with local people were hardly helped by inept air attacks called for by the army and made by Bristol Blenheims of 11 Squadron on four villages in the Kiswe area, 'where there were no military objectives whatsoever'. Twenty-one people were killed. Damage was extensive. Tedder also noted a sortie over Suweida (As-Suwayda in southwest Syria) by Blenheims of 11 and 45 Squadrons on 11 July 1941, the day before the Vichy surrender. The light bombers were charged with dropping leaflets advising local people of the military situation. For some reason, someone saw fit to drop a 'farewell bomb' that killed two people as they rushed to pick up the leaflets, 'a display of high spirits that was, of course, in direct defiance of instructions. This gave a very unfavourable impression.'

What had been impressive was the success of RAF fighter attacks. During the brief campaign – concluded on 12 July, when General Dentz sought an armistice shortly after the 21st Australian Brigade was about to enter Beirut – Tedder recorded fifty-five enemy aircraft destroyed on the ground. In addition, 107 were damaged during sorties by Hurricanes, flown by George Westlake and his colleagues, and RAAF (Royal Australian Air Force) Curtiss P-40 Tomahawks. Tedder believed the strikes could have been even more successful if the Tomahawks had been fitted with radio transmitters. This would have made it easier for pilots to be able to identify friendly and enemy soldiers on the ground. Tedder had also been concerned that the fighters' attention had been diverted all too frequently to protect the Royal Navy cruiser fleet operating along the Lebanese coast. The fighters were in danger of spreading their wings too thinly.

On the positive side, British and Commonwealth pilots were learning how to attack ground targets protected by anti-aircraft guns, how to work in close co-operation with one another and with troops on the ground, and how to adapt to different climates and temporary makeshift living conditions. Being born and brought up in Rangoon, George Westlake was familiar with heat, mosquito nets and the need to guard against malaria. And it was fun to fly in shirt sleeves and shorts. For many of his colleagues, all this was quite new. The presence and banter of colleagues aside, one of the most familiar and reassuring aspects of this new life in the eastern Mediterranean was the imperturbable thrum of the V12 Rolls-Royce Merlin engines of their Hawker Hurricanes.

During the campaign, Westlake shared the shooting down, along with the Potez 630 he shared with Roald Dahl, of an American-built Vichy French Martin 167 medium bomber over Palestine. He also destroyed a Dewoitine D.520 fighter and shared a victory over a second of these nimble machines. He strafed Vichy airfields, destroying aircraft on the ground. The French, he learned, lost a total of 179 of the 289 aircraft they dedicated to the fight from Syria before dispatching survivors to Rhodes, an Italian possession from the end of the First World War.

Shortly before the Free French were in harness in Syria and Lebanon, George was posted to Cyprus. The British aerodrome at Nicosia was a daily target for Italian and German bombers. On 7 July, now back with 213 Squadron, George scrambled to intercept Junkers Ju-88s with 'bombs bursting on either side of the runway'. On 9 July, he took off 'with bombs crumping behind'. On 10 July, he flew a third patrol – 'volunteered...thro' boredom'. Just as well. A German raid 'developed into a "Pukka" Blitz. Aerodrome bombed. Another petrol dump and runways'. On 18 July, 213 was scrambled to intercept Savoia-Marchetti SM.79 tri-motor bombers over Nicosia. Chasing and catching one, eighty miles from the coast and very low over the water, George shot it down into Morphou Bay in front of a cheering and waving Cypriot fishing fleet.

Sir William Battershill, the island's Governor and Commander-in-Chief, who had served in the First World War as a young army officer in India and Iraq, got hold of the tale. He presented George with a bottle of whisky, promising a crate if he could down a second enemy bomber. He did, a tri-motor Italian CANT Z.1007 *Alcione* (Kingfisher) near Capo Greco, a rocky headland on which falcons, harriers, buzzards and kestrels, oblivious of war, rested on their annual migrations. The machine-gun bullets of George's Hurricane sawed through the wooden spars of the bomber's wings. Like a sheet of paper, one wing folded, sending the aircraft spinning to the ground near the port of Larnaca. George had to make do with just the one bottle of whisky. Sir William had left Nicosia the previous day to take up an appointment with the Colonial Office in London.

Things happened quickly out here, every day a surprise. Sent to intercept a 'hostile' flying in from the north of the island towards Kyrenia, George was met by the extraordinary sight of a green Soviet-built Catalina seaplane bomber complete with a red star on its tail. Told to force it down, he escorted it to Morphou Bay, where it landed abruptly. Astonishingly, the NCO at the controls proved to be a deserter from Sevastopol. He had never flown before, but had taken his chances, crossing the Black Sea and Turkey on the way. A spirited combat pilot in the making, he was handed over to the Soviet authorities, much to the RAF airmen's dismay, his fate sealed.

Now a part of the Western Desert Air Force (WDAF), 213 Squadron was redirected to Alexandria to protect the Egyptian harbour before heading west into the desert to tackle German and Italian fighters. This was air-to-air fighting once again, flying four and even five sorties a day, with Bf 109s 'pecking' in pairs at the Hurricanes as they had done over the Sussex coast and the English Channel. What was different – climate and landscape aside – was the fighting style of Italian pilots. Instead of 'pecking' and vanishing like their German partners, Italian pilots flew their agile Macchi C.200 and C.202 monoplane fighters below the Hurricanes before pulling up in front just out of range of their guns and performing theatrical upward rolls. These, George learned quickly, were invitations to dogfight. The Italians certainly had panache. Hurricane pilots were grateful that the Macchis were so lightly armed. Spitfires, a match for any dogfighter, had yet to arrive in North Africa. George and his fellow pilots would have loved to have flown gymnastic Spitfires into battle against Italian and, more so, German fighters. It wasn't to be.

Flying in Syria, Lebanon and now North Africa had allowed George to evaluate close up and in extreme conditions the efficacy of the different aircraft supplied to the WDAF. The Hurricane he knew so well was a fine all-rounder. Bigger and heavier than the supremely elegant Spitfire, it was more rugged than its Supermarine compatriot and so a good aircraft, especially with its wider undercarriage, to bring down to land on rough-and-ready airstrips. It could out-turn both the Spitfire and the enemy's Messerschmitt Bf 109. Its thick wings made it slower than the Spitfire – both fighters powered by Rolls-Royce Merlin engines – but these could be fitted with heavier and more impactful guns.

In June 1942, Hurricane Mk IIds of 6 Squadron went into action in Egypt. Known as 'flying can openers', they were equipped with pairs of 40mm tank-busting Vickers cannons mounted beneath each wing. While the guns restricted the top speed of the fighters to 288mph, the tank-busting

Hurricanes proved to be highly effective. In attack, they were flown very low, and none lower than the Mk IId of Flight Lieutenant Philip 'Pip' Hillier. His DFC citation read,

> In June 1942, this officer participated in 2 sorties against a column of enemy armoured vehicles near Sidi Rezegh. On his first sortie, in the face of heavy fire, he made 4 low level attacks on the target, hitting several tanks. On his second sortie, he flew so low that part of the tail unit snapped off on the turret of one of the vehicles he attacked. Despite the damage sustained to the aircraft he flew it safely to base. Flight Lieutenant Hillier played a gallant part in the operations which were attended with much success.

The Spitfire was designed as a lithe, high-flying interceptor and was, without a doubt, superb in this role. It was the aircraft that as a fighter-bomber pilot you would want as an escort on ground-attack missions, ready at any moment to twist up, away and around to tackle encroaching enemy fighters. Always in demand, the Spitfire was developed continuously throughout the war. The aircraft, though, that George Westlake and his colleagues would fly with great success up through Italy and until the end of the war was the Curtiss Kittyhawk.

First flown in 1938 and produced in huge numbers – 13,738 – from 1939 to 1944 at the Curtiss-Wright factory in Buffalo, New York, the P-40 was known as the Warhawk by the USAAF (United States Army Air Force) and the Tomahawk by foreign air forces, including the RAF and the RAAF. While some early models had been shipped to

England from February 1941, its modest high-altitude performance meant that, as a frontline combat fighter, it equipped just one squadron – 403 RCAF (Royal Canadian Air Force) – and, even then, was replaced by Spitfires after just twenty-nine sorties.

Outside the US, later versions from the P-40D onwards were known as Kittyhawks. The RAF's P-40Ms were designated Kittyhawk Mk III. George Westlake would get to know the Mk III well. The Kittyhawk had virtues hidden from RAF pilots until their experience in North Africa. It was dependable and easy to maintain. It was highly manoeuvrable. It was notably hardy. And it could be dived at high speed, recovering well as it pulled up full throttle from daringly low altitudes. It became popular, replacing Hurricanes in the Mediterranean theatre, its growing appeal enhanced by the paintwork adopted, at first by the Tomahawks of WDAF's 112 Squadron, with the nose of the aircraft appearing to gape open like a shark and revealing rows of fearsome teeth. The idea had been adopted from twin-engine Luftwaffe Messerschmitt Bf110 fighter-bombers. It became hard to imagine P-40s without their shark noses.

In North Africa, George shot down five confirmed enemy aircraft – a C.202, two Bf109Fs, a Messerschmitt Bf 110 fighter-bomber and a Junkers 87 dive bomber – and damaged three others. Throughout two years of intense and incessant frontline action, as the huge land armies of the Axis and Allied forces seesawed back and forth across vast desert distances below, his own aircraft were never hit. In September 1942, a month after Spitfires finally arrived to join the fight over the desert, he was awarded the DFC. The citation read:

Ft. Lt. Westlake is a daring and tenacious fighter pilot. As a flight commander he has proved a great success. On the occasion when he has led the squadron, he has shown brilliant resource coupled with a high degree of accuracy. He has destroyed at least eight enemy aircraft.

The Spitfires, though, were to make all the difference. Whatever their virtues, Hurricanes and Curtiss P-40 Kittyhawks were hard pressed by the Luftwaffe's finest fighters and their expert pilots. On 3 June 1942, the livewire German ace *Hauptman* Hans-Joachim Marseille, nicknamed *Stern von Afrika* (African Star), had dived his lone Bf109E into a formation of sixteen P-40s, shooting down six from 5 Squadron SAAF (South African Air Force), three of them flown by aces. On 1 September, flying three sorties in a Bf109F, Marseille destroyed seventeen Allied aircraft, eight of them within ten minutes. An exceptional fighter pilot, Marseille died on 30 September, failing to jump clear of his Bf109G after its engine caught fire during a sortie escorting Ju-87s Stuka dive bombers over Egypt near Sidi Abdel Rahman. His total tally was 157 enemy aircraft destroyed. He had been awarded the Knight's Cross of the Iron Cross with Oak Leaves, Swords and Diamonds and the Gold Medal of Military Valour. A veteran of the Battle of Britain, he was twenty-two when he died.

British Spitfire veterans of the Battle of Britain like twenty-two-year-old Wing Commander Hugh 'Cocky' Dundas DFC took a moment or two to adjust to the desert war. The primitive tents instead of coddling Neo-Georgian officers' messes. The narrow wire mesh strips rolled across sand that served as runways. The heat, of course, and the informality of RAF life in North Africa. Officers arriving fresh from England in crisp blue uniforms, collar and tie were met by fellow pilots, some of them looking as if they might have been fighting with Lawrence in the Arabian desert.

The Western Desert Air Force (WDAF) was forged in the heat of this fight against Italy and Germany in Egypt, Libya and Tunisia. As head of RAF Middle East Command from June 1941, Air Marshal Arthur Tedder did much to turn large sections of British and Commonwealth air forces flying in North Africa into a 'flying artillery'. His technique for ground support was for his aircraft to carpet bomb narrow and shallow areas in front of advancing troops. The 'Tedder Carpet', as the press dubbed it, proved hugely effective. Tedder was certainly the man for the job. The highly intelligent and widely experienced RAF officer, who we met in the Syria–Lebanon campaign, had read History at Magdalene College, Cambridge, studied German in Berlin, served in action as a frontline pilot and a squadron commander with the Royal Flying Corps on the Western Front in 1916–17, flying Bristol Scout Cs and Sopwith 1½ Strutters. Among his decorations was the Italian Silver Medal for Military Valour. He held senior posts throughout the Empire, including Director General for Research in the Ministry of Aviation in 1938–9.

Tedder was more than ably assisted by Air Vice Marshal Arthur 'Mary' Coningham. Australian by birth but raised in New Zealand – hence his nickname, 'Maori' mispronounced 'Mary' by the linguistically challenged British – Coningham shaped the WDAF, formed in November 1941, into a hard-hitting tactical air force, its crews drawn mostly from Australia, Britain and South Africa and working in increasingly close cooperation with the Eighth Army. A First World War Royal Flying Corps ace, Coningham had flown dozens of missions in Royal Aircraft Factory SE5 biplane fighters strafing enemy aerodromes, gun positions, troop movements, trains and ground transport. Imagine what they could have achieved with radio. And then Coningham brought radio to bear in North Africa. Forward air controllers, positioned in mobile radio stations or riding in leading tanks, armoured cars and light army-cooperation aircraft could, thanks to Coningham, call up support at very short notice from 'cab ranks' of circling fighters and fighter-bombers, the Hurricanes of 213 Squadron among them.

Speed. Daring. Close co-operation. Accuracy. British and Commonwealth fighter and fighter-bomber pilots – they had yet to be joined by the Americans – were learning lessons that were to stand them in good stead in later months as they fought up the Italian peninsula and were charged with attacks on and near densely populated and historic cities.

The airmen also learned the art of moving from improvised airfield to improvised airfield at the drop of a side cap. The Desert War was rarely less than fast moving. Challenging, too. It was a world of makeshift tents, bully beef, hardtack biscuits, tinned potatoes, tinned jam, tea, sand in everything, scorpions, flies and more flies, hot days, cold nights, slapdash bathing and whatever alcohol was going. When the hot desert winds blew, and unless properly filtered, the sand flew into every exposed nook and cranny of aircraft, guns and equipment.

91

Having completed two tours of duty – 400 flying hours – George was rested by being appointed a land-based 'fighter controller', directing fighters and dive bombers to 'targets of opportunity' in close cooperation with ground forces across Egypt, Libya and Tunisia. Promoted Squadron Leader, he controlled the radio unit at the critical Second Battle of El Alamein in October–November 1942, positioned in front of hundreds of British twenty-five-pounders. It was noisy to say the least, and decidedly 'hairy' when the enemy fixed the British artillery positions, bombarding them with 80mm shells from disturbingly accurate *Granatwerfer* mortars.

After General Montgomery's victory at El Alamein in November 1942, the British pursued the Germans and Italians back across the deserts of Libya and Tunisia, meeting up with Allied armies – British, US and Free French – that had landed on 7–8 November in French North Africa under the auspices of Operation Torch, commanded by US Lieutenant General Dwight D. Eisenhower. British victory had been key to showing the Americans what the armed forces of their new allies were capable of.

Operation Torch was as much a political as a military breakthrough. It brought the Americans into a land war, fighting side by side with their Allies. The Americans had been protected as they landed by Seafires, Hurricanes, Martletts, Fulmars and Albacores flying from the Royal Navy aircraft carriers HMS *Furious*, *Biter* and *Dasher* and by WDAF's fearsome multirole twin-engine Beaufighters and its Wellington bombers.

Operation Torch spelt the end of the pro-Hitler Vichy regime in French North Africa. Most of all it meant the cooperation of British and Commonwealth and US armed forces. A brooding fug of Anglophobia among American general staff and Washington politicians, together with an abiding belief that the US should commit to military intervention in Europe alone, and not some African sideshow, had delayed Operation Torch until Franklin Roosevelt, as *de jure* US Commander-in-Chief, issued a presidential decree enforcing the invasion of North Africa rather than southern France.

From now on, Rommel, his Afrika Korps and Italian allies were very much on the back foot. The RAF's increasing command of the air had threatened and then destroyed German and Italian shipping ferrying essential supplies of fuel, weapons and ammunition from Italy. Straws that broke the Axis camel's back had been the sinking of *Prosperpina*, a tanker brimming with fuel, and *Tergestea*, a motor freighter carrying 1,042 tons of ammunition, both outbound from Taranto, as they neared Tobruk on 26 October. Beaufighters of RAF 47 Squadron, and possibly Blenheim Mk Vs of SAAF's 15th Squadron, did for both ships. The Beaufighters were caught in action by German newsreel cameras. It is astonishing to watch, if just for a few black-and-white seconds, these powerful aircraft hurtling towards the ships at great speed, their big propellers barely above the water. German supply ships could no longer fetch through.

In early February 1943 all Allied air forces, by order of Eisenhower, now the Allied supreme commander, were put under the command of his deputy, Air Marshal Tedder. General Alexander was to command all Allied land forces in the Mediterranean theatre. In March, Spitfire Mk IXs arrived, late in the day perhaps, but here was a fighter superior to any other on either side in North Africa. Ground crews, it should be noted, had performed superbly, easily bettering their German and Italian rivals in terms of the number of serviceable aircraft available at any time to pilots and crew.

The African game was up. On 9 March, Field Marshal Rommel flew back to Germany on sick leave, less than three months after Field Marshal Friedrich Paulus had surrendered what remained of his frozen and half-starved 6th Army to the Russians at Stalingrad. The Germans, even Joseph Goebbels, Reichsminister for Public Enlightenment and Propaganda, referred to this, the final bloody encounter in the failed North African campaign against the combined British and US forces, as 'Tunisgrad'. The hard-fought Battle of Tunis had been a disaster, with 260,000 Italian and German soldiers made prisoners of war, and the Luftwaffe losing huge numbers of aircraft it badly needed in Europe on both the Western and the Eastern Front. After Stalingrad and 'Tunisgrad', Hitler and his once seemingly unstoppable military machine were on the defensive.

Promoted Wing Commander, George Westlake was now closely involved in planning air support, from mobile operations rooms, for the upcoming invasion of Sicily and, from there, to the Italian mainland. This was, Winston Churchill liked to say, the 'soft underbelly of Europe'. The more German forces that could be diverted to the Italian peninsula, the fewer divisions Hitler would have to oppose the long-mooted Allied invasion of Western Europe.

Curiously, it was at this moment that WDAF was renamed the Desert Air Force (DAF), a strange name for the multinational force, now including the USAAF 57th and 79th Fighter Groups, flying the Curtiss Warhawk (a Kittyhawk by another name), that was to operate up through Italy and into Austria and Yugoslavia. But then the WDAF name had always been a little misleading, its aircraft and crews flying over the Mediterranean and the Atlas Mountains as well as the deserts of North Africa.

George landed in Sicily on 5 September 1943, two days after the Eighth Army had waded ashore, itching to get back into the air in something more aggressive than the Percival Proctor and Miles Magister spotter planes he had been flying on recent forward control and reconnaissance missions. At least he had been up in the air again.

And then fate, or mosquitos to be exact, intervened. As General Montgomery's Eighth Army and US General Patton's Seventh Army battled towards Messina – pushing the Germans and Italians into a corner at the port on the north coast of the island within thirty-eight days of landing in Sicily – George went down, as did so many other Allied soldiers, with a nasty bout of malaria. Missing the invasion of Italy, he was in hospital in at first Tripoli and then Cairo for what would have been for him three very long months.

While recuperating, George had time to think about both his war to date and the war in general. The war was like a virus, a malaria of sorts infused with cordite that was spreading rapidly. His own war, when he thought about it, was one fought over sea and desert for the most part, from those early patrols over the Isle of Wight when he shot down his first bandit – that Bf109 off Selsey Bill – to the fast-paced action in Egypt, Libya and Tunisia. To date, he had not been asked to attack targets within the boundaries of a town or city, and yet millions in civvy street across Europe had faced days, weeks and even months of bombing and from all sides.

One had to admire the boys in Bomber Command, giving hell to Jerry and Herr Hitler, yet it was common knowledge that the horrific raid on Coventry, destroying the old city, was in part a tit for tat after our bombers' raid – Wellingtons and Hampdens – on Munich a few days earlier. They were after the railway yards, but, so the rumours went, they may well have tried to have a crack at the beer hall where Adolf was ranting that evening. Missed, sadly. Australian pilot on the next bed says the beer hall is owned by the local Löwenbräu brewery. Expensive German lager. They used to stock it on *The Flying Scotsman*. More than twice the price of a bottle of Bass…

What George missed, flying ops aside, was a new turn in Allied operations: the destruction of historic towns that, serving as Axis military strongholds, stood in the way of the advance on Messina on the northeast coast of Sicily. The last of these was Randazzo, with a population of about 10,000, close by Mount Etna. Many fled and many were killed as Randazzo was bombed to bits. On 11 August, twenty-year-old Lieutenant John Woodhouse (he was to become a distinguished post-war SAS officer) of the 1st East Surreys, 78th Division, wrote home:

My dear mum
I am on a hill with crowds of refugees sheltering nearby, they are half starved and ridden with disease, we have fed out of stuff left over from our rations… the devastation is

absolutely staggering, the Luftwaffe is a child's toy compared with the Allied Air Forces out here.

In hospital, George learned that his beloved Rangoon had been bombed, too. After the fall of Singapore in February 1942, the Japanese had slashed their way north up through Burma. They bombed Rangoon for three months before seizing the city in March. Smashed the docks and the nearby streets and houses he knew so well. What George didn't know was that, on 8 November 1943, as he whiled away his days in Cairo, an RAF raid on the Rangoon docks, now in Japanese hands, had hit the Botahtaung Pagoda, the exquisite 2,500-year-old shrine built to house relics, including a single strand of the Buddha's hair. The pagoda George had known so well as a boy had been blown to pieces.

Chin up. Soon enough, George would be in Italy.

Troops from 51st (Highland) Division unloading stores from tank landing craft on the opening day of the Allied invasion of Sicily, 10 July 1943.

FIVE

SICILY TO CALABRIA
AND THE GUSTAV LINE

Messina Strait, 11 August 1943

A ring of dazzling searchlights lit the night sky above the port of Messina. Allied aircraft bold or mad enough to fly into this aerial trap faced the criss-crossing fire of three hundred German and Italian anti-aircraft guns positioned on either side of the narrow stretch of water separating Sicily from mainland Italy. Flak, aircrews said, was worse than it was over the Ruhr. Over six ensuing nights, between 40,000 and 60,000 German and more than 60,000 Italian troops along with tanks, heavy guns, military vehicles and 2,000 tons of ammunition were spirited across the two-mile Strait of Messina to mainland Italy on board a flotilla of vessels. These included armed catamaran ferries, some powered by BMW aeroengines, designed by the aircraft engineer Ernst Siebel, a Luftwaffe colonel, for Operation Sea Lion, the postponed 1940 invasion of England. This escape, although more successful, was reminiscent of the evacuation of the British and French armies from Dunkirk in May and June that year.

The narrowness of the Messina strait, and the power of the heavy guns protecting it, made it next to impossible for the Royal Navy to attack the German flotilla crossing to Calabria. Over six nights, German losses amounted to a single motor raft. The only other vessel put out of action was the diesel-electric train ferry *Cariddi*, scuttled as the Allies closed in. This modern ship, launched from Trieste in 1932, had ferried 3,000 troops at a time back and forth across the strait. Resurfaced, rebuilt and recommissioned after the war, *Cariddi* served as a train ferry again until 1991. (I made several crossings on board *Cariddi* by both day and sleeper trains between Rome and gloriously Baroque, if still evidently war-damaged, Palermo.)

The German and Italian escape from Messina was meticulously planned and organised. So, for the most part, had been the Allied invasion of Sicily from North Africa. Again, in scenes that connected events in Sicily 1943 with those in Britain in 1940, Air Vice Marshal Sir Keith Park, who had led Fighter Command's 11 Group defending London and southeast England in the Battle of Britain and had, more recently, established RAF air superiority over Malta, sent waves of fighters from Malta, Gozo and Pantelleria (captured on 11 June) in support of the Allied armies and navies.

Under the overall command of US General Dwight D. Eisenhower, and with General Sir Harold Alexander as second-in-command, General Sir Bernard Montgomery was in charge of the British Eighth Army and Lieutenant

General George S. Patton the US Seventh Army in the assault on Sicily launched on 9 July. Following the German and Italian defeat in Tunisia, Allied bombers had begun strategic attacks on ports not only in Sicily – notably Messina and Palermo – but also on Naples and Cagliari in Sardinia. The multiple attacks were planned in part in the hope of confusing Kesselring's generals. Might the Allies invade Sardinia first or even bypass Sicily altogether?

The most successful bluff was realised through Operation Mincemeat. It seems appropriate that, not so long after the end of the war, this extraordinary episode was turned first into a hugely successful thriller, *The Man Who Never Was* (1953), and second, into the 1956 film of the same name directed by Ronald Neame, whose later films included *The Odessa File* (1974), based on Frederick Forsyth's 1972 thriller concerning the whereabouts of a former SS concentration camp commander protected by Odessa, the Organisation for Former Members of the SS.

Former Royal Navy officer Lieutenant Commander Ewen Montagu was the author of *The Man Who Never Was*. Together with Flight Lieutenant Charles Cholmondeley, an RAF Intelligence officer seconded at the time to MI5, a plot was hatched whereby on 30 April 1943, the submarine HMS *Seraph* launched the body of a drowned Royal Marines officer, Captain (acting Major) William Martin, off the coast of Heulva in southern Spain. Attached to the Captain's waistband was a case containing top-secret documents revealing that Greece and Sardinia, rather than Sicily, were the targets of a proposed Allied invasion of Europe following the victory in North Africa. This made sense. Greece especially. Punching up through the Balkans, the Allies would be able, all going well, to meet the Red Army and so fight Germany in strength from the east.

Washed ashore, the body of the drowned captain was found by local fishermen. Soon afterwards, the case and its documents were handed over by the nominally neutral Spanish to German intelligence. Hitler was informed. Field Marshal Rommel and three German Panzer divisions, one from France and two from the Eastern Front were dispatched to Salonika. The Greek coast was mined. Cholmondeley and Montagu's ruse had worked. Captain Martin had been a fiction, as were his secret documents and forensically thought-through personal effects, including a letter, with accompanying photograph, from his imaginary 'fiancée'. The uniformed corpse was, in fact, that of Glyndwr Michael, a homeless man originally from Aberbargoed in South Wales, found dead in a King's Cross warehouse in central London. His last meal had been a slice of rotting bread spread with rat poison.

At this stage in the embryonic Italian campaign, a host of new characters in new and even unprecedented roles began to join the Allied wagon train: intelligence officers and civil servants in ever growing numbers; press and public relations officers; and, especially important in the story of Venice and other art-historical Italian towns and cities, experts whose role was to identify and (in whatever way possible in the heat of battle) to protect and save invaluable works of art, including buildings. Known as the Monuments Men, and drawn mostly from Britain and the United States, they formed a loose-knit team of architects, art historians, artists, archivists and archaeologists, mostly in early middle age, assigned to MFAA (Monuments, Fine Arts and Archives Unit) and packed off to, at first, North Africa and then Sicily. Commissioned as captains and majors, they performed their work in onerous and often downright dangerous conditions. The initiative had support at the very highest level. Both President Roosevelt and Winston Churchill were keen advocates.

Starting in Sicily, the 'Monuments Men' worked under the auspices of the newly established Allied Military Government of Occupied Territories (AMGOT), known by those on combat duty as Aged Military Gentlemen on Tour. This was set up under Major-General Francis Rodd and his US counterpart, Colonel Charles Poletti.

Rodd was a polyglot former First World War artillery officer who had moved on to the Diplomatic Service and then the Bank of England, through which he met Mussolini in Italy. He befriended his hero, Colonel T. E. Lawrence of Arabia fame. Recommissioned in June 1940, he took part in the invasion of Sicily before his AMGOT appointment. Rodd was an ideal choice, as he was fluent in Italian, having spent a part of his childhood in Rome, where his father was British Ambassador, and part of his adult years as a diplomat in the city. He had come to appreciate Italian art, architecture and culture and had a measured understanding of the country's rival and sometimes violently opposed political factions. He also understood the role of the Mafia – 'less a secret society,' he wrote, 'than an attitude of mind'. All of this was key to understanding the military governance of occupied Italy.

Charles Poletti, son of working-class Italian immigrants, had only recently been Governor of New York. A Harvard-trained lawyer fluent in German and Italian, he had also studied at the universities of Rome and Bologna. He proved to be highly effective in reconstruction in the wake of the slow and destructive Allied advance north through Italy.

Before the invasion of Sicily, heavy Allied raids on the island's cities had wreaked terrible damage on its venerable churches and palaces. Palermo, a strategic port supplying the Italian military in North Africa, had been under attack by the RAF, based in Malta, since January 1941. Palermo was also an architectural jewel box bursting at its seams with memorable and glorious buildings. Bombs raining down on the port and shipping berthed there often went astray, hitting the densely occupied streets, squares and buildings of the city.

From early 1943, US B-17 Flying Fortress and B-24 Liberator bombers operating from French North Africa made heavier and more destructive raids. On 9 May, 211 US bombers sent to hit the harbour and railway marshalling yards did great damage to the city, killing at least 373 citizens. On 30 June, a US raid on the Boccadifalco airbase hit the city's university and main hospital. The following day, the RAF struck the Palazzo dei Normanni, Europe's oldest royal residence, initiated in 1072 just six years after the Norman Conquest of England. Several weeks earlier, RAF bombers had badly damaged the Norman and Baroque church of Santissimo Salvatore and smashed the interior of San Francesco Saverio, a Baroque Jesuit church designed by the brilliant Jesuit architect Angelo Italia – what a name – who shaped masterpiece after masterpiece and even entire town and city centres following the devastating Sicilian earthquake of 1693.

Almost as soon as Palermo was taken by the US Seventh Army on 22 July 1943, the *Regia Aeronautica* and Luftwaffe began bombing the city. By this time, civic and residential areas including Borgo Vecchio and San Pietro alla Cala had been blitzed into near oblivion, with terrible loss of life. They had been that bit too close to the port. All told, eleven major historic buildings were completely destroyed, and eighty-six churches, twenty *palazzi* and thirteen civic buildings were severely damaged. Imagine Venice on the receiving end of such brutal treatment.

'Palermo, when I came to it in 1943,' wrote AMGOT officer Major Lionel Fielden, 'was a town terribly and most unnecessarily wrecked by Allied bombardment. Looking at the houses along the lovely waterfront, who would not ask what purpose had been served by such barbaric destruction? The Liberation of Italy! The liberation of a rose by a sledgehammer.'

Major Fielden shared a 'tiny and very hideous villa' in the city with the exuberant Captain Edward 'Teddy' Croft-Murray, one of the most effective of the British Monuments Men. Fielden and Croft-Murray had met by chance on board the crowded SS *Aorangi*, a 17,500-ton transpacific liner and refrigerated cargo freighter launched in 1924 and commandeered by the Ministry of War Transport at the outset of the war. In a previous life ending in 1940, the newly commissioned forty-seven-year-old Major Fielden, a friend of Mahatma Gandhi and Lord Reith, had been Director General of All-India Radio.

Finding most of the men squeezed into *Aorangi* boorish, this sophisticated aesthete was delighted to find Teddy Croft-Murray in the crush while waiting to be assigned shared cabins on the once elegant ship, with its Louis XIV-style dining room and Jacobean smoking room. Fielden wrote that the officer in charge had said, 'Very well then, I want one major to go with seven colonels… Somebody let out a smothered gust of laughter. I looked around and caught the twinkling eye in a large face attached to the most untidy imaginable body. Somebody else had visualized a major perishing under the weight of colonels sevenfold. I wasn't alone on the ship. So I shifted around and spoke for the first time to Teddy Croft-Murray, the most intelligent and endearing character who ever went to Italy under the banner of AMG(OT).'

A fellow Oxford graduate, forty-five-year-old Croft-Murray, who liked to call himself an 'Ancient Monument', was Assistant Keeper of Prints and Drawings at the British Museum. His first assignment on arriving with the invasion force was to report damage to works of art in Sicily, including historic buildings. While coastal towns around the island were badly hit, precious inland sites like that of the Greek temple of Segesta, which had escaped destruction by the Carthaginians during the Greek–Carthage wars more than two thousand years before, tended to survive undamaged.

Operation Husky was the biggest amphibious invasion of the Second World War, with 180,000 soldiers landed in Sicily, compared with the 156,000 landed in Normandy on D-Day (6 June 1944). With support from the USAAF, RAF, the US

Navy and the Royal Navy – fronting six battleships, ten cruisers and two aircraft carriers and bombarding coastal defences and enemy tanks on or near coastal roads – the 7th and 8th Armies moved quickly up towards Messina, despite fierce fighting, 40°C summer heat, virulent malaria and the rivalry and misunderstandings between Patton and Montgomery. 'This is a horse race,' noted Patton, 'in which the prestige of the US Army is at stake.'

The fighting could be confused and messy. On 11 July, an armada of 144 Douglas C-47 transport planes flew towards Gela on the south coast, ferrying the US 504th Parachute Infantry Regiment and the 376th Parachute Field Artillery Battalion. They were fired on by Allied ships and ground troops newly established on the Sicilian beaches. Twenty-three C-47s were shot down. Eighty-one paratroopers were killed, 229 injured. There was a lot to learn.

And much to ignore, including, along with cases of rape and sexual assault, the massacring of civilians and prisoners of war by American troops. On 14 July, Sergeant Horace T. West, a cook with 180th Infantry Regiment, executed thirty-seven Italian and German prisoners with a Thompson sub-machine gun near Biscari airfield. That same day and near the same airfield, Captain John T. Compton of the 180th had thirty-five Italian prisoners shot and killed. Both Sergeant West and Captain Compton were reported by an officer. When told of the crimes by General Omar Bradley, General Patton noted in his diary, 'I told Bradley that it was probably an exaggeration, but in any case to tell the Officer to certify that the dead men were snipers or had attempted to escape or something, as it would make a stink in the press and also would make the civilians mad. Anyhow, they are dead, so nothing can be done about it.'

Something was done about it. Both men were court-martialled for war crimes. Initially sentenced to life imprisonment, West was back in service in November 1944 after serving jail time in North Africa, while Compton was acquitted. He was killed while fighting later in the Italian campaign. Reassigned to the 399th Infantry Regiment in France, after serving a fourteen-month prison sentence, West served as a sniper, claiming to have killed 130 German soldiers with 'Mabel', a Springfield rifle with a telescopic sight he had named after his wife.

Brutality grew as the war entered a new phase. Many level-headed soldiers on all sides of the conflict would have been horrified by the savage bombing of Naples, hit harder by the British and Americans than Palermo. A major port, the city harboured large parts of the Italian navy. It was an important rail hub, a home to industries – notably petroleum and steel – that fed Italy's and Germany's war machines. It was also densely occupied, beautifully set and home to a cheek-by-jowl scrum of slums and architectural magnificence. Poorly equipped for defence and with few conventional air raid shelters – there was a network of sorts of tunnels beneath the city – it was an easy target for Allied bombers.

While attacking the extensive port, bombers ravaged close-by neighbourhoods including Bagnoli, San Giovanni a Teduccio and Pozzuoli. By mid-1942, Naples was subject to carpet bombing. By the following January, and with the USAAF in action over the city, raids were made daily, the biggest of all taking place on 4 August 1943, a week before the Germans abandoned Sicily. Four hundred B-17s flew over the city at 20,000 feet in a ninety-minute raid to bomb a submarine base. The Flying Fortresses dropped incendiaries as well as high-explosive bombs. Neapolitans were particularly saddened by the torching of the impressive Baroque interior of the basilica of Santa Chiara.

With news that on 3 September the Allies had landed on the mainland and that the Italian government had surrendered, it seemed possible that Naples would be liberated from what was effectively German rule sometime quite soon. With Italian Fascist politicians, officials and generals in civilian dress already abandoning the city, that rule was gathered to a disconcerting degree in the hands of Colonel Water Scholl, a former Afrika Korps officer who seems to have adopted his moral compass more from Heinrich Himmler than Erwin Rommel. Scholl's, and indeed Hitler's, fear was that Naples would make an excellent base for the Allies. As such, plans were entertained for the hungry and increasingly ragged city's destruction.

And then, in a spontaneous and chaotic fashion, the people of Naples took violent action against their German masters. Following deadly attacks on German soldiers, Scholl decreed that 100 civilians would be executed for each one of his soldiers killed. Public executions took place with local people forced to attend. All Neapolitan men aged eighteen to thirty-three were to be transported to work camps in northern Italy and Germany. The city's port was to be destroyed. Scholl declared a curfew and a state of siege. The civilian tide broke. Neapolitans – men, women and children, released prisoners and the city's countless street urchins among them – joined in an attack on the Germans known as the Four Days of Naples. Between 27 and 30 September, citizens fought quite literally tooth and nail for their freedom. Gangs of children pinned isolated German soldiers to the ground, hammering nails into their heads with large stones. Corpses of their comrades were covered in human bite marks.

The Germans abandoned the city. In an act of pure spite, they torched the city's *Grande Archivio di Stato*, housed, since 1835, in the cloisters of the monastery of Santi Severino e Sossio and dating back to the tenth century. 'The extent of the disaster is enormous,' wrote Riccardo Filangieri, Superintendent of Archives. 'In that depository I had collected all the most precious series of documents coming from the various archives of the south of Italy. And their destruction has created an immense void in the historical sources of European civilization, a void which nothing will ever be able to fill.'

Scholl damaged the water supply and had booby traps set across the city. On 1 October, the tanks and armoured cars of the 1st King's Dragoon Guards and the Royal Scots Greys rumbled into shattered Naples. The Germans began aerial bombing. The physical damage to the city and, to a disturbing extent, the moral vacuum created by an assault on Naples now by the Germans, now by the Allies and then the Germans again were caught to darkly satirical effect in Curzio Malaparte's *La pelle* (*The Skin*), published in 1949. This independent-minded Italian journalist and liaison officer observed the European war, on both the Western and the Eastern Front, with unnervingly detached eyes.

In a brutally ravaged Naples, who was friend and who was foe? Neapolitans, observed Malaparte, jump 'for joy amid the ruins of their houses, unfurling foreign flags which until the day before had been the emblems of their foes, and throwing flowers from their windows on to the heads of the conquerors'. When the Americans arrive, Neapolitans sell them and their North African allies anything – *anything* – they want. Savagely ironic and shocking still, *The Skin* was banned on publication by the city of Naples and the Catholic Church. But Malaparte – a play on Bonaparte, his real name was Kurt Erick Sickert – was a brilliant writer who captured the horror of war in his own, slyly memorable way.

An artist, too. In *The Skin*, he tells the story of Field Marshal Rommel visiting his exquisite house on the edge of Capri not long before the Battle of El Alamein:

> I offered him a glass of Vesuvian wine from the vineyards of Pompeii. 'Prosit!' he said, raising his glass, and he drained it at a single draught. Then before leaving, he asked me whether I had bought my house as it stood or whether I had designed and built it myself. I replied – and it was not true – that I had bought the house as it stood. And, with a sweeping gesture, indicating the sheer cliff of Matromania, the three gigantic rocks of the Faraglioni, the peninsula of Sorrento, the islands of the Sirens, the faraway blue coastline of Amalfi, and the golden sands of Paestum, shimmering in the distance, I said to him: '*I* designed the scenery.'

Malaparte also designed, in quasi-fictional terms, the terrifying scenery of Naples as it was in the last two years of the war. Fiction, however, could only go so far in portraying the sheer horror.

While Italian and German soldiers would fight the British and Americans another day, and soon, they faced a dramatically changed political and military landscape in southern Italy. A heavy bombing raid made on Rome on 19 July 1943, the day after approval had been given for the Allied invasion of mainland Italy, had determined the fate of Benito Mussolini. More than five hundred USAAF bombers raided Rome's Ciampino and Littorio airports and the railway freight yard and steel works in the city's San Lorenzo district. Bombs struck apartment blocks along with the Papal Basilica of San Lorenzo, killing 3,000 people, many of them civilians. Pius XII wrote to President Roosevelt, calling on him not to make war on civilians. A week later a vote of no confidence in Mussolini was held by the Grand Fascist Council. The country was under threat. The dictator, who had lost his much-vaunted African empire, was evidently unable to defend the Eternal City.

On 25 July, King Victor Emmanuel III dismissed Mussolini and had him arrested. On 28 August, the deposed Italian leader was sent to the D-shaped (D for Duce) Hotel Campo Imperatore – Room 220, second floor – a ski resort 6,990 feet up on the challenging slopes of Monte Portella in the massif of Gran Sasso d'Italia. On 12 September, Mussolini was rescued on Hitler's orders. Led by *Hauptsturmführer* Otto Skorzeny, SS commandos and paratroopers flew to the remote mountain location in ten DFS 230 gliders. Operation Oak (*Unternehmen Eiche*) was one of the most daring rescue missions of the Second World War. Mussolini was bundled into a lightweight Fieseler Storch liaison aircraft that had landed close by, while Skorzeny stormed the hotel, and flown to Pratica di Mare airfield near Rome.

From Rome, Mussolini flew on via an overnight stop in Vienna to the *Wolfsschanze* (Wolf's Lair), Hitler's concrete bunker headquarters hidden in the forests of East Prussia. Here, the Duce was offered an impossible choice. Either accept the role of head of a newly decreed Italian Social Republic, a German puppet state, or else be witness to the wholesale German destruction of Milan, Turin and Genoa. Italy's prime industrial powerhouses, these were also historic cities of universally acclaimed art, culture, architecture and learning. They had, of course, been hit heavily by British bombing raids, the biggest to date on Milan on the night of 12 August, when 478 RAF Lancaster and Halifax heavy bombers hammered and scorched the city.

While Mussolini had been confined to the Hotel Campo Imperatore, the British had landed on the Italian mainland at Reggio di Calabria and Marshal Pietro Badoglio, the new Italian Prime Minister, had signed an armistice with the Allies. Hitler responded by attacking and disarming Italian forces and invading Italy. On 13 October, the Kingdom of Italy declared war on Germany. With two governments, Italy was plunged into what very soon became a vicious civil war. A month later, Field Marshal 'Smiling Albert' Kesselring, as the Allied soldiers knew him, whose own view was that the Allies should allow Italy to withdraw from the war, adopt a neutral stance and spare itself further loss of life and devastation, was appointed supreme commander of German forces in Italy.

Fully aware of Kesselring's military prowess, the Allies had already raided his headquarters at Frascati. USAAF General Jimmy Doolittle's order could not have been more to the point. 'Heavies [heavy bombers] will destroy the town of Frascati – this target is important and must be destroyed.' On the morning of 8 September, 131 B-17G Flying Fortresses equipped with the latest bomb-aiming equipment had flown over Frascati, southeast of Rome, at between 18,000 and 20,000 feet. According to the National Museum of the United States Air Force, the Norden bombsight, developed as early as 1932 for US Navy aircraft but fitted only slowly to USAAF bombers, allowed bombardiers to 'enter data about wind direction, airspeed and altitude into the bomb-sight's analog computer, which calculated wind drift and provided the correct aim point. An internal gyroscope provided the stability necessary for using the telescopic sight at high altitudes. When connected to the Sperry C-1 Autopilot, the Norden bombsight provided unprecedented accuracy.'

The historic town was wrecked. Four hundred and eighty-five civilians were killed. The raid was a calling card. Since Operation Torch, the USAAF had linked wings with DAF. Kesselring was unharmed.

While the Frascati raid had been relatively accurate, the sheer number of American bombers flying over the city was probably the main reason why it was so badly ravaged. (American newspapers repeated the claim made for the Norden bombsight that it was so accurate it could 'drop a bomb into a pickle barrel'.) A month on from the Frascati raid, 250 B-17s dropped bombs on ball-bearing factories at

Schweinfurt, Bavaria. Despite using Norden bombsights, just one in ten bombs fell within 500 feet of their target. The raid failed completely. Sixty bombers and 600 crewmen were lost.

Even so, the Germans decided it best to move their headquarters unceremoniously into the Soratte Bunker, a web of tunnels dug three miles into and up to 985 feet under Monte Soratte, a mountain ridge in the Tiber Valley thirty miles north of Rome. In *The Path to Rome* (1902), Hilaire Belloc, who had been on a walking pilgrimage from northern France, described Monte Soratte as standing up 'like an acropolis, but it was a citadel for no city. It stood alone, like the soul that once haunted its recesses and prophesied the conquering advent of the northern kings.'

Although complete with dormitories, kitchens, stores, heating and a communications centre, this soulless place was not somewhere any regular German soldier wished to spend any more time than necessary. Built by Italian military engineers, in case Rome came under siege, it remained Kesselring's HQ until June 1944.

For Kesselring, greater threats than bombing raids had been what he continued to perceive as the wholesale disorganisation of the Italian armed forces, their almost palpable lack of military drive and a chain of command that, nominally, had made German generals – Kesselring himself in Italy, Rommel then in North Africa – subordinate to their Italian counterparts. Rommel had been at loggerheads with Marshal Ettore Bastico, Governor General of Tripolitania. The Italians, Kesselring was sure, had been holding back vital military supplies. Rome itself, meanwhile, seemed wholly unaffected by the war.

Worse still for Kesselring was Hitler's continued reluctance to take the Mediterranean war as seriously as he believed Germany needed to. Before the Allied invasion of Italy, the capture of Malta had been Kesselring's strategic priority. If the British had lost the island, their supply route to North Africa would have been cut. If so, Rommel may well have triumphed. Focused on the Eastern Front, the Führer would not be drawn on the matter. Finally, Kesselring faced Hitler at the *Wolfsschanze*. Tempers ran high. Germany must take Malta. At the end of the meeting, Hitler grasped Kesselring's arm. 'Keep your shirt on, Field Marshal Kesselring,' he rasped. 'I'm going to do it.' He didn't.

Defended by the Hurricanes and Spitfires of the RAF commanded by Air Vice Marshal Keith Park, Kesselring's counterpart in the Battle of Britain, and supplied by the Merchant Navy guarded by the British Fleet, Malta did not fall. The supply route to North Africa stayed open. The British and Commonwealth armies there grew in strength and confidence. Now ashore on the Italian mainland, they believed, as did the Americans, that they would be able to march rapidly up the leg of Italy towards the Alps.

Progress, however, proved slower – much slower – than expected. By December, though, the Allies (Montgomery's Eighth Army on the east, US General Mark Clark's Fifth Army to the west) had liberated Naples, seized the vital airfields at Foggia on the Adriatic and reached Kesselring's Gustav (Winter) Line, a sequence of determined defences up to twenty miles deep set coast to coast across the Apennines guarding the very few approaches to Rome and land routes north. At its centre stood the venerable and revered Benedictine abbey of Monte Cassino.

Here, the Allied armies, supplied in large part from the port of Bari south of Foggia, ground to a halt as a brutal winter set in. It had not been for a lack of trying. If the Gustav Line had a weak point, it was surely on the Adriatic coast, where the mountains gave way to plains criss-crossed by rivers giving on to the sea. When, though, on 23 November the Eighth Army crossed one of the principal rivers, the Sangro, it had swollen, from its normal width of 80 feet to 300 feet. According to General Montgomery, 'the troops were quite magnificent... the water was icy cold and heavy snow fell in the mountains where the river rised. Many were drowned.' This horrible crossing had been made with the assistance of DAF employing its increasingly effective Rover David Cab rank system, devised by Group Captain David Haysom.

Self-sufficient Mobile Opps Room Units, each comprising eighteen-strong teams comprised of two officers, a sergeant, a radio operator, cipher clerk, technicians, drivers, mechanics, cook and guards travelling in an armoured car and trailer, a light truck and three Jeeps with trailers, worked with the army to locate ground targets such as enemy gun emplacements, fortifications, tanks, field artillery and heavy troop dispositions. Using VHF radios, Rover David officers called down waiting DAF fighters and fighter bombers, their pilots using the same large-format grid maps as their colleagues on the ground. The system worked well and was to be used to devastating effect. The weather at the eastern flank of the Gustav Line was, however, more than a match for the Eighth Army, DAF and Rover David. Driving rain, flooded rivers and fierce German resistance held the Allies at bay.

And there had been danger from the air when least expected. On the afternoon of 2 December, the day DAF Spitfires, Warhawks and Kittyhawks flew 340 sorties on behalf of the Eighth Army and a further seventy with Warhawks in support of Yugoslav partisans, Air Vice Marshal Coningham called a press conference at Bari, a long way south of the Gustav Line and considered by now to be out of reach of a dwindling Luftwaffe. The German air war, said Coningham, was over. 'I would consider it a personal insult if the enemy should send so much as one plane over the city.' At 7.30 p.m. that evening, bombs fell down on the port from the fuselages of 105 Ju-88s commanded by Field Marshal Wolfram von Richthofen, cousin of the legendary First World War flying ace, Manfred von Richthofen – the 'Red Baron' – with whom he flew in combat during the First World War. Kesselring had wanted to bomb also the Foggia airfields now occupied by large numbers of Allied bombers, fighters and fighter-bombers, but he was persuaded by Richthofen to go all out for Bari.

German reconnaissance revealed the city's docks were clearly visible after sunset (there was no black-out; they were apparently oblivious to air raids), while Allied ships were unloaded late into the night. Richthofen's Ju-88s sunk twenty-eight of them, damaging a further twelve. The port was put out of action. Unexpectedly, the badly damaged US Liberty ship SS *John Harvey* carrying a top-secret load of 2,000 mustard gas bombs exploded, releasing its terrifying cargo into the air and into the water. Allied soldiers, sailors, merchant seaman, dockers and civilians died horrible deaths. Washington and London insisted on a cover-up, even though Field Marshal Harold Alexander, Allied Commander-in-Chief, insisted on pursuing and discovering the truth. A fragment of an M47A1 mustard gas bomb was discovered in the wreckage of SS *John Harvey*. Not content with dispatching mustard gas to Italy, to be used, Washington said, in retaliation if the Germans initiated gas attacks, which they never did, the Americans were shortly to use napalm.

Records are unclear as to whether napalm was dropped on mainland Italian targets during the Second World War. The first combat demonstration of this terrifying chemical weapon, however, was made in Sicily in August 1943, when US troops torched a wheatfield thought to be sheltering Germans with flamethrowers. Invented the year before by the chemist Louis Fieser at Harvard University, napalm was a self-igniting fuel-gel mix with great visco-elasticity, meaning it could be projected over long distances. Moreover, it stuck to targets, ensuring enduring destruction, horrendous in contact with human skin.

The American historian Robert M. Neer has written of the ultimate use of napalm in the Second World War, to immolate entire cities in Japan:

On the night of March 9, 1945, about 690,000 pounds of flaming napalm from M-69 bombs burned 15 square miles of central Tokyo. A supernatural open chimney of flames and smoke rose 18,000 feet over the city amid gale-force winds. Official tabulations recorded 87,793 people dead from the firestorm – more than from the nuclear explosions at Hiroshima or Nagasaki – and 40,918 injured, over 1 million homeless, 267,171 buildings wrecked, and 18 percent of Tokyo's industrial area and almost two-thirds of its commercial district destroyed. Airmen gagged and vomited from the smell of burning flesh penetrating their B-29s. Tail gunners saw a red glow from the burning city 150 miles away on the flight home.

Mustard gas, napalm, the wanton destruction of Naples by the Germans as they abandoned the city, the massacre of Italian POWs in Sicily by US infantry under the command of General Patton and whatever the SS were up to north of the Apennines – General Alexander, a cultured man who spoke Italian well, along with French, German, Russian and Urdu, now understood that the war in Italy would indeed be much less 'clean' than it had been in the North African desert.

Harold Macmillan, British Minister in Residence in the Mediterranean, found the atmosphere of Alexander's mess at the former royal palace of Caserta, a Baroque masterpiece to the immediate north of Naples and built for the Kings of Italy, to be like that of the high tables of Oxbridge colleges. Over dinner, the General preferred to discuss Roman military campaigns and architecture. He enjoyed painting historic Italian townscapes. He remembered being torn between art school and Sandhurst. What he did not want to address was the increasingly brutal destructiveness facing him in what would be a prolonged fight to push the Germans from Italy.

Quite how far the destruction of Italy's heritage could be allowed to go was an increasingly tricky and morally trying question. The limit as to what could be bombed to prosecute the war had been reached, some thought, that summer, when news had reached HQ that Pompeii had been bombed overnight on 24–5 August 1943. This was during the intense Allied campaign aimed at knocking out German and Italian supply routes, factories and other targets that, if destroyed, would ease the passage of the 15th Army Group into mainland Italy.

Speaking on the morning of 25 August, Amadeo Maiuri, Pompeii's Superintendent of Archaeology at Pompeii, said,

At 10 p.m. in the evening of yesterday, twenty-fourth of the current month, the excavation site at Pompeii was struck by three bombs during an aerial bombardment of nearby towns in the Vesuvius area: one bomb fell on the Forum area, another on the house of Romulus and Remus, causing considerable structural damage; a third bomb fell on the Antiquarium, with serious damage to archaeological material, which is only partially salvageable. In view of the continuation and intensification of aerial attacks in the area, I believe it is necessary to call for intervention by neutral countries to prevent the blinkered and brutal violence that threatens to destroy Pompeii, an inviolable monument to all human civilization. Visiting the site in person, I ascertained the damage and took remedial measures. I applaud the exemplary conduct of the night watch staff.

The number of bombs that fell on Pompeii that night may well have been many more than Maiuri's 'three'. Thirty, according to some accounts. Whatever the tally, Pompeii was hit again by USAAF, RCAF (Royal Canadian Air Force) and RAF bombers a further nine times, with somewhere between 150 and 170 bombs striking the Ancient Roman town, partially destroyed and partly preserved in lava in 79AD, when Vesuvius erupted. There was much for the custodians of Pompeii to fear. Aside from Allied bombs, the threat of invasion had prompted gangs of thieves to plunder the site, damaging the fabric of the ancient buildings as they did so. Rumours spread in military circles to the effect that German troops might have been hiding among the ruins of Pompeii. This proved to be untrue, yet the rumour was finally squashed only when Allied soldiers entered the site on 29 September, and the bombing stopped. By then, more than a hundred Roman-era buildings had been damaged.

With Rome itself in mind, late in the year the Allies planned Operation Shingle, a major landing on the beaches at Anzio on the west coast, north of the Gustav Line. The brainchild of Winston Churchill, it would, if all went to plan, outflank Kesselring's defences and open a clear path to Rome. The operation's commander, US Major General John Lucas, had remarkably little faith in the mission. In his diary, he confided, 'They will end up putting me ashore with inadequate forces and get me in a serious jam... Then, who will get the blame?' He added, the operation 'has a strong odour of Gallipoli and apparently the same amateur was still on the coach's bench'. He meant Churchill, who had been key to the planning of the wretched Gallipoli campaign in the First World War that, from the first British imperial assault on the Turkish beaches, led to the deaths of a quarter of a million soldiers on both sides and a victory for the Turks.

When Lucas landed at Anzio, he appeared reluctant to move out to fight the German 10th Army behind the Gustav Line. This gave Kesselring the time he needed to move his tanks and artillery around Anzio. 'I had hoped we were hurling a wildcat onto the shore,' said Churchill, 'but all we got was a beached whale.' The cautious Lucas was replaced by Major General Truscott, but the Allied breakout was not happening any time soon.

On 16 February 1944, the Germans launched Operation *Fischfang* (Fishing), an all-out attack supported by fearsome Tiger tanks along the course of the Via Anziate leading from Anzio towards Rome. The loss of American and British life was horrific. Among those killed was Second Lieutenant Eric Waters, 8th Battalion Royal Fusiliers. Nearly sixty years later, his son, Roger Waters of Pink Floyd fame, wrote and recorded a song called 'When the Tigers Broke Free' in memory of his father. Like Gallipoli, Anzio remains an unstaunched wound.

On 17 March 1944, Vesuvius, which of course had destroyed Pompeii in the first place, erupted, damaging three villages, killing twenty-six people and displacing 12,000 others. As if asserting its pre-eminence, and in revenge for US bombing raids, it also destroyed eighty-eight twin-engine B-25 Mitchells of 340th Bombardment Group based at Pompeii air base. Destruction, directed and wanton, was in the air and all around.

'Air raid at Monte Cassino, February 1944' by Peter McIntyre, New Zealand's official war artist.

SIX

FIGHTING IN A MUSEUM

Monte Cassino, 14 February 1944

Allied guns blasted leaflets over the abbey of Monte Cassino and the small town below. Believing, mistakenly, that this great testament to Western civilisation, sited 1,700 feet above the valley road leading to Rome, was a makeshift German fortress at the heart of the Winter Line obstructing their painfully slow advance north, the Allies announced their intention to bomb it. Monks, if they were still there, would be given a safe passage from the abbey on 16 February.

On the cold blue morning of 15 February, a fleet of USAAF bombers (Boeing B-17 Flying Fortresses, North American B-25 Mitchells and Martin B-26 Marauders) from the US 12th and 15th air force bases at Foggia, dropped not leaflets but 1,150 incendiary and high-explosive bombs on the monastery, founded in the early sixth century by Saint Benedict. Stormed in earlier centuries by Vandals – their name synonymous from their sacking of Rome in 455 with wilful destruction – Lombards, Saracens and Normans, Monte Cassino had survived Goths and the 'Dark Ages' to nurture such profound theologians as St Thomas Aquinas, while treasuring invaluable literary works, among them the last surviving manuscript of Tacitus's *Histories*. The abbey also housed historic archives and cherished works of art.

Around one in ten of the bombs dropped by the US bombers hit their target. Those that did were enough to blow the abbey to kingdom come. That afternoon, 746 artillery pieces firing 200,000 rounds pounded the ruins. Dive bombers, among them RAF Kittyhawks of DAF's 239 Wing, continued the destruction on 16 and 17 February. There had been no Germans there. Allied commanders had been misinformed. Some 250 civilians, including women and children who had sought refuge in the abbey, were killed, many of them crammed into a stairwell behind the abbey's main door. German positions behind and above the abbey were untouched. As the dust settled, battle-hardened Luftwaffe *Fallschirmjäger* paratroopers moved in. The ruins made excellent gun-emplacements. Thousands of Allied soldiers were to die here – there were 55,000 casualties – in the ensuing months before the abbey was finally seized by Polish troops. By its end, the prolonged fight for Monte Cassino over five blood-soaked months was, at best, a Pyrrhic victory for the Allies.

The forty or so people who survived the bombing of the abbey, a miracle in itself, made their way out early in the morning of 17 March, led down a mule path across lines of fire by the seventy-nine-year-old abbot, Gregorio Diamare.

Reciting the rosary, they came across a German first-aid station where the badly wounded were taken to hospital by ambulances. The monks, all except one, were driven to the monastery of Sant'Anselmo all'Aventino in Rome. The missing monk was eighty-year-old Fra Carlomanno Pellagalli, seen by German paratroopers by the tomb of St Benedict. Some thought he was a ghost. *Obergefreiter* (Senior Lance Corporal) Karl Schonauer, the first German soldier to climb into the ruins after the bombing, offered him a blanket. In the general confusion, Fra Carlomanno disappeared. He was not seen again.

In the aftermath of the bombing, it was found that a junior British intelligence officer seems to have mistranslated an intercepted German radio message. Asked if the 'abt' was in the abbey, a German paratroop officer had replied in the affirmative. By 'abt' he meant the abbot and not, as the British intelligence officer thought, a battalion. That mistaken 'abt' set the fuse for the destruction of the abbey. Perhaps, of course, 'abt' for battalion was the word Allied commanders had wanted to hear. Their soldiers had fought for all too long in the shadow of the abbey in wretched conditions exposed to heavy artillery fire they believed was directed by spotters in the monastery, if not by guns installed there. Numerous reports from officers on the ground agreed, communicating their assertions to their C-in-C, General Alexander.

Even then, there had been qualms. Initially, Lieutenant General Mark C. Clark, in command of the US Fifth Army, refused to sanction the bombing raid. Many of his soldiers were Roman Catholics. Responding to a request by Brigadier

H. K. Dimoline of the 4th Indian Division, Lt General Sir Bernard Freyberg VC, DSO and three bars (meaning three further DSOs), commanding Indian and New Zealand battalions of the British Eighth Army, and who in 1922 had spent his honeymoon in Italy, called for raids by 239 Wing fighter bombers. These would blast holes in the 150-foot-high, ten-foot-thick abbey walls, allowing his 4th Indian Division to storm the citadel without destroying it. General Alexander gave the order, delegated to the uncertain General Clark, to bomb Monte Cassino. In a Pontius Pilate-like gesture, Clark told Alexander, his superior officer, 'You give me a direct order and we'll do it.'

While many soldiers who had been fighting in some of the worst conditions encountered in Western Europe cheered as the US bombers rained hell on the heavenly abbey, others were dismayed. Rather than fighter-bombers, the USAAF flew wave after wave of medium and heavy bombers. When they roared away, the battalions of Freyberg's 4th Indian Division were unready to follow through, allowing the crack German 1st Parachute Division to occupy the smouldering ruins. When the 4th Indian Division finally attacked, scrambling on all fours up the jagged slopes of what soldiers called 'Monastery Hill', its men were cut down by German machine guns.

A lack of preparedness, however, had not been the 4th Division's fault. There had been no warning of the exact time of the attack. This was treated as an exclusively air force matter with no proper communication with the army. Brigadier Osmond de Turville Lovett of the 7th Indian Brigade recalled, 'I was called on the blower and told that the bombers would be over in fifteen minutes... even as I spoke the roar [of aircraft] drowned my voice as the first shower of eggs [bombs] came down.' At the HQ of the 4/16th Punjabis, the adjutant wrote, 'We went to the door of the command post and gazed up... there we saw the white trails of many high-level bombers. Our first thought was that they were the enemy. Then somebody said, "Flying Fortresses!"'

The following day, the raid by fifty-nine Allied fighter-bombers caused further destruction and, doubtless, confusion and danger for Indian troops. Freyberg's New Zealand Corps, which was meant to storm Monte Cassino alongside Indian Army troops, was still two days from the battle scene.

In Britain, the public had been prepared for an attack on the abbey before the misreading of the German 'abt' signal. On 11 February, the *Daily Mail* ran an army-fed lead story: 'Nazis Turn Cassino Monastery into Fort', adding to reports splashed in the *New York Times* of German observation posts, German uniforms hanging from a clothesline in the abbey courtyard and artillery positions sited fifty yards from the abbey walls. The newspaper may well have got its 'facts' from Lieutenant General Ira C. Eaker, Commander-in-Chief of the Mediterranean Allied Air Forces, who had flown over Monte Cassino with Lieutenant General Jacob L. Devers, deputy to General Sir Henry 'Jumbo' Maitland Wilson, Supreme Allied Commander of the Mediterranean Theatre based in Algiers. But Major General Geoffrey Keyes, US II Corps commander serving under General Mark Clark, had flown over the abbey several times. He had seen no evidence of German occupation. Of Eaker's and Devers' reports, Keyes said, 'They've been looking so long they're seeing things.' Eaker and Devers had watched the raid, taking pride in the efficacy of their bombers and in the tight formations they flew in over the doomed abbey.

The Allies had given their word to Pope Pius XII that Monte Cassino would not be attacked. At the time, Alexander believed that the Germans had broken their word by occupying the abbey and thus justifying the bombing raid. Lying on the ground less than two miles from the abbey, Alexander witnessed the destruction. General Clark refused to join him. Clark, however, experienced the effects of the raid by default. Sixteen bombs intended for Monte Cassino fell on the Fifth Army compound at Presenzano, *seventeen miles* from their intended target, exploding near the trailer the American general was working in.

Eaker and Devers' efforts were certainly appreciated by Major General Francis Tuker of the 4th Indian Division. From a hospital bed in Caserta, fifty miles south of Monte Cassino, where he was recovering from a recurrent bout of tropical fever, Tuker called for a 'blockbuster' bomb attack to reduce the supposed German garrison in the abbey 'to helpless lunacy'. In Naples, the general had found a book dating from 1879 detailing the massive construction of the abbey. What was required was 'sheer unending pounding for days and nights by artillery and air'. Although feverish, Tuker's appeals touched a nerve with Allied commanders. Even if the abbey was not in German hands, it may well be soon enough. Best to get rid of this bulwark standing in the way of the Allied advance on Rome.

Whatever the immediate circumstances, those fated to destroy Monte Cassino were able to fall back on a letter written by their Supreme Commander:

Allied Force Headquarters
Office of the Commander-in-Chief
29 December 1943
Subject: Historical Monuments
To: All Commanders

Today we are fighting a country which has contributed a great deal to our cultural inheritance, a country rich in monuments which by their creation helped and now in their old age illustrates the growth of the civilisation which is ours. We are bound to respect those monuments so far as war allows.

If we have to choose between destroying a famous building and sacrificing our own men, then our men's lives count infinitely more and the buildings must go. But the choice is not always so clear-cut as that. In many cases the monuments can be spared without any detriment to operational needs. Nothing can stand against the argument of military necessity. That is an accepted principle. But the phrase 'military necessity' is sometimes used where it would be more truthful to speak of military convenience or even of personal convenience. I do not want it to cloak slackness or indifference.

It is a responsibility of higher commanders to determine through A.M.G. officers the locations of historical monuments whether they be immediately ahead of our front line or in areas occupied by us. This information passed to lower echelons through normal channels places the responsibility on all Commanders of complying with the spirit of this letter.

Dwight D. Eisenhower
General, U.S. Army
Commander-in-Chief

Eisenhower would have been aware of the 1907 Hague Convention prompted by US President Theodore Roosevelt. This proved to be the last international agreement made before 1939 concerning the legalities of bombardment in war. Although the Convention was held just four years after the Wright brothers demonstrated sustained powered flight, a number of its Articles could refer to any form of warfare. Article 25 said, 'The attack or bombardment, by whatever means, of towns, villages, dwellings, or buildings which are undefended is prohibited.' Article 26 added, 'The officer in command of an attacking force must, before commencing a bombardment, except in cases of assault, do all in his power to warn the authorities.' And Article 27 stated, 'In sieges and bombardments all necessary steps must be taken to spare, as far as possible, buildings dedicated to religion, art, science, or charitable purposes, historic monuments, hospitals, and places where the sick and wounded are collected, provided they are not being used at the time for military purposes. It is the duty of the besieged to indicate the presence of such buildings or places by distinctive and visible signs, which shall be notified to the enemy beforehand.'

Few or none of these guidelines were abided by in either the First or the Second World War. At the outset of war in 1939, US President Franklin Roosevelt had got an agreement from the major European powers including Germany not to bomb civilian targets outside combat zones. This, though, was so much 'Jaw Jaw'. Soon enough, Britain and Germany were bombing their enemy's cities with abandon.

There were then, of course, as there always have been and perhaps always will be, those who argue that concerns for works of art and architecture in time of war are somehow decadent and wrong-headed. What matters is human life. It is important to remember, though, that all the many historic buildings and the works of art within them standing in the way of tanks and bombers, and in range of broadsides from Allied warships, too, in December 1943 were the work of humans. They embodied more than something of the best of us. They *were* civilisation made tangible, who we were, who we are, expressed in brick, stone and marble. And built by human hands.

Churches are prayers in stone. While there have long been clergy who have argued that the Church itself has no need of buildings, humans do build and always have done – both for essential shelter and to shape places where people can gather protected from the elements and share and celebrate their beliefs and rituals. Over centuries, churches somehow absorb and reflect the faith of those who built them, of those who have nurtured them. Their loss is as much intangible as tangible.

Addressing Congress immediately after the bombing of Monte Cassino, President Roosevelt quoted Eisenhower's letter. German propaganda had a field day, revelling in its depiction of the barbaric nature of its enemies. Although the Pope himself was silent, his Cardinal Secretary of State, Luigi Maglione, told Harold Tittmann, a US Vatican diplomat, that the attack on the abbey was a 'colossal blunder...gross stupidity'.

The Germans came out smelling of incense. In December 1943, Kesselring had ordered German units not to use the abbey as a defensive position despite its strategic location in his defensive Gustav Line stretched west to east across the Italian peninsula to hold up the Allied advance on Rome. Kesselring informed both the Vatican and the Allies. More than this, in autumn 1943 the treasures of Monte Cassino were transferred to the safekeeping of the Vatican and Castel Sant'Angelo in Rome. This ambitious scheme had been proposed by two officers of the Hermann Göring Panzer Division, Captain Maximilian Becker, an army medic, and Lieutenant Colonel Julius Schlegel. Despite Abbot Gregorio Diamare's initial doubts, within three weeks that November, Becker and Schlegel transported 800 papal documents, 80,500 volumes from the abbey's libraries, 100,000 prints, 200 parchment manuscripts and 500 block-printed medieval pamphlets, along with old master paintings, including Titians, Goyas and an El Greco in 100 lorry convoys, accompanied by monks, to Rome and the Vatican.

Perhaps inevitably, several crates made their way to Carinhall, the country seat of Hermann Göring in the Schorfheide Forest, northeast of Berlin. At Monte Cassino, a mass was celebrated in the abbey church followed by a presentation of signed parchment scrolls in Latin to General Paul

Conrath, commander of the Hermann Göring Panzer Division, in tribute to Schlegel and Becker.

The fighting immediately before and immediately after the Allied occupation of the ruins of Monte Cassino was as unholy as it was destructive. Mountain and hillside villages and small towns were ravaged. A post-war count showed that 96 percent of the buildings of Cisterna di Latina had been destroyed in the fighting between January and March 1944 as General Clark's Fifth Army encountered a blistering German counter-attack, as the Americans tried to push inland from the surprise landing on the beaches of Anzio made on 22 January. This was both a bid to attack Kesselring's Gustav Line from behind and to cut off the retreat route of the German 10th Army, should Kesselring pull it back from Monte Cassino.

The destruction of their homes and even, as in the case of Cisterna di Latina, entire villages, was, however, just one of the tragedies inflicted on civilians. According to Norman Lewis, a second lieutenant with the 1st King's Dragoon Guards,

> The French colonial troops ('Goumiers', that is Berber, Arab and Senegalese irregular auxiliary troops – most were from exclusively Moroccan units – serving with French Expeditionary Force of Italy) are on the rampage again. Whenever they take a town or a village, a wholesale rape of the population takes place. Recently all females in the villages of Patricia, Pofi, Isoletta, Supino, and Morolo were violated. In Lenola, which fell to the Allies on 21 May, fifty women were raped, but – as these were not enough to go

135

round – children and even old men were violated. It is reported to be normal for two Moroccans to assault a woman simultaneously, one having normal intercourse while the other commits sodomy. In many cases severe damage to the genitals, rectum and uterus has been caused. In Castro di Volsci doctors treated 300 victims of rape, and at Ceccano the British have been forced to build a guarded camp to protect the Italian women.

According to a report in *Il Corriere delle Regioni* (14 March 2021) sourcing documents from the National Association of Civilian Victims of War,

In S. Andrea, the Moroccans raped 30 women and two men; in Vallemaio two sisters (aged 15 and 18) had to satisfy a platoon of 200 goumiers. In Esperia, 700 women were raped out of a population of 2,500 inhabitants. Even the parish priest, Don Alberto Terrilli, in an attempt to defend two girls, was tied to a tree and raped for a whole night. He died two days later from internal lacerations. In Pico, a girl was crucified with her sister. After the gang violence, she [was] killed. Pollica reached the pinnacle of bestiality... girls and old women were raped; the men who reacted were sodomized, shot dead, emasculated or impaled alive.

In January 1947, the French government made compensation payments to 1,488 victims of sexual violence for crimes committed by French colonial troops. In 2019, the Italian Senate launched its own investigation, finding that 2,000 women and 600 men had been raped. In *The Skin*, Curzio

Malaparte tells of Neapolitan women selling their 'merchandise' on street corners. 'This consisted of boys and girls of eight or ten, whom the soldiers – Moroccans, Indians, Algerians, Madagascans – caressed with their fingers, slipping their hands between the buttons of their short trousers, or lifting their dresses. "Two dollars the boys, three dollars the girls!" shouted the women.'

Who knew? General Charles de Gaulle, leader of the Free French, was seen decorating French soldiers in some of the very villages where these atrocities were enacted. Did anyone tell him? Probably not. A number of passing American soldiers did know but were told not to intervene – on the side of the angels – as their job was to fight the Germans, not the French. German atrocities were all too common. By this stage of the Italian campaign, there was not much that American and British soldiers hadn't seen. While not always angels themselves, certain incidents proved too much to bear. When Lieutenant John Warrender and his Royal Scots Greys tanks, in Italy between September 1943 and January 1944, had on one occasion encountered German soldiers, whom they caused to surrender, sporting women's underwear around their necks, it was impossible for the young officer to restrain his men. The Germans were shot.

The psychological complexities and moral ambiguities involved in fighting a brutal, exhausting war were all too real if not always or indeed often understood by those involved. On landing at Salerno on 9 September 1943, Lieutenant Warrender's tank had been hit by a German shell while attempting to drive onto the beach in water that was simply too deep. His driver was mortally wounded. Warrender had pulled him out. The NCO driver, a fellow Scot – from the East End of Glasgow – had been with the Lieutenant in their fight through North Africa and Sicily. He asked Warrender, who had no idea until then that his comrade was a Catholic, to offer him the Last Rites. Warrender did so, and as he did, he pledged himself to the Roman Church. There was a God, but whose side was he on?

General Clark was simply too busy to concern himself with the morality of rape and butchery. He was certainly having quite a war. On 28 January 1944, the patrol torpedo boat ferrying him to the beachhead at Anzio had been fired on accidentally by the US Navy, killing and wounding several sailors around him. There was, of course, the occasion of the bombs meant for Monte Cassino dropped on his HQ on 15 February courtesy the USAAF. On 10 June, while being flown in a Stinson L-5 Sentinel liaison aircraft over Civitavecchia, not far from Rome, his pilot hit the cable of a barrage balloon and span around it. The Sentinel broke free and its pilot, Major John T. Walker, was able to crash land in a meadow. The men were uninjured.

By then, Clark was in Rome, for which he was much criticised by his senior officers. General Alexander's plan, once the Germans were driven off Monte Cassino, had been for Clark to trap and contain the German 10th Army and to wait for the arrival of the main body of the Fifth Army and Montgomery's Eighth Army to arrive. The destruction or surrender of General von Vietinghoff's 10th Army may well have foreshortened the war in Italy by some months. Clark, however, had other plans. With his press and PR team in tow, he split his VI Corps in two. The smaller part was charged with holding up the German retreat from Monte Cassino; his – the larger part – headed northwest to Rome. The German 10th Army meanwhile was on its way to join arms with the 14th Army and thus to present a formidable defence against the Allied armies as they pushed doggedly north.

General Clark entered Rome on 4 June 1944, two days before D-Day. Propaganda leaflets had been dropped on the city that morning by order of General Alexander. Romans were called upon 'to stand shoulder to shoulder to protect the city from destruction'. Hitler, meanwhile, had ordered that the destruction and vandalism caused by German forces retreating from Naples in autumn 1943 were not to be repeated in Rome. On 14 August 1943, the Italian government had declared Rome an Open City. It had, in other words, abandoned all defensive efforts and should be occupied peacefully by the Allies.

Allied aerial raids on the city had begun on 19 July 1943, when Rome, then in German hands, was targeted by 521 bombers. In the morning, they hit a steel factory and railway yards in the San Lorenzo district, in the process wrecking nearby apartment blocks – killing 1,500 people – and damaging the venerable Papal Basilica of San Lorenzo fuori le Mura, the shrine of Saint Lawrence martyred in 258 AD. The Pope and many American Catholics condemned this and later raids that, despite the Open City declaration, continued until 18 March 1944, a day when 100 citizens died.

Adolf Hitler had visited Rome, along with Naples and Florence, in May 1938. A highlight of his tour was a visit to the Pantheon, the remarkably intact circular temple commissioned by Emperor Hadrian and completed in 126AD. 'For a short while I stood in this space [the rotunda] – what majesty! I gazed at the large open oculus and saw the universe and sensed what had given this space the name Pantheon – God and the world are one.'

Back in Berlin, Hitler charged his architect, Albert Speer, to draw up plans for a supersized Pantheon for Berlin, at 950 feet high. The oculus, or roof light, in the centre of the dome, at 150 feet in diameter, would have been so big that Michelangelo's dome of St Peter's could have been lowered through it. Only test foundations of this building, to be called the Volkshalle, were built before the war put an end to the project. Hitler remained in thrall to Italy. At dinner on 21 July 1941 – he had visited frontline troops in Latvia that day – he remarked, 'The magic of Florence and Rome, of Ravenna, Siena, Perugia! Tuscany and Umbria, how lovely they are! The smallest palazzo in Florence or Rome is worth more than all Windsor Castle. If the English destroy anything in Florence or Rome, it will be a crime. In Moscow, it wouldn't do any harm; nor in Berlin, unfortunately.'

Hitler may well have raised an eyebrow if he had been shown a translation of an article published in the popular *Sunday Dispatch* newspaper (19 January 1941) and written by H. G. Wells, Stalin apologist and author of *The War of the Worlds*, calling for the bombing of Rome:

Every common-sense person in the world must be asking this question. Three facts stand out. First, raiders have bombed Buckingham Palace, St. Paul's and Lambeth Palace, and have shattered valuable stained glass in Parliament and

Westminster. Secondly, the Italians confess that they shared in these feats. Thirdly, Rome is within easy range of the British Fleet and the Naval Air Arm, and it would be the most practicable thing in the world to treat St. Peter's, the Vatican, the Duce and King Victor Emmanuel to an enlarged version of this mischief which is being inflicted with impunity on London... I cannot see why Roman citizens, who perhaps do not possess our vulgar Cockney spunk, should not spend a few thoughtful hours underground. It would be so educational for them.

After a rambling anti-Catholic rant, Wells concluded, 'I appeal to you to drop this idea of some peculiar sacredness about Rome, justifying its present immunity, its right to strike and not be stricken. Rome has become an Ally of our enemies. I am sorry, but those who cut must expect to be slashed.'

Well before General Mark Clark's entering Rome on 4 June 1944, Hitler had been ambivalent about the prosecution of war in Italy. When the Allies invaded the mainland, he was confused by the conflicting advice given by Field Marshals Rommel and Kesselring. Rommel argued for an immediate pull-back of German forces to the north of the country. Fighting in Italy would be a waste of German lives and resources. Rommel had a low opinion of the Italian military. Kesselring, the Italophile, overall confidence in the combined German–Italian war effort until the surrender in July 1943. His belief was that it was worth fighting the Allies in a slow retreat north of Rome, holding up their armies at consecutive defensive walls, like the Gustav Line, stretching from coast to coast. Hitler chose to place his confidence in Kesselring's hands. With the German 10th Army free to move unmolested north from Monte Cassino as General Clark made his glory-bid for Rome, Kesselring would delay the progress of the Allied armies for many, brutally fought months to come.

Alan Whicker, war correspondent with the British Army's Film and Photo Unit, who had reported from Monte Cassino, was incredulous when he learned that, just four miles from closing the trap on von Vietinghoff's 10th Army at Frosinone, Clark had diverted a major part of the Fifth Army from there to Rome. The US General, Whicker recalled,

> was so eager that the world should see pictures showing him as the liberator of Rome, that he allowed the armies of a delighted Kesselring to escape. He had ignored the orders of Field Marshal Alexander in a decision as militarily stupid as it was insubordinate. This vainglorious blunder, the worst of the entire war, lost us a stunning victory, lengthened the war by many months and earned Mark Clark the contempt of other American and British generals. They saw an operation that could have won the war in Italy, thrown away at the cost of many Allied lives, because of the obsession and vanity of one man. If General Mark Clark had been in the German Army, Hitler would have had him shot.

Clark's glory days in the media spotlight were short-lived. Two days after the press conference he held in Rome, D–Day witnessed the Allied invasion of France. News from Italy was relegated to the back burner. Significant numbers of Allied soldiers who had fought in Italy up to this point were transferred in preparation for Operation Dragoon, the invasion of southern France.

Despite Clark's diversion to Rome, and this new depletion of the Fifth Army, the Allies had won a victory, costly and confusing though it was, over the Germans, as Kesselring was the first to admit. His forces pulled back, in a fighting retreat, under increasing attack from the Desert Air Force and, as they backed towards the Gothic Line, from a new enemy behind their backs – the Italian partisans. Clark's prospects, meanwhile, were undimmed by his opportunistic drive on Rome. At the end of the year, when General Alexander was promoted Field Marshal, taking overall command of the vast Mediterranean Theatre, Clark was appointed Commander-in-Chief of the 15th Army Group.

While the fighting and the terrible destruction, loss of lives and atrocities accompanying it might have seemed a long way from Venice, 400 miles northeast of Monte Cassino, the Veneto region was under attack during these gruelling months. A passenger train had just pulled in from Venice on 16 December 1943 when bombs from the second of two raids on Padua that day fell close by the station. Dozens of passengers were killed or injured. The 15th Air Force had been aiming for the railway marshalling yard but hit monuments including the Tempio della Pace (Temple of Peace). Completed in 1934 to designs by Antonio Zanivan, this Neo-Romanesque church had been built by the city to thank God and its patron saint, Anthony, for sparing Padua from invasion in 1917 by Austro-Hungarian forces after the Battle of Caporetto. The church was struck again on 30 December, when the bones of those who had fought and been entombed here were scattered through its shattered nave.

The Scrovegni Chapel, with its cherished cycles of frescoes painted by Giotto at the beginning of the fourteenth century, stands about a third of a mile from the Tempio della Pace. Until Giotto, said Kenneth Clark in his book *Civilisation* (1969), 'Italian painting was really only a less polished form of Byzantine painting. It was a flat, flowing linear style based on traditional concepts which had changed very little for five hundred years. For Giotto to break away from it and evolve this solid, space-conscious style was one of those feats of inspired originality that have occurred only two or three times in the history of art.' A second or two's mistiming by the American bombers may well have meant the obliteration of the Scrovegni Chapel. While the fabric of the building might have been rebuilt, those captivating Giottos were wholly irreplaceable.

Giotto or not, the assault on Padua was to be relentless. On 11 March 1944, an aerial armada of 111 B-17s destroyed, among much else, Andrea Mantegna's late fifteenth-century frescoes adorning the Ovetari chapel of the church of the Eremitani. The Cathedral was hit on 22 March. By March 1945, just 4 percent of the buildings of the city's Arcella district, which had housed 8,500 people before December 1943, remained standing.

The Allies' 1943 Christmas present to Vicenza, forty miles from Venice, was a bombing raid attacking the airfield, killing over thirty people in the city's San Bartolo and San Francesco districts. Among the buildings badly damaged by RAF bombers attacking Vicenza's marshalling yards on 18 March 1945 were two masterworks by the great Venetian architect Andrea Palladio, the Basilica Palladiana (Palazzo della Ragione) and the Palazzo Valmarana.

Venice itself was home to two of Palladio's finest buildings, the churches of San Giorgio Maggiore, rising from the island of the same name, commenced in 1565 and, from 1577, Il Redentore (The Redeemer) on the Giudecca. Palladio's hugely influential book *I quattro libri dell'architettura*, published in 1580, took his ideas north and west to the British Isles and the United States and north and east to Germany and Russia. Who would ever wish to damage or destroy a building by Palladio? And yet only the wondrous façade of the Palazzo Valmarana, featuring double-height Composite pilasters rising above a rusticated base almost preconfiguring the Baroque, was to survive wholly intact.

Some 2,000 civilians were killed in Vicenza and Verona by Allied bombing raids. Even at the very late stages of the war, bomber forces struck loose and free over civilians and civic treasures, even when not deliberately targeting these. Throughout the slow, if resolute, Allied push from the land-ing on the Italian mainland to the Gustav Line and beyond, the Monuments Men had been in frantic action. Lionel Fielden recalled Teddy Croft-Murray dashing from site to site in a worn 1930s Fiat Balilla saloon (top speed 53mph) with US Captain Mason Hammond, a Harvard professor of Latin, and Lieutenant Perry Cott, an assistant curator at Worcester Art Museum, Massachusetts.

Croft-Murray, who had been busy in Palermo, sifted through the wreckage of Monte Cassino, initiated repair work on some 700 buildings and supervised the removal of 500 paintings, 1,000 pieces of furniture and 20,000 books for safekeeping from the Palazzo Reale, Caserta, until very recently the Italian Aviation College occupied by both Italian and German soldiers and now the headquarters of Allied forces in Italy.

Sometimes, the fate of small towns that, through no fault of their own, stood in the way of the Allied armies as they slogged and shelled their way up the Italian peninsula was in the hands, if not of serendipity, then, quite remarkably, of a single work of art. This is certainly the case with Sansepolcro, a small town in the vicinity of Arezzo, birthplace of Buitoni pasta and Piero della Francesca. Aldous Huxley, who had recently made his name with his first novel, *Crome Yellow* (1922), visited Sansepolcro, where, after a meandering seven-hour bus ride from Urbino, he saw 'a little town surrounded by walls, set in a broad flat valley between hills; some fine Renaissance palaces with pretty balconies of wrought iron; a not very interesting church, and finally, the best picture in the world'. Some claim.

The world's best picture was a fresco on the wall of a room in Sansepolcro's medieval town hall. It was the *Resurrection* by Piero della Francesca. Huxley wrote a slightly over-wrought essay, 'The Best Picture', including it in his Italian travel book *Along the Road*, published in 1925. 'Raptures,' he wrote, 'depend largely upon the stars in Baedeker [the pre-eminent travel guide of the time], and the stars are more freely distributed to works of art in accessible towns than to those in the inaccessible.' Hidden away in off-the-beaten-path Sansepolcro, Piero's *Resurrection* was relatively little known at the time beyond small coteries of art historians and connoisseurs. In 1944, Piero's picture saved Sansepolcro from destruction.

Oddly enough, Baedeker Guides had given their name to the infamous 'Baedeker Raids' made on historic British cities by the Luftwaffe in April–May 1942. In response to the wholesale destruction of Lübeck on the German Baltic coast by RAF Bomber Command in March 1942, the Luftwaffe struck Exeter, Bath, Canterbury, Norwich and York, aiming specifically for targets of cultural and historic value. Joseph Goebbels noted that Hitler shared his view that 'cultural centres, health resorts and civilian centres must be attacked... there is no other way of bringing the English to their senses. They belong to a class of human beings with whom you can only talk after you have first knocked out their teeth.'

The story of the Sansepolcro miracle was told twenty years later by H. V. Morton in his capacious and engaging book *A Traveller in Italy* (1964). A while before its publication, Morton happened to be in Cape Town, where he visited Clarke's bookshop on Long Street to buy a scarce tome on Florence. He was soon in conversation with the shop's owner, Tony Clarke. In 1944, Lieutenant Clarke had been a troop commander in the 1st Regiment, Royal Horse Artillery. He had fought across North Africa against Rommel's Afrika Korps and up through Sicily and Italy. Moving north from Città di Castello, Clarke's job was to establish an observation post overlooking Sansepolcro. Told over the wireless that the town was occupied by Germans, he was given an order to shell it. Clarke lobbed a few cursory shells while scanning the town through his binoculars. There may well be Germans there, but he was unable to spot one. At that point a ragged boy leading a dog approached the Lieutenant's tank, signalling that the *Tedeschi* had left town and were heading for the hills. It was at that moment Clarke remembered reading Huxley's essay.

'So I fired no more,' he told a rapt Morton.

The next day we entered Sansepolcro unmolested. I asked immediately for the picture. The building was untouched. I hurried inside and there it was, secure and magnificent. The townsfolk had started to sandbag it, but the sandbags were only about waist-high. I looked up at the roof: one shell, I knew, would have been sufficient to undo the admiration of centuries. And that is that. Sometimes I wonder how I would be feeling now if I had happened to destroy the *Resurrection*. At one time I thought of writing to Aldous Huxley. The incident might, I suppose, be a fine illustration of the power of literature, and that the pen is mightier than the sword.

An Italophile and an art lover, Clarke kept a diary through his war years. He wrote of his shock as he drove below the walls of the ravaged monastery at Monte Cassino. Over the centuries, warring regimes around the globe have deliberately targeted the enemies' prized architecture, works of art, religious symbols, cultural artefacts, schools and libraries in bids to destroy the heritage and very soul of those they deem to hate and wish to crush. What was so odd about this war was the destruction of the expressions of the very civilisation the Allies were meant to be fighting for.

Sansepolcro was rebuilt in dull fashion after the war. On the edge of town, there is an inconsequential street named Via Anthony Clarke. There ought to be a principal street in Chartres named after US Colonel Welborn Barton Griffith Jr. Like Lieutenant Clarke, there were many US servicemen and women who questioned the destruction of cultural monuments across Europe. In Griffith's case, the target of US artillery was the Cathedral of Notre Dame, Chartres, a glorious and profound medieval church that on 16 August 1944 was reported to be a profane sanctuary for German troops. Snipers were said to be hiding in its twin west towers, although no one could say for sure if they had heard, much less seen, a shot fired from either one. The order was given to shell the cathedral. Just before the tanks and artillery pieces let rip, Texan-born Colonel Griffith made a dash to the Cathedral's main entrance in company with a single enlisted soldier.

Moving at a pace through the numinous nave, choir and transepts and finding no Germans there, Griffith dashed up the spiral stairs to one of the bell towers. No snipers. He rang the bells to signal 'all clear, don't fire'. Griffiths had saved Chartres Cathedral. Whether or not he had God on his side it is hard to say. He was killed later that same day by enemy fire some miles from the French city. The French themselves, in the guise of fervent revolutionaries toppling the *ancien régime*, had wanted to demolish the Cathedral in the late 1790s, just as Napoleon, their promising young general, proved keen on ravaging Venice.

At much the same time as Clarke in Italy and Griffith in France fought on behalf of Western European civilisation,

Field Marshal Kesselring sought to protect Florence, heart of the Italian Renaissance, as the Allied armies closed in on the city.

At 2150hrs on 11 March 1944, a huge explosion in the centre of Florence marked the beginning of Operation *Feuerzauber* (Magic Fire), the destruction of bridges over the Arno. The Allies would soon be here, their progress through the city and across the Arno delayed by Kesselring's 'Magic Fire' as the retreating Germans sped north to the Field Marshal's new Gothic Line, 300 miles north of the by now abandoned Gustav Line. The blasts continued until 5 a.m. the following morning. The treasured Ponte Vecchio alone remained standing, although the venerable streets leading to the covered medieval bridge at either end were reduced to rubble.

Kesselring, however, had no intention of wrecking the city, and nor, in fact, had Hitler. 'Florence is too beautiful a city to be destroyed,' the Führer told Rudolf Rahn, German Ambassador to Italy, at a meeting in November 1943. Rahn had been pressed to discuss the fate of the city with Hitler by his friend Gerhard Wolf, the German Consul. The two diplomats had been secretly rescuing political prisoners and saving Jews from persecution. 'Do what you can to protect it,' Hitler instructed Rahn. 'You have my permission and assistance.' Hitler had visited Florence in May 1938. He had looked out over the Arno from a window created for the occasion at the centre of the fourteenth-century Ponte Vecchio. A secret passage above the buildings spanning the bridge created by Giorgio Vasari – artist, architect and author of *The Lives of the Artists* (1550) – allowed members of the all-powerful Medici family to cross the river without having to mingle with crowds and potential assassins. According to Florentine legend, the two circular windows Vasari set in the passage, known as the 'eyes of Florence', gave the Medicis an opportunity to spy on citizens. More recent legend says partisans made frequent use of the passageway during the Second World War, although as Hitler had been shown the secret passage, this might not have been such a good idea after all.

While the Nazis had looted works of art from the city, its fabric was considered unassailable. There was, though, to be no guarantee for the safety of art-historical Italian towns and cities, neither to the north or south of Kesselring's Gothic Line. If anything, the obdurate defensive line constructed to delay the Allied advance into the Po Valley only increased the chance of their being badly damaged.

From 6 June 1944, as Allied forces battled their way east from Normandy beaches, and after the final breaching of the Gustav Line following the fourth and final Battle of Cassino, Allied ground forces now faced the challenge of the much tougher Gothic Line behind which Kesselring's armies had retreated. Beyond that jagged defensive line lay Milan, Turin, Genoa, Venice and, not far beyond, Austria and the Balkans – the underbelly of Nazi Germany. At the time, there was one certain way of crossing the seemingly impregnable Gothic Line and striking at the Germans encamped on and behind it. Over the sea and from the air. More than ever, commanders, crews and individual pilots would need to work in the very closest cooperation.

2nd Lieutenant Gerry Teldon, 85th Fighter Squadron, 79th Fighter Group with his P47-D 'Mr Lucky', 1944.

SEVEN

THE DESERT AIR FORCE IN ITALY

Nettuno, 6 June 1944, 2100hrs

Captain Rex Dunkerley banked his Mk V Spitfire over the Tyrrhenian Sea. Wheels and flaps down, throttle back, he nosed towards Nettuno airfield, a makeshift military strip laid only recently by engineers of the US 12th Air Force. It had been a hot day – 32°C at noon – but the weather was closing in now with low cloud forming and the threat of squally rain. The airfield was dimly lit. Dunkerley could make out, on steel plank parking areas beside the single asphalt and wire-reinforced hessian runway, the distinctive profile of a USAAF P-38 Lightning – he knew a squadron of these twin-engine fighters was due to arrive here any day soon – and, just feet from the ground, tents, supply dumps and gasoline drums.

This, for one last night, was to be home for the thirty-four-year-old South African Air Force (SAAF) pilot. With the recce op he had flown over the Terni and Rieti industrial area sixty miles northeast of Rome completed in a matter of seconds, he would, debriefing aside, be on leave. Dunkerley was thinking of his wife, Thelma, at home 5,000 miles away in Benoni, a gold town in the Transvaal.

Captain Dunkerley was a highly experienced pilot. A skilled workman, he had signed up in Pretoria on 1 November 1939 and had served with 40 SAAF Squadron from its formation on 30 May 1940, flying Hawker Hartbees, South African-built ground attack versions of Sydney Camm's Rolls-Royce Kestrel-powered Hawker Hart light bomber. Dunkerley trained fellow South African recruits before transferring to Hurricanes – he'd had an accident with Hurricane Z4270, the same aircraft George Westlake had flown over the Med to Alexandria – and Spitfires with the Desert Air Force in North Africa, Sicily, and now mainland Italy. For his skills as an instructor, he had been awarded the AFC (Air Force Cross). His citation read, 'As Group and Flight Commander and Instructor…he has at all times been a pattern to the other Pilots…A very good Pilot and Instructor who turns out pupils whose general flying is of a very high standard. Instructional flying hours: 1,074.'

As Dunkerley touched down, a USAAF P-47D Thunderbolt, following him in, crash landed on top of the Spitfire. The beefy American aircraft weighed twice as much as the lithe British fighter. It was as if a London bus had ploughed at speed into a 1930s sports car. Pulled from the wreckage, Rex would never make it home to Thelma and the Transvaal. Terribly injured, he died from his wounds on 11 June.

Pilots of the US 79th Fighter Group assigned to fly with the RAF's Desert Air Force (DAF) had only recently converted from the Curtiss P-40 Warhawk – Kittyhawk in RAF parlance – that they had flown in North Africa and the early stages of the Italian campaign south of Rome to the mighty Republican P-47D Thunderbolt. The difference between the Kittyhawk and the Thunderbolt can hardly be exaggerated.

Longer and wider than the older plane, the P-47D was, at the tip of its enormous four-bladed propellers, 14 feet 8 inches high – taller than a London double-decker – dwarfing the 10-feet 8-inch P-40. Its eighteen-cylinder, forty-six-litre Pratt & Whitney R-2800 Double Wasp air-cooled radial engine generated 2,000hp. The P-40 could call on 1,240hp from its liquid-cooled, twenty-eight-litre V12 Allison 1710. In level flight, the Thunderbolt was 100mph faster than the Kittyhawk. Fully laden, the P-47D weighed up to eight tons – heavier than a contemporary London double-decker – this figure including the aircraft's formidable armament: eight .50-caliber Browning machine guns and ten five-inch rockets or a 2,500lb bombload. The Thunderbolt's armoured cockpit was spacious, its instrumentation orderly and the view from its bubble cockpit generous.

Converting to the giant Thunderbolt from smaller, lighter fighters, however, was not easy. Many young pilots died in the process. It was better if it was the first operational fighter they flew. Initially many, if not all, P-40 veterans took against the massive Thunderbolt, saying they had hoped for the lighter and lither Rolls-Royce Merlin-powered North American P-51D Mustang.

Twenty-year-old Lieutenant Gerry Teldon, born in the Bronx and raised on Long Island, went into action for the first time, from Foggia on the Adriatic Coast, with the 85th Fighter Squadron of the 79th US Fighter Group six months after Captain Dunkerley's death. A diet of early Hollywood war movies and a boyhood plane ride over New York City – a prize for selling the most subscriptions to the Long Island *Newsday* newspaper – had triggered a desire to fly. Turned down by the Navy ('I could not think of anything more exciting than landing an airplane on a boat that's bobbing up and down in the ocean'), Gerry was accepted by the USAAF. He imagined the high life, leaping into cockpits and flying balletically to and from club-like air bases. The reality proved to be slightly different.

'I was eighteen when I joined the Army Air Force. After going through flight training, I went to Pocatello Idaho to check out in a P-47, had a crash landing on the lava beds adjacent to the airport. It hit the ground so hard that the engine separated from the body and flew fifty yards ahead of me.' Then he went to Italy, where there were no permanent runways, much less Hollywood-style air force clubhouses. Thunderbolts, Mustangs, Kittyhawks and Spitfires took off from and landed on readily movable twelve-foot sections of pierced-steel planking joined together at each side.

As frontlines moved, the fighters and their temporary airfields moved with them, with Jeeps serving as mobile control towers. On his first 'show', as he had learned to call ops from British and Commonwealth colleagues, Gerry spotted a train, not knowing whether its carriages were filled with troops or supplies. Turning to riddle it with machine-gun fire, he unleashed his rockets, one narrowly missing his own flight leader. Gerry pulled up just above the tree line, or so he thought.

After landing, his crew chief met the plane, whistled a greeting and began removing branches from the engine cowling. Out of alignment, the Thunderbolt's rocket tubes were stained green. Gerry realised that he had come very close 'to becoming a part of the Italian scenery'. British and Commonwealth crews thought the Americans wild and even dangerous.

Low flying day in, day out was, to say the least, dangerous. On another op, Gerry told me, he was

> just coming out of a strafing run [a low-level air-to-ground attack] doing about 140, and for some reason looked left and between the first and second gun [on his left wing] there was a stream of tracers and nothing I could do. I could only see my death approaching as the tracers ripped through my wing. Didja ever hear of the saying 'the last nine yards'? It came about because when loading the bullets for the machine guns, the tape was nine yards long. Well, I wouldn't be here if, as I'm watching the tracers creeping towards the edge of the wing, the last nine yards [of the German gun] stopped and here I am! When I returned to base and told my crew chief, he painted 'Mister Lucky' on the engine nacelle. And thereafter that's what I was called.

Flying close to the ground at high speed led to any number of untoward and tragic incidents. Everything happened, as Thunderbolt pilots said, very fast indeed. Sometimes, it was hard to know quite what your target was. In January 1943, P-47s of USAAF 306th Wing had mistakenly strafed the 239 Wing Adriatic airbase at Cutella shooting up three P-51 Mustangs and killing ground staff and crew. The US captain's intended target was fifty miles away. Australian pilots based at Cutella said they wanted to 'bomb up and pay them a return visit'.

It was not difficult then to understand why a Thunderbolt crash-landed on Rex Dunkerley's Spitfire. This was not the Battle of Britain, much less a Hollywood movie. The 79th Fighter Group, equipped with P-47s from February 1944, was charged with assisting the British Eighth Army in providing tactical ground support, which, in practice, and as Gerry Teldon knew, meant blasting away at everything in sight that looked remotely like a legitimate target, with several missions flown on any one day. It was all a bit intense. As the Germans retreated north from the Gustav Line, the 79th Fighter Group and their British and Commonwealth DAF partners chased after them incessantly.

A practising Jew, Gerry Teldon had felt slightly less out of place with each nautical mile his dogged ship, the *Victory*, had steamed from Manhattan to the Bay of Naples. Pilots aside, the ship's passengers were Black American ground troops. Gerry was one of just two Jews in the fighter group. He said at no time, neither at sea nor in combat, did he hear an anti-Semitic remark. And on Rosh Hashanah (Jewish New Year), September 1944, he was given a special pass to attend a service in Rimini, where the Chief Rabbi from Palestine presided. Did he know about the Nazi extermination camps? And, if he did, would this knowledge have made him want to fight even harder, if such a thing were possible? 'Strange you should ask. During my stay there, no one in the group knew of anything that was taking place at that time. The concentration camps or the killing of Jews and others. The *Stars and Stripes* newspapers never had any details. The first I knew of anything happening was after the war ended; we were posted to Austria in case we had to fight the Russians.'

Other DAF pilots, flying under the banners of the Royal Air Force (RAF), the Royal Australian Air Force (RAAF), the South African Air Force (SAAF) and the United States Army Air Forces (USAAF), knew a lot more about the savagery of Nazi Germany than young Gerry Teldon. Among British, Australian, New Zealand, South African and US personnel were pilots and crews, many of them Poles, who had fought the Germans in 1939 and had escaped Nazi-occupied Europe.

Newly equipped with the latest fighters, the squadrons, groups and wings of all nationalities were only as good – even when the aircraft were among the best in terms of design, specification, weapons and performance – as the young men who flew them, and the ground crews who serviced them, patched them up and kept them flying. Six further Spitfires were lost the day Rex Dunkerley was killed at Nettuno, as were at least six P-47Ds and eight P-40s. Flak, machine-gun fire, target explosions, bad weather, getting lost, trees – these had all been killers. Flying over the North African desert had been one thing, fighting in the air over the rugged Italian landscape pockmarked with enemy gun emplacements quite another.

On 9 June, three days after Captain Dunkerley's death, George Westlake had been posted to RAAF 3 squadron initially at Sant'Angelo near Foggia – the squadron's base moved several times within the next few weeks – flying Kittyhawks. He had been instructed earlier in the art of dive bombing with Kittyhawks by Australian pilots of 450 Squadron based at RAF Abu Suier in the Nile peninsula. The Kittyhawks were to take on a ground-attack and a dive-bombing role from the invasion of Sicily onward. Theoretically, the dive bomber itself, developed successfully by the Germans with the advent of the Junkers Ju-87 Stuka championed by Albert Kesselring, offered a form of 'surgical' destruction, whether the target was an enemy gun emplacement, tank, munitions depot, warship or a dock in a historic city.

The Stuka, however, had also been designed to terrorise civilians. A pair of air-induced sirens known as 'Jericho Trumpets' howled demonically as it dived. This was, the Luftwaffe claimed when the Ju-87 went into service in 1936, to help pilots know when they were up to speed in a dive. Even then, this was nonsense. With its vampiric profile and screaming siren, the Stuka was a machine for instilling fear and used as such throughout the Second World War. Britain, as we have seen, had played its part in the development of this feared machine.

The dive bomber, however, was vulnerable. Hurtling toward its intended targets at precise trajectories – ninety-degree angles in the case of the Stuka, sixty degrees with the Kittyhawk – and then, bomb released, climbing away as immense G-forces caused pilots to lose vision temporarily and even to black out altogether, the dive bomber could be an easy target for enemy fighters. Flak, too. This vulnerability meant that dive bombers needed protective cover from accompanying fighters. Most fighter-bomber attacks, however, were made not in such extreme and unflinching plunges towards the ground, but in sketchy shallow dives and zigzagging flight to avoid flak and sudden attack from behind. There was, though, little time for finesse. This was total war, with Allied aircraft of every type attacking ground targets with a relentless fury, with low-altitude Italian skies criss-crossed by tracer bullets, rockets, parachutes and burning aircraft.

Even the Spitfire, that superb fighter, was drawn into dive bombing. Major Cecil Golding DFC recalled flying SAAF 3 Squadron Spitfires over Italy. The Spitfire, he pointed out, had no air brakes, meaning it was hard to slow in a dive. It was, of course, a machine that, 99 percent of the time, could fly itself out of trouble through sheer balletic dexterity. It was also capable of very great speed as it hurtled towards the ground. Word had got around in spring 1944 that a Spitfire had come close to breaking the sound barrier. Indeed, it had. During a series of test dives conducted by the Royal Aircraft Establishment, Farnborough, on 27 April 1944, a Mk IX Spitfire flown by Flight Lieutenant 'Marty' Martindale reached the unprecedented speed of 606mph – a little under Mach 0.9 – in a forty-five-degree dive. In the rush, the Spitfire's engine gave up the ghost and its propeller broke up. Martindale, a skilled test pilot, glided the fighter down to a safe landing.

In the heat of battle, how might a less experienced Spitfire pilot cope if speed in a dive rose to 500mph and more? The trick, Major Golding learned, was to begin the dive with the Spitfire very close to a stall, flying in other words as slowly possible in the hope that the maximum speed would be significantly less than 'Marty' Martindale's on 27 April. Even then, there was the chance that the 250lb bombs – one under each wing – might fail to drop. If this was the case, it would be very hard work indeed pulling the Spitfire up from the bottom of its dive and, after this nerve-wracking experience, trying to land back at base on a narrow makeshift airstrip with the bombs ready to explode if the pilot made the slightest error. It was never a good idea to attempt a landing with a primed bomb still in place under a wing, yet if such a bomb was impossible to shake off, a pilot had little choice but to attempt a landing, aiming ideally for the far end of a landing strip away from fellow airmen and hoping to get out before the thing blew.

George Westlake was finally back in a cockpit on 3 May 1944. He needed to know, as did his colleagues, that he was ready for the rigours of dive bombing, after his long stay in hospital and convalescence. He flew North American Harvard trainers for four days, three accompanied by a fellow pilot, one solo. In rapid succession, he practised low flying, close-formation flying, spins, aerobatics and ground attacks. Dive bombing, pilots said, was like playing a game of chicken with the ground, or sea. It took nerves of steel. If their luck was out, the ground would win.

Flying Kittyhawks from June with 3 Squadron's steely Australian pilots from Sant'Angelo, Guidonia, near Rome, George dive bombed ammunition dumps, roads, trains, gun emplacements and enemy headquarter buildings in and around Chiusi, Cortona, Arezzo and Perugia, each a jewel box of historic architecture and works of art. George flew Rover David Cab rank ops, called from ground controllers to hit targets identified by the army. By this stage of the Italian campaign, sightings of enemy aircraft, particularly German day fighters, had become increasingly rare. The last recorded pitched encounter between Allied and German fighters had been over Rimini and Pesaro on 28 April.

If the threat from German if not Italian fighters had faded, there were plenty of other ways DAF pilots could lose their way or their lives over this complex and ever moving battlefield up, over and around southern and central Italy, and the Gothic Line. Friendly fire. The blast from bombs dropped from their own aircraft. Engine failure. Flying into barely visible power lines. Hitting trees. Bad weather. Disorientation. Fatigue. Small arms fire. Flak.

Of these, flak remained the greatest danger. This four-letter word, derived from *Flugabwehrkanone* (aircraft defence cannon), appeared again and again in George Westlake's logbooks. Gerry Teldon faced flak on his first operational mission with the 85th Fighter Squadron and had found it 'strangely hypnotic'. Unveiled in 1928 by Krupp, the colossal industrial and armaments manufacturing empire founded in Essen in the early nineteenth century, the 88mm 'Flak' cannon fired 20lb shells, one every three or four seconds, 26,000 feet into the air. When an 88mm projectile exploded at altitude, it sent out jagged metal fragments that tore through aircraft. It also left a characteristic black cloud hanging in the sky.

Flak was often so thick, pilots and bomber crews said you could get out and walk on it. To understand what it was like flying through flak, here is former USAAF 8th Air Force Flying Fortress navigator Lieutenant Frank Murphy (*Luck of the Draw: My Story of the Air War in Europe*, 2001):

When we entered the flak, it was an almost uninterrupted cloud of swirling black smoke filled with angry red explosions. Plainly, any one of those exploding shells could obliterate an aircraft and its crew without warning. When the group ahead of us entered this inferno, they all but disappeared. My heart felt as if it would stop. It did not appear possible that anyone or anything could fly into that hell and come out alive on the other side. But somehow, despite being buffeted by thunderous explosions and the incessant clinking, clanging, and pinging of shell fragments striking our airplane, we made it through.

I quickly learned to hate flak – it frightened the life out of me. We could not see it coming, nor could we fight back as we could with enemy fighters... The din inside the airplane was horrific – the continuous roaring of our four Wright Cyclone engines was almost deafening. Still, we could easily hear the muffled explosions of nearby flak bursts, and if they were really close, they made loud, cracking sounds like near-miss lightning strikes or breaking tree limbs. Dust and threads of insulation flew about the airplane, and shrapnel from flak, which varied in size from as big as baseballs to as small as gravel, rained on and often penetrated the thin skin of the airplane. Inside the Plexiglas nose of the airplane, it was as if we were in a fishbowl in a shooting

164

gallery five miles up in the sky in an already-unforgiving environment. It is difficult to describe how exposed and unprotected we felt.

Developed throughout the war, late models of flak cannon could fire in tandem and with great accuracy. The 88s could also be employed, as they were to be along the Gothic Line, as tank-busting artillery. Lighter 40mm, 37mm and 20mm anti-aircraft guns, German or Italian, were equally deadly for low-flying aircraft. It took courage and youthful bravado to nose an aircraft towards a target protected by flak. George felt that flying down into flak was like diving into gun barrels.

No sooner than he had got into his stride with 3 Squadron, in mid-July 1944 George was dispatched to Campo Vesuvio, an airfield behind the famous volcano that had erupted with spectacular and destructive force that spring, as the USAAF knew to its cost, losing eighty-eight B-25 Mitchell bombers and a number of A20-Havocs to red-hot rocks and searing lava. George's role was to take temporary command of 10 Group *Quattro Stormo* (flight) of the newly constituted *Aeronautica Cobelligerente Italia* (ACI). Following the Armistice of September 1943, the Italian air force was split into two, with the royalist ACI fighting from the south of the country on the side of the Allies and the *Aeronautica Nazionale Reppublicana* (ANR) operating in the north on behalf of Mussolini's Italian Social Republic.

In the south, Italian pilots had flown their remaining M.202 and M.205 fighters to Brindisi-Casale and then Lecce-Galatina airfields. To boost their fighting strength, they were re-equipped in June 1944 with 170 Bell P-39N and P-39Q Airacobra fighters, drawn from a stock of surplus and often battle-worn USAAF aircraft stored at Napoli-Capodichino airfield.

At Vesuvio, George found himself in command of three squadrons of Airacobras, a Spitfire squadron and two squadrons of Martin Baltimore light bombers. There were airmen from the RAF, technicians from the USAAF and Italian interpreters from Malta working around the clock. George found the Italian pilots to be an extraordinary bunch. Most had fought in Spain, Abyssinia and Libya before the Second World War, then against the British over Malta, Sicily and Italy. Lieutenant Teste, passed over for promotion because he disapproved of fascism, had been a fighter pilot for the past nineteen years. Captain Graziani was a nephew of the 'Butcher of Ethiopia' – Marshal Rodolfo Graziani – whose Italian 10th Army had been destroyed by the British Eighth Army in Egypt. Captain Graziani had sunk twenty-three British ships. The fortunes of war. How quickly enemies had become allies.

Baron Franchetti was from a wealthy Jewish family who until the 1920s had owned a magnificent Gothic palazzo on the Grand Canal in Venice. Count Piccolomini was a descendant of the Renaissance Pope Pius II. He said he could arrange a private audience for George with the current Pope, Pius XII, and was as good as his word. George received a blessed rosary from the Pope that he sent to a young fan, Shirley Boulter from Wallesey, much taken by a photo of the Wing Commander that had appeared recently in the *Daily Mail*. In return, although without asking, George received weekly rations of Players No. 3 Virginia cigarettes and the *Weekly Daily Mail* from Shirley's Catholic family.

The senior Italian officer, Lieutenant Colonel Diulio Fanali, with fifteen kills to his name, was small, dark, intense and dynamic. When George arrived at Vesuvio, Fanali flew a precise and daring display with his Macchi C.205 *Veltro* (Greyhound) that was as good as any the British pilot had yet witnessed. Having shown what he could with it, Colonel Fanali allowed George to fly the C.205. It was, he thought, the 'nicest aircraft' he had piloted so far during the war.

Group Captain Wilfrid Duncan-Smith, from November 1943 Commanding Officer 324 Wing flying Spitfires in combat over Italy, recalled, 'In general the standard of flying of the Italian pilots was very high indeed, and in encounters with Macchi 205s particularly we were up against aircraft that could turn and dogfight with our Spitfires extremely well.' Captain Eric Brown, the hugely experienced Chief Naval Test Pilot and commanding officer of the Royal Aircraft Establishment's Captured Enemy Aircraft Flight, described the C.205 as 'one of the finest aircraft I ever flew... Oh, beautiful. And here you had the perfect combination of Italian styling and German engineering. It was really a delight to fly, and up to anything on the Allied programme... it came just before the Italians capitulated, so it was never used extensively.' Just as well. To add to the glamour of Vesuvio, Umberto, the Crown Prince, was a regular visitor. Unassuming and friendly, he had, George thought, a wonderful sense of humour.

As for the Bell Airacobras, these were a poor substitute for the impressive Mario Castoldi-designed Italian air-superiority fighters. Although an ingenious design, with its Allison V12 engine installed behind the cockpit to make space for a 37mm, armour-piercing cannon firing through its nose, the P-39 lacked the high-altitude performance of the justly revered Italian, British and German fighters – C.205, Spitfire, Bf109 – that made them ideal for aerial combat. Like the P-40 Kittyhawk, however, the P-39 Airacobra proved to be a fine ground-attack fighter. Soviet pilots, whose missions were made for the most part at low level in support of Red Army ground operations, swore by their *Kobrushka* (Little Cobra).

In ways other than its weapon-priority design configuration, the P-39, which stood upright on the ground on tricycle landing gear, would have seemed strange to both Italian and British pilots. Its cockpit was accessed through car doors complete with wind-down windows (the Airacobra's T9 cannon was manufactured by Oldsmobile), while in a spin, the P-39 could tumble tail-over-nose due to the change in weight distribution when the thirty weighty shells of its tank-busting cannon had been expended. This was something even the most experienced pilot would have found alarming.

The Italian pilots were not exactly enamoured with the P-39. Aside from anything else, its Anglo-Saxon instrumentation was unfamiliar, as was the action of the throttle. Where RAF and USAAF pilots would expect to push the throttle lever forward to increase power, Italian pilots pulled back. While getting the hang of the correct way to use a throttle might seem simple enough, it is all too easy to push a lever the wrong way in the heat of action. Anyone who has driven a classic or vintage car, for the first time, with a centre throttle – where you expect the brake pedal to be – when heading downhill at speed towards a roundabout will understand.

There were several fatal accidents. Among those killed was the Italian 'ace of aces', Sergeant Major Teresio Martinoli. George, however, enjoyed the Airacobra, as he did his brief command of the charismatic *Gruppo Stormo* 4. The Italian squadrons flew in missions over the Balkans – successfully so – so as not to clash with fellow Italian aircrews serving with the ANR (*Aeronautica Nazionale Repubblicana*). Every attempt was made to confine the threat of civil war in Italy.

George was destined to fight up and over Italy itself. On 9 September, he was appointed Wing Leader, 239 Wing Desert Air Force, and was quickly in frontline action once again, flying Kittyhawks, with a bombing raid on a factory in Rimini on 12 September. In the following days he logged his own direct hit on a bridge near Casena, an assault on gun positions near Rimini and attacks on military repair depots. Along with 'Excellent Bombing', his logbook for these September ops notes 'Flak Bad' and, tellingly, 'Too Much Flak'.

The Wing comprised 3 RAAF, 5 SAAF and 260 RAF squadrons newly equipped with the Rolls-Royce Merlin-powered North American P-51 Mustang (Mk III and IV) and 112, 250 and 450 RAAF squadrons flying Kittyhawks. The fighter-bomber wing was given a roving commission to seek out and destroy enemy targets. Tanks. Transport. Railway bridges. Ships. Patrol craft. Gun positions. Troop concentrations. From Foggia to the Gothic Line and along the Adriatic to Yugoslavia, its attacks became increasingly accurate. Spitfires of 244 Wing gave the fighter-bombers cover.

Although during the day enemy aircraft were notable by their absence, on 3 September, Squadron Leader Neville Duke, 145 Squadron, brought down two Bf109G night fighters – equipped with radar, they could 'see' in the dark – with his Spitfire IX between Ravenna and Lugo. Two days later, as his II.JG77 squadron left for Germany, *Oberfeldwebel* Max Volke, an ace with thirty-seven victories, became the last German day fighter pilot killed in action in Italy. His Bf109G was shot down over Mirandola, forty miles north of Bologna, by a gunner firing from a USAAF B-25 Mitchell of the 321st US Bomber Group, on a mission to destroy the bridge over the Po at Polesella north of the Gothic Line.

Conditions on the ground for DAF pilots were decidedly rough and ready. Primitive even. For many months until the end of the war, DAF's principal bases were in and around Foggia by the Adriatic coast. The landscape was flat – good for airfields – but bleak in the wretched winter months of 1943–4 and 1944–5. This was not a realm of art-historical hill towns or jewel-like Gothic cities kissed by the Renaissance. In the mud and driving rain, the airbases became positively primeval. British and Commonwealth airmen, four or five together, were often billeted in canvas tents measuring twelve by six feet and four and a half feet high, sharing their meagre accommodation with spiders, beetles, mosquitoes, moths and grass snakes. For many, there were no beds, no sleeping bags. They made do with straw palliasses.

Set in wheatfields and olive groves around perforated temporary steel airstrips, tents were prone to flooding. Dysentery, jaundice and stomach upsets were par for the course. Lorries delivered chlorinated water in jerrycans. Makeshift stoves heated water for washing and shaving. Lavatories, such as they were, comprised tents with benches and buckets in trenches below them. In the North African desert, camping out by airstrips had not been so very bad, pilots flying in shorts and shirts, sleeves rolled up and suede desert boots. But here, as the days grew colder, and rain turned to snow in late 1944, camping by the Adriatic coast was a challenge. So, too, was landing from over the sea, to avoid flak, especially late in the day. Without lights, the very basic airstrips could be all but impossible to see as darkness fell.

George Westlake was all too aware that one of 239 Wing's former COs, twenty-seven-year-old Group Captain John 'Jackie' Darwen DSO, DFC & Bar, had taken off into heavy rain the previous October. He was not to return. 'Jackie' had been one of the Wing's most driven pilots. During an air raid on London in March 1941, the Café de Paris, where he was dancing with his young wife, was hit. She died in his arms.

Hot meals of fried corned beef, Spam, tinned Maconochie stew (a Scottish confection of turnips, carrots, beef and fat) and eggs – swapped with locals for cigarettes – were cooked on metal grilles with fires lit below and washed down with stewed tea sweetened with condensed milk. Hard liquor, when available, was exchanged with American colleagues for the luxuries of tinned chicken, ham, doughnuts, ice cream and real fruit.

The Americans enjoyed a little more comfort than their British colleagues, yet pilots fresh from the States were often shocked by the primitive conditions they were expected to endure in and around Foggia. For Gerry Teldon, the worst of it was that there were no hot showers. Because it was so cold and damp for much of their fighting lives, the US airmen lived around the clock in their flying suits and flying boots. Fortunately for Gerry and his once clean-cut 79th Fighter Group colleagues, 'they all smelled the same, everyone from Group Commander to crew chiefs. It wasn't too distressing.'

As part of DAF, the three Thunderbolt squadrons of the 79th FG shared these improvised airbases with SAAF and RAAF pilots. Gerry found Australians and South Africans to be fearless, hard drinking and rough playing. They flew sometimes still drunk after the barest minimum of sleep. Most, Gerry discovered, were superstitious. He was, too, making a point of urinating on his Thunderbolt's tail wheel 'for luck' before take-off, even though he was 85th Squadron's 'Mister Lucky'. Pilots who survived twenty ops were driven to Sorrento for a few days' leave. Gerry stayed at the Minerva Hotel overlooking the Gulf of Naples. It's still there.

Pilots had to be lucky. Gerry Teldon arrived in Italy in autumn 1944, when bad and then atrocious weather set in for months ahead. But even in the high days of a southern Italian summer, low flying and the sheer intensity of combat led to deaths that might be prefaced by the word 'unnecessary' today.

Three days after that P-47-D crash-landed on top of Captain Dunkerley's Spitfire at Nettuno, another Thunderbolt, flown by 2nd Lieutenant Stuart Bartlett, hit a house while strafing a target near Foligno-Spoleto, and he was killed. On 19 June, a Spitfire shot down a USAAF Airacobra, the pilot thinking he was attacking a Focke-Wulf 190. On 30 June, six Spitfires of 2 SAAF Squadron were jumped on at 8,000 feet above Arezzo by seven Thunderbolts, their leader opening fire. The nimbleness of the Spitfires allowed their pilots to escape.

Flak, though, was increasingly the main culprit. Some pilots bailed out, struggling from the cockpits of stricken aircraft – no life-saving explosive canopy bolts and ejector seats then – while praying their parachutes would open and, one way or another, if safely down on the ground, hoping to find their way back to base. In steep dives, pilots were often hurled back onto the tails of their machines, their parachutes entangled with airframes. Some were able to nurse their stricken aircraft home. Some were captured and made prisoners of war. Many died.

Pilots of 239 Wing scrubbed up for a visit by one General Collingwood on 26 July. No one had heard of 'General Collingwood' before, but he was clearly a very important person. Escorted by Spitfires of 1 Squadron SAAF, the General arrived. The men recognised him instantly. General Collingwood was King George VI. The King's visit was well-timed. The focus of the media in both Britain and the United States has been trained very much on the Allied landings in Normandy and the skirmishes and battles fought across France in their wake. D-Day – 6 June – was also the day Captain Dunkerley was killed at Nettuno. Servicemen fighting in Italy felt overlooked, forgotten even. The situation was made worse when someone in England – gossips named Viscountess Astor, the American-born socialite and Tory MP – was said to have described those serving in Italy as 'D-Day Dodgers'. A song pretty much every English-speaking soldier serving in the prolonged and brutal Italian conflict remembered for years afterwards was 'D-Day Dodgers', written in rebuttal by Lance-Sergeant Harry Pynn of the Tank Rescue Section of the 19th Army Fire Brigade, a unit that had been in the thick of the fighting with the 78th Infantry Division since North Africa. Pynn set his song to the tune of that British and German soldiers' favourite, 'Lili Marlene'.

We're the D-Day Dodgers out in Italy
Always on the vino, always on the spree...
We landed at Salerno, a holiday with pay,

Jerry brought the band down to cheer us on our way
Showed us the sights and gave us tea,
We all sang songs, the beer was free.
We are the D-Day Dodgers, way out in Italy.

And so on, to

Once we had a blue light that we were going home
Back to dear old Blighty, never more to roam.
Then somebody said in France you'll fight.
We said fuck that, we'll just sit tight,
The windy D-Day Dodgers, out in Sunny Italy.

Now Lady Astor, get a load of this.
Don't stand up on a platform and talk a load of piss.
You're the nation's sweetheart, the nation's pride
We think your mouth's too bloody wide.
We are the D-Day Dodgers, in Sunny Italy.

Italy was far from sunny as the British and Americans began what was to be a prolonged assault on Kesselring's Gothic Line, a solid barrier of mountainous terrain stretching from La Spezia on the west coast across the Apennines to the Adriatic between Pesaro and Ravenna on the east coast of the Italian peninsula. To its north lay the great agricultural flatlands of the Po Valley, the economic powerhouses of Milan and Turin, the ports of Genoa and Venice. The Gothic Line was to hold out against the 'D–Day Dodgers' for many terrible and trying months.

Tuskegee airmen, Marcellus G. Smith and Roscoe C. Brown, 332nd Fighter Group, service a P51-D Mustang, Ramitelli, Italy, March 1945.

EIGHT

THE GOTHIC LINE

22 August 1944, Vergato

From 21 August 1944, the 320th Bombardment Group of the US 12th Air Force was directed to target road and railway bridges in and around the Gothic Line. The following day, a B-26 Martin Marauder twin-engine bomber of the Group's 441st Bombardment Squadron was hit by flak while on a mission to attack a bridge at Vergato. 1st Lieutenant Robert Dinwiddie turned back to base at Decimomannu, Sardinia, ditching safely just off the Corsican coast. Following a short spell raiding targets in southern France, the 320th's Marauders were back in action over the Apennines in September.

References I have found to the bombing of Vergato, a small Apennine town between Bologna on one side of the mountains and Florence on the other, are few and far between. Vergato, though, is one of the towns destroyed almost completely by Allied bombing as Field Marshal Kesselring's Gothic Line came under sustained aerial attack. The results of what were at least thirteen air raids on Vergato are clear to see even today. While the town, an hour's train ride from Bologna, is set in a magnificent landscape, and the streets leading from its railway station are hospitably tree-lined, the buildings are pretty much all post-war Italian — that drab, matter of fact, *centesimo*-plain style of shops and offices and apartment blocks common to towns and cities of the era.

A single venerable building remains, the handsomely named Palazzo di Capitani della Montagna, a fifteenth-century town hall, rebuilt in the late nineteenth century in a style that might have pleased John Ruskin, and restored thirty or so years ago.

Vergato's 'captaincy of the mountains' spelt its ill-fortune. The town, on that rail route to and from Bologna, was a gateway for supplies to German positions stretched along the Gothic Line. German fortifications and gun emplacements can still be seen less than an hour's walk from the town centre. Climbing up Monte Pero, a ridge leads to these ghostly concrete sentinels. German guns here could fire down on the road that led through Vergato. The fortifications wove their way along and above this road, and today the local authorities promote walking tours along and above stretches of the SS64 and west across the mountains.

After a pincer movement of the Fifth and Eighth Armies stormed across and around the Apennines in April 1945, little of Vergato remained. This is true of other Apennine villages and small mountain towns up and across the Gothic

Line's harsh embrace of the region. Trekking from one to another is an unsettling experience. While the scenery is mostly magnificent, the small towns, rebuilt awkwardly after the war, tell a story of devastation, of a military drive up through these mountain valleys by the Allied armies fought inch by inch in the teeth of stubbornly fierce German opposition.

In October 1944, the US 91st Infantry Division took Livergnagno – they called it 'Liver'n'Onions' and 'Little Cassino' – a small town standing in the way of its advance along a twisting road leading north more or less parallel to the road on which Vergato stood, separated from it by high mountain ridges. Photographs of Livergnagno taken that month show what looks like a lunar landscape. Such a characterful town, much of it with its colourful medieval houses built into rockfaces smashed to a stone and plaster pulp. The first assault on the town at 0600hrs on 13 October comprised the non-stop firing of 2,120 mortar rounds.

Vergato, Livergnano. These, according to the 91st's official history,

are only the names the public knows. These are the places the spotlight has caught. But there are hundreds of houses, crossroads, hills and draws where the men of the 91st fought and died to make the capture of more famous places possible. There are miles of road the Engineers swept for mines, scores of streams they bridged or by-passed so the Division could move forward. There are miles of roads, dusty or muddy, frozen hard or running with water over which the service forces brought food and ammunition to the support of the drive. And sometimes there were no roads, and men and mules carried supplies over narrow precipitous trails. Over the same trails and roads the litter bearers evacuated the wounded swiftly and skillfully. Behind these names lies the courage, determination and combat wisdom of each individual infantryman and each individual artillery man. Again and again the story repeats itself: the artillery blasted a path for the infantry, drove the enemy into his holes and the infantry followed up to dig the dazed and shaken enemy from the holes.

What must villagers have made of the extraordinary multi-national force storming their way? The Fifth Army's 442nd Infantry Regiment was Japanese-American, its soldiers released from internment camps in the US to sign up. Many of these second-generation American immigrants hailed from Hawaii. In December 1941, the surprise Imperial Japanese attack on Pearl Harbor on the Hawaiian island of Oahu had brought the US into a war against Japan and into Europe. It must have been confusing to see Japanese troops, led mostly by white officers, fighting with the Americans against Axis forces. What Italian villagers would not have known, even if they had access to radios, was that families of the 442nd Regiment remained in internment camps as their menfolk fought what is officially recognised as a heroic war in Italy from late June 1944.

They would have encountered African American soldiers of the 92nd Infantry Division, segregated like the Japanese Americans, and also commanded by white officers. And then there were the unsegregated Brazilians with their Black and

Japanese soldiers. Many Brazilian soldiers were second-generation Italian immigrants. There were fellow Italians – the Legnano Division led by Lieutenant General Umberto Utili – and named after the Battle of Legnano of 1176, when the armies of the Lombard League led by Guido da Landriano defeated those of Friedrich Barbarossa. Barbarossa was the charismatic German king who in one of his five incursions across the Alps into Italy had been proclaimed King of Italy and Holy Roman Emperor. In 1944–5, the Italians fought under the Legnano banner. The legendary battle featured either directly or by implication in Italy's official national anthem, *Marcia Reale*, adopted in 1861 when the newly united Kingdom of Italy was founded, in the unofficial Fascist anthem *Giovinezza* and in *Canto degli Italiani*, the song Italians had sung since it was written in 1847, whichever regime held the reins of power. It became the new national anthem in 1946. Its fourth verse begins

Dall'Alpi a Sicilia
dovunque è Legnano
(From the Alps to Sicily,
Everywhere is Legnano)
The *Marcia Reale* had,
L'Alpe d'Italia libera,
dal bel parlare angelico,
piede d'odiato barbaro
giammai calpesterà
(The Italian Alps will be free,
angelic speech will reign,
the hated barbarian

will never set foot here)
And *Giovinezza,*
Sorgi, o popolo sovrano,
Su dall'Alpi di Salvore,
Fino al siculo vulcano,
Che or si vince oppur si muor.
(Arise, o sovereign people,
Up from the Alps of Salvore
As far as the Sicilian volcano,
When now you conquer or you die.)

Hitler had chosen Barbarossa as the name for his June 1941 invasion of Russia. Now, with the help of multinational armies, Italians – some, not all, of course – were fighting to liberate their country and to push the hated barbarians back across the Alps. Aside from the Americans and British and those drawn from across British dominions – among them Black Africans, West Indians, Indians, Gurkhas, Australians, New Zealanders, South Africans – other foreigners fighting in Italy from autumn 1944 included Poles, Czechs, Greeks and Brazilians. Italy was a centre of global attention.

The Gothic Line held for a long time. Approaching the Apennines from the south, you can see why. The mountains form a natural barrier across Italy. And where the mountains give way to a stretch of level land to the east, this is scored by river after flood plain after river, making it difficult to cross and especially so for heavyweight tanks. Within the deep mountain wall, engineers of the Organisation *Todt* (responsible for the construction of the Atlantic Wall defences in France under the direction of Field Marshal Rommel) assisted by

15,000 Italian soldiers and prisoners of war and 18,000 German sappers, installed some 4,000 concrete pillboxes, 479 rapid-firing 20mm cannons along with mortars and assault guns, 2,375 machine gun posts, swivelling *Panzertürme* – 88mm-gun tank turrets mounted on concrete foundations – 16,000 sniper stations, more than 95,000 landmines, anti-tank ditches and 70 miles of barbed wire.

There were innumerable concrete-lined dugouts, command posts and bunkers. The work took ten months, sabotaged, when possible, by an understandably recalcitrant and often downright hostile workforce and held up at times by deliveries of unusable concrete made deliberately badly in Italian cement works.

In this great mountain fortress seasoned German soldiers waited. Kesselring's ground forces were still, in terms of numbers, at least as strong as the combined might of the 5th and 8th Armies. For those confronting the Germans, there was something haunting, provocative and slightly sinister in the very deliberate name Gothic Line (*Gotenstellung*). It called to mind the fierce nomadic Gothic tribes who had invaded the Roman Empire in 376 and brought Rome to its knees in 476 when the Germanic king Odoacer deposed eleven-year-old Romulus Augustulus, the last emperor of the Western Empire. This is the moment in European history when the classical world might be said to have yielded to its medieval successor, an era we readily associate with Gothic architecture, the triumph of northern Europe and rule by the sword. If Gothic also called to mind mist-wreathed pine forests, snow-capped mountain peaks, vertiginous fortifications and a certain horror, the Gothic Line had all of these.

Hitler himself was unsure about the Gothic Line, and its name, too. The Allies, he said, might be able to outflank it, and if they did, they would use its name as proof that they had now advanced into German territory. In deference to Hitler, Kesselring changed the name to Green Line, although pretty much everyone on either side of and within the mountains knew it by Kesselring's original name. Its fundamental weakness, however, became clear once DAF had achieved mastery of the Italian skies, and supplying the Gothic Line became increasingly difficult. With trains and road transport unable to move in daylight for fear of being trounced by Thunderbolts, Mustangs, Spitfires and Kittyhawks, and decreasing supplies of fuel, spare parts and ammunition from Germany, the Gothic Line was more precarious than it had first seemed for either those charged with defending it or those trying to take it from the south.

The winters of 1944, though, the worst in fifty years, brought heavy snow, savage winds, below-freezing temperatures, torrential rain and mud, mud, mud. Conditions, often much worse than those experienced on the Western Front in the First World War, were such that troops relied on horses, mules and oxen more than motor transport to fetch and carry. The animals got stuck in the mud, too.

Who, though, would blink first? 'Operation Olive', a determined attempt to breach the Gothic Line from 25 August 1944, prompted 373 Allied air attacks made from 13 September on Rimini, the Adriatic town feted, aside from its many other attractions, for its well-preserved Roman bridge, commissioned by Tiberius, and completed during

Jesus' lifetime. Flying a P-40, George Westlake dive bombed a factory there, strafed anti-aircraft gun positions ('Flak bad'), demolished a military transport depot and workshop and made a recce ('Too much flak') of the road pointing like an arrow from Rimini towards Bologna, behind the Gothic Line.

Lieutenant-General Oliver Leese, who had replaced Montgomery as commander of the Eighth Army when, in December 1943, the Field Marshal was posted to Northern Europe, said the Battle of Rimini was one of the hardest yet fought by the Eighth Army, as fierce and prolonged as El Alamein and Monte Cassino. In Rimini itself, 98 percent of the buildings were damaged or destroyed. Tiberius's bridge at least was still standing when the 3rd Greek Mountain Brigade led by Colonel Thrasyvoulos Tsakalotos occupied the city centre. And yet, after so much sound, fury, expenditure of lives, livestock and weaponry, and sheer destruction, the Gothic Line held.

For Kesselring, though, these were particularly testing times. From September, OKW (*Oberkommando der Wehrmacht*, German military high command, Berlin) ordered divisions of his 10th and 14th Armies back north of the Alps to defend postions there. At the same time, the Field Marshal was under pressure from Hitler to counter-attack. This would have been suicidal. Kesselring held his ground. While his soldiers remained resilient, Allied air superiority left him little room for manoeuvre. His armies were also under increasing attack by Italian partisans, bands of irregular, guerilla soldiers and those serving with them in various roles as messengers and saboteurs in countryside and cities alike, their name adopted from the dialectial northern Italian *partezan*, a 'part' or member of a faction.

Since September 1943, the resistance movement against the Germans and Italian Fascists had been organised into highly active partisan bands. By the time of the Battle of Rimini there were as many as 100,000 partisans in guerrilla combat, with large concentrations fighting in the Apennines. As many as a further 100,000 partisans, including 35,000 women, operated as saboteurs and couriers in towns and cities. Among them, aside from Italians of every political hue and social background, were Yugoslavs, Russians, Ukrainians, Dutch, Spaniards, Greeks, Poles, British and Americans – escaped POWs for the most part – and German defectors and deserters.

In the Alps, north of Milan, Squadron Leader Count Manfred Czernin DFC, an SOE (Special Operations Executive) operative, who had flown Hurricanes with 213 Squadron together with George Westlake and who went on to become a Battle of Britain ace, was parachuted into enemy-held territory in northern Italy to help coordinate partisan attacks. Czernin is a further reminder of just how complex loyalties in the war against Hitler in Italy were.

Born in Berlin and partly brought up in Italy – his Italian was fluent – Czernin was the son of an Austrian diplomat. His English mother was the daughter of Lord Grimthorpe, a Boer War cavalry officer, Tory MP (until he inherited the Grimthorpe peerage) and banker. An Italophile, in 1904 Lord Grimthorpe bought a historic villa near Ravello on the Amalfi Coast and turned it into a splendid, fortified mansion, complete with Moorish and Venetian Gothic details, which he called Villa Cimbrone, and where he is buried at the foot of his circular Temple of Bacchus, inscribed with these lines of Catullus:

O quid solutis est beatius curis
cum mens onus reponit, ac peregrino
labore fessi venimus larem ad nostrum,
desideratoque adquiescimus lecto?

Oh what freedom from care is more joyful
than when the mind lays down its burden,
and, weary, back home from foreign toil,
we rest on the bed we longed for?

(Translation: A. S. Kline)

Among pre-war guests languishing at Villa Cimbrone were Virginia Woolf, E. M. Forster, John Maynard Keynes, D. H. Lawrence, T. S. Eliot, Greta Garbo, Leopold Stokowski and Winston Churchill.

And Squadron Leader Czernin did indeed coordinate partisans operating in the mountains between Venice and Milan. Dropped by parachute behind enemy lines near Edolo some sixty miles north of Bergamo on the night of 21 March 1945, his task as a Senior British Liasion Officer was to coordinate the activities of scattered partisan units into a unified command. First, he had to reach them. This required his crossing of the 8,000-feet high Passo del Diavolo. After two unsuccessful attempts, Czernin finally fetched through with a determined, frost-bitten twenty-four-hour slog through snow up to six feet deep. He was soon in action with the partisans, personally forcing the surrender on 26 April of three enemy garrisons at San Pellegrino, Zogno and Sedrina, while other forces under his command that same day eliminated or captured garrisons in Isola, Bordogna, San Martino del Calvi and San Giovanni Bianco. By 1300 hours, the Val Brembana, north of Sedrina had been cleared of the enemy. Bouyed up by adrenalin and extraordinary self-confidence, Czernin decided to move into Bergamo itself, the heavily defended headquarters of *SS-Obergruppenführer* Wolff. Czernin's DSO citation reads,

On 26 April 1945, Squadron Leader Czernin, with a large Union Jack draped over his car, and with the leader of the Partisan forces, drove into Bergamo to demand the unconditional surrender of the German forces. The Germans opened fire and Squadron Leader Czernin was forced to withdraw. He immediately ordered the Partisans to attack the city and arranged for the underground elements in Bergamo to rise simultaneously. By midday on the 27th, only a small area in Bergamo was still in enemy hands and at 7.00 a.m. on 28th, 1945, Squadron Leader Czernin obtained an unconditional surrender from General Ebeling of all enemy troops in the Bergamasco.

For the most part, the partisans fought a guerilla war, notably in the mountains as Czernin's units did, although they also faced German troops openly in the streets of Florence, and between 28 July and 3 August 1944 fought a pitched battle in open countryside in and around Montefiorino, a hill town fifteen miles from Modena and core of the short-lived

'Republic of Montefiorino'. While ultimately no match for the Germans, the partisan force was some 3–4,000 strong, comprising farm workers from the surrounding area and factory workers from Modena.

In September 1944, a group of 250 partisans of the Garibaldi Brigade occupied Monte Battaglia, high on the south side of the Gothic line. In pouring rain, the Germans responded immediately. With the help of at first the US 350th regiment and, later, the 1st Welsh Guards, the partisans drove the enemy back. Time and again over five days, German attacks supported by artillery fire, mortars and flamethrowers were repulsed in bayonet charges, grenade duels, hand-to-hand combat, hurled rocks and slashing knives. By now, partisan attacks had made it difficult for high-ranking German officers to move with certainty through the Apennines. *Generalleutnant* von Senger took, he said, to travelling in a Volkswagen with 'no general's insignia of rank – no peaked cap, no gold or red flags'.

Kesselring's response was to order the execution of at least ten Italians for every German death attributable to partisans. This was not the Field Marshal's finest hour, although, as he later claimed, 'my soldiers were ambushed; they were hunted; they were burned, the wounded soldiers in Red Cross ambulances were burned; their bodies nailed to window frames, their eyes struck out, their noses and ears were cut off, also their sexual organs; they were put into barrels which were filled with water and afterwards machine gunned, and, last but not least, in Pisa as a sign of gratitude that we supplied the children with milk, the wells were poisoned'.

Certainly, there was pressure from Karl Wolff, the former public relations and advertising executive who had been appointed Supreme SS and Police Leader Italy in September 1943. He became responsible for anti-partisan warfare. The retaliatory methods employed by the SS against partisans and civilians alike had been highlighted in a truly terrifying manner in Rome, three months before General Clark and his Fifth Army drove into the newly liberated 'Open City'.

Twenty-eight soldiers of an SS column marching and singing through Piazza di Spagna into Via Rasella were killed by a partisan bomb hidden in a rubbish cart. The same night, an order, directly from Adolf Hitler, was given for the execution of ten Italians for every German soldier killed. Kesselring decided that this could mean the execution of Italians already sentenced to death. In the event, 335 Italians from all walks of life, among them seventy-five Jews, were rounded up and driven in lorries to disused quarries in a rural suburb beside the Via Ardeatina, the Ancient Roman road. Led into a cave in groups of five, they were forced to kneel and shot in the back of the head by SS officers.

Father Pietro Pappagnello, an anti-fascist priest, was among those killed, as was Major General Simone Simoni, a First Word War hero and now a resistance leader, whose eldest son Captain Gastone Simoni had been killed at the Second Battle of El Alamein. Held by the SS for fifty-eight days, the General, who admitted nothing, had been tortured with a blowtorch. Colonel Giuseppe Montezemelo, a staff officer decorated with the German Iron Cross for bravery at the Battle of Tobruk in North Africa, loyal to the King of Italy and known personally by Kesselring, had his teeth and fingernails pulled out by SS interrogators before his murder in the Ardeatine cave. His captors had learned nothing from him.

Kesselring had thought long and hard about how partisans should be dealt with. The order he had signed on 17 June in 1944 was unequivocal. It was addressed to 'GHQ Staff 10th Army, GHQ Staff 14th Army, Army Group V Zangen, General Plenipotentiary German Armed Forces in Italy, HQ Luftflotte 2; German Naval High Command, Italy, Supreme Head of SS and Police, Italy, General i/c CTPT, Italy, Plenipotentiary of the Greater German Reich with the Italian Government, Ambassador Rahn'. Here are its three key paragraphs:

1. The partisan situation in the Italian theatre, particularly in Central Italy, has recently deteriorated to such an extent, that it constitutes a serious danger to the fighting troops and supply lines as well as to the war industry and economic potential. The fight against the partisans must be carried on with all the means at our disposal and with the utmost severity. I will protect any command who exceeds our usual restraint in the choice of severity of the methods he adopts against partisans. In this connection the old principle holds good, that a mistake in the choice of methods in executing one's orders, is better than failure or neglect to act. Only the most prompt and severe handling is good enough as punitive and deterrent measures to nip in the bud other outrages on a greater scale. All civilians implicated in anti-partisan operations who are apprehended in the course of reprisals,

are to be brought up the Assembly Camps which are being erected for this purpose by the Quartermaster General C-in-C South West for ultimate despatch to the Reich as workers.

2. The combat against partisans consists of passive and active operations with the centre of gravity on the latter. The passive combat consists of protection of important buildings of historic or artistic value, railways and roads, as well as essential installations such as power stations, factories, etc. Even these passive operations must be conducted within the local boundaries; for example, Recce Troops will constantly guard the foreground of an installation to be protected. Active operations will be conducted especially in partisan-overrun districts, where it is vital to maintain the lifeline of the Armed Forces. These partisans will have to be attacked and wiped out. Propaganda among partisans (as well as use of agents) is of the utmost importance.

3. The responsibility for the entire operations against partisans in the Italian theatre and the fundamental instructions for same [sic] continue to be valid with the following amendments: GHQ 10 and 14 Armies are responsible for all operations against partisans within their Army Sectors and Army Group V Zangen within the coastal belt for 30km. The task entrusted the GOC in C Operational Zone Adriatic Coast in connection with coastal defence (in accordance with Fuehrer Instruction No. 40) are not affected by this ruling. In the remainder of the Italian Theatre the Supreme Head of the SS and Police conducts the operations against Partisans on his responsibility, in accordance with my instructions.

The SS, Waffen-SS and the Brigate Nere interpreted Kesselring's instruction very much their own way. Together in August they murdered 560 villagers and refugees in the Gothic Line village of Sant'Anna di Stazzema. The victims included eight pregnant women, one of whom – Evelina Berretti – had her womb cut open with a bayonet to allow a soldier to kill her baby in front of her while she was still alive. After three hours of death and destruction, the SS soldiers sat down to lunch on the edge of the burning village. This was certainly not a clean war.

Nor was it a simple case of Allies and partisans good, Germans very bad indeed. Eric Newby was a twenty-two-year-old lieutenant serving with the SBS (Special Boat Service), the Royal Navy's clandestine commando unit. Captured off the coast of Sicily in August 1942 after an operation to sabotage an airfield swarming with Ju-88 bombers ready and waiting to attack British Mediterranean convoys went wrong, he was held as a POW at first at Chietinear Pescara and then at Fontanellato near Parma. Having escaped in September 1943 at the time of the Armistice with the help of the young Slovenian woman (Wanda Škof) – whom he married in 1946 – and her father, a First World War Austrian army officer, Newby was spirited into the Apennines, where he lived and worked on farms with anti-Fascists. Late one morning while climbing high into mushroom woods, he lay down in a grassy hollow and was lulled to sleep by the humming of bees, the buzzing of insects, the clanking of sheep bells and the warmth of what must have been the Angelus sun, with church bells calling solemnly to one another across the valley below him.

Newby woke, or so he recalled in his enchanting book *Love and War in the Apennines* (1971), 'to find a German soldier standing over me', an officer, of much his own age, in summer battledress carrying an old-fashioned civilian haversack and a large butterfly net. *Oberleutnant* Frick, Education Officer, guessed that Newby was English and offered him a bottle of German beer. He explained that he was based at the headquarters spa town of Salsomaggiore in the foothills of the Apennines, where his job was 'to give lectures on Italian culture, particularly the culture of the Renaissance, to groups of officers, and any of the men who are interested. It is scarcely arduous because so few are.'

He continued:

I must confess that there are some aspects of my countrymen's character that I cannot pretend to understand. I do not speak disloyally to make you feel more friendly to me because, no doubt, you, also, do not understand your own people, but surely only Germany would employ a professor of entomology from Göttingen with only one lung, whose only interest is *lepidoptera*, to give lectures on Renaissance paintings and architecture to soldiers who are engaged in destroying these things as hard as they are able. Do you not think it strange?

Newby replied, saying that the British and the Americans did the same sort of thing. Frick told Newby that, although it would take a long time, Germany would lose the war. 'We shall hold you here, at least through this winter and perhaps we could hold you through next summer [1944]. What is going on in Russia is more than flesh and blood can stand.

We are on the retreat from Smolensk; we are retreating to the Dnieper. According to people who have just come from there we are losing more men every day than we have lost here in the Italian peninsula in an entire month.' The two men shook hands. Frick asked for his beer bottle back, as these were in short supply, and then he ran down towards the valley 'making curious little sweeps and lunges as he pursued his prey... I was sorry to see him go.'

It hardly matters whether Newby's beguiling story is true or not. It captures the absurdity of armed forces on both sides of the Italian war doing their best to destroy the very civilisation championed by their leaders, Nazi, Fascist or nominally democratic. And it conveys the sense that Kesselring's prolonged defence of Italy was futile, with soldiers on both sides knowing this to be true. There is also something touching in the portrait of a kindly young German officer flitting between the atrocities of the Apennines in pursuit of neither communists nor POWs on the run, but of Titania's fritillaries, Piedmont ringlets and Alpine blues.

At the end of Lewis Milestone's 1930 film *All Quiet on the Western Front*, based on Erich Maria Remarque's novel of the same name published the previous year, the young German student conscript Paul Baümer is shot dead by a French sniper as, artillery rumbling in the background, he reaches out from the rampart of a fortification towards a harmless butterfly. One can readily imagine a partisan hidden among the trees shooting Newby's *Oberleutnant* Frick dead as he chased an equally beautiful insect.

If he was real, Frick may have seen *All Quiet on the Western Front* before it was banned, first by the Weimar government fearful of the effect of Nazi protests and then in 1933 by the Nazi regime itself. For the Nazis, the problem with the film was twofold. It depicted German defeat in the First World War and it was directed by a Jew. During its premiere and early screenings in Berlin, Joseph Goebbels had Brownshirts yelling *Judenfilm!* while clearing cinemas using such puerile pranks as stink bombs, itching powder and live mice running between seats, before they took to beating cinemagoers taken for Jews.

'Within ten minutes, the cinema resembles a madhouse,' noted the future Minister for Public Enlightenment and Propaganda in his diary after one such screening.

> The police are powerless. The embittered crowd takes out its anger on the Jews. The first breakthrough in the West. 'Jews out!' 'Hitler is standing at the gates!' The police sympathize with us. The Jews are small and ugly. The box office outside is under siege. Windowpanes are broken. Thousands of people enjoy the spectacle. The screening is abandoned, as is the next one. We have won. The newspapers are full of our protest. But not even the *Berliner Tageblatt* dares to call us names. The nation is on our side. In short: victory!

★

The Italian partisans were no angels, yet for DAF airmen, as with any other Allied soldier, it was not a good idea to fall into the hands of Italian Fascists. Throughout the Gothic Line stalemate, DAF flew numerous strike and armed reconnaissance ops high and very low over northern Italy. On 29 August, Sergeant Arthur Banks, who had been with 112 Squadron for three weeks, was over Rovigo to the north of Ferrara when his Mustang III was hit by flak. Banks crash-landed successfully, set fire to the aircraft and began walking. He was lucky, at first, to encounter the 'Boccato' partisans, whom he joined, becoming an invaluable member of the group.

In the hope of reaching Allied lines, and with the promise of resupplying the Boccato group, presumably from the air, Banks attempted to escape in a fishing boat through the Po estuary. Betrayed by a double agent, he was caught in a set-up operation by German Field Police and Italian militia. Beaten and tortured for six days, Banks remained silent save for offering his name, rank and number. Frustrated, the Germans handed Banks over to the Brigate Nere (Black Brigades) fascist paramilitary group. His savage torture was supervised by two fanatical women. Still, Banks remained silent. Finally, they poured petrol over his horrifically scarred naked body, throwing him into the River Po before flames took hold.

Astonishingly, Banks found the strength to swim across the river, but – how could he know? – it was to a bank where waiting Brigate Nere militia dragged him back to the barracks where he had been tortured. An Italian officer there shot him in the back of the head. The airman's dead body was thrown on a dung heap. It was rescued by townspeople and buried in a local cemetery. At the end of the war, Banks received a posthumous George Cross, his body reinterred in the Argenta Gap War Cemetery. The cemetery, designed by Louis de Soissons, a Canadian-born British architect with a great fondness for eighteenth-century Italian architecture, is set in fields, a forty-five-minute walk from the railway station at Argenta, two hours by train from Venice.

Arthur Banks's headstone reads, 'The Righteous are in the hand of God and there shall no torment touch them.' Sergeant Banks was twenty-two.

Had he made it back to Allied lines and 112 Squadron, Banks may well have flown on Operation Bowler. He would have liked Venice. At school, St Edward's, Oxford, he was Captain of Boats. Kenneth Grahame, author of *The Wind in the Willows* (1908), had been a pupil at St Edward's, and Banks must surely have read his enchanting book. Here is the Sea Rat from *The Wind in the Willows* relating his ventures to Rat, captivated by the lure of the warm 'South':

> Thence we turned and coasted up the Adriatic, its shores swimming in an atmosphere of amber, rose, and aquamarine; we lay in wide land-locked harbours, we roamed through ancient and noble cities, until at last one morning, as the sun rose royally behind us, we rode into Venice down a path of gold. O, Venice is a fine city, wherein a rat can wander at his ease and take his pleasure! Or, when weary of wandering, can sit at the edge of the Grand Canal at night, feasting with his friends, when the air is full of music and the sky full of stars, and the lights flash and shimmer on the polished steel prows of the swaying gondolas, packed so that you could walk across the canal on them from side to side! And then the food – do you like shellfish? Well, well, we won't linger over that now.

Another pupil, four years above Banks, whose name is forever associated with water, was Wing Commander Guy Gibson VC, DSO & Bar, DFC & Bar, who led 617 Squadron's famous Dambusters Raid. Gibson was killed in September

1944 when the Mosquito he was flying back from over Mönchengladbach crashed outside Steenbergen in the Netherlands, and when Arthur Banks was enduring horrendous pain in Italy.

The DAF kept up relentless raids on enemy targets throughout the autumn. Young American pilots like Gerry Teldon and British Battle of Britain veterans alike were intrigued to find themselves flying in an ever-more international Allied air war. Brazil had declared war on the Axis on 26 August 1942 and the Brazilian Air Force, trained in the US, was now flying bomber escort and ground strafing missions with P-47s.

As wild as ever, Gerry Teldon's 85th fighter group engaged in mock dog fights with US fighter squadrons escorting bombers home on the last legs of their missions, sometimes encountering the red-tailed P51-D Mustangs of the all-Black 99th Fighter Squadron. The 'Tuskegee Airmen' had been in action in Italy since June 1943. The 85th usually got the worst of it. The 99th's Mustangs had a better turn ratio than the Thunderbolts while, Gerry believed, their pilots, as fighter interceptors, were used to pulling higher 'Gs'. They also had a style very much of their own. Flying a 324 Wing Spitfire, Group Captain Wilfrid Duncan Smith picked up a radio transmission from the 99th:

'Red leader calling. Target three o'clock below. Get ready to dive bomb. Blue Leader to go on down first. Over.'

Silence.

'Red leader calling Blue Leader. Ain't you heard me? Dive bomb. Go!'

'Blue Leader to Red Leader. Man, look at all that flak. Y'all go on down. You've got the Distinguished Flying Cross, so let's see you do some distinguished flying.'

★

Kesselring's armies, distinguished and formidable fighting units though they were, were saved time and again by the, as yet, impermeable Gothic Line and by the turn in the weather. By the late autumn of 1944, it was truly wretched. General Alexander called off army operations. In a radio broadcast he asked partisans to take a winter break. As for the Desert Air Force, its name seemed increasingly inappropriate.

Snow fell. Soldiers of the 5th and 8th Armies were exhausted. Embedded in the mountains, the Germans were suffering too. But, if Allied ground troops had yet to breach the Gothic Line, the DAF and its Italian confederates had. Railways, roads, freight yards, bridges and viaducts had been pummelled and destroyed the length and breadth of the Po Valley, into northeast Italy and also – with the long-range Mustangs – into Yugoslavia. German supply lines had been shredded. This threatened not just the German 10th and 14th Armies holding on to northern Italy, now under the command of General Heinrich von Vietinghoff following Field Marshal Kesselring's accident in late October, but also the industrial powerhouses of Turin, Brescia and Milan, already ravaged by Allied bombing raids launched from England.

Moving to Fano between Ancona and Pesaro on the Adriatic coast, 239 Wing's crews and pilots were billeted in a convent and nearby houses. They were unable to count their blessings. The Wing had barely settled in when one of 5 SAAF's Mustangs returned to base with a 1,000lb bomb that had failed to drop over its target hanging perilously from one of its wings. Before the Mustang could land, the bomb worked itself loose and, falling into Fano's busy midday central square, killed four civilians and four members of a South African Signals unit. Bad weather and increasing fatigue led to further accidents.

DAF, however, fought through any gap in the weather during the long months of the assault on the Gothic Line, and on operations far beyond it. If Sergeant Banks could have heard news about his squadron that terrible autumn, he would have learned that 112's Mustang IIIs had strafed a German airfield at Grado near the Gulf of Trieste, hitting eight Ju-87s, Fw-190s and Bf-109s. They had bombed bridges east of Rimini and near San Felice. On Saturday 21 October, they went train spotting, destroying twenty-eight locomotives. Sergeant Arthur Jones was hit by flak. Baling out thirty miles from the Adriatic shore, he was rescued by Walrus and Catalina seaplanes. News was good and bad. The following day, Lieutenant John Lund was shot down and killed by flak while strafing German tanks southwest of Ravenna.

With flying conditions deteriorating over Italy, 112 Squadron headed further afield. Pilot Officer Robert Deeble was shot down and killed by flak over Slovenske Konjice, Yugoslavia, on 6 November. Two days later, Pilot Officer George 'Knobby' Clark was killed when his Mustang was shot down near Cavanella d'Adige, seventeen miles south of Venice. His target had been in Yugoslavia, but fog there prompted him to seek a new target near Venice. After dropping his bomb, he turned back to inspect the damage and was blown out of the sky. Flying Officer Jacques Roney from East Sheen in Surrey died of his wounds after engine failure on take-off caused his Mustang to strike a pair of 24 SAAF Squadron B-26 Marauders and a petrol bowser (tanker).

On 5 September, the 79th Fighter Group entered German air space – one up to the Americans – its Thunderbolts strafing Freiberg airfield, destroying a Heinkel He III and damaging twelve other aircraft. That same day, 87th Squadron flew as far as Mulhouse in the Alsace close to the German and Swiss borders, destroying four He IIIs, two Bf 109s and a Stuka on the ground. Three 250 Squadron Kittyhawks were shot down by flak between 18 and 23 September, their pilots wounded or simply shaken up, but all returning safely.

Seven Spitfires of 72 Squadron flew an armed reconnaissance mission over Venice on Saturday 21 October. They were engaged over Lake Garda by eight Bf109s of ANR 2 *Gruppo*, a sharp reminder that, while the Luftwaffe had ceased daylight operations over northern Italy, the Fascist *Aeronautica Nazionale Repubblicana* was still up for a fight. The Spitfires drove the Messerschmitts away, shooting down one for certain, possibly a second and damaging a third. Spitfire pilots, however, could not afford to be cocksure. Things could go suddenly wrong without their even knowing quite why. Captain A. W. Meikle, Acting CO of 7 SAAF Squadron, damaged his Spitfire IX in a rocket attack over the Adriatic. He was picked up safely by a Catalina.

Some Allied pilots shot down were rescued and returned safely by Italian and Yugoslavian partisans. Others were attacked, yet again, by trigger-happy Americans who, away from the heat of intense aerial combat, should have known better. On 22 November, a British Westland Lysander 'spy plane' flying the clandestine Operation Templar to Tramonti di Sopra near Udine, taking three undisclosed passengers into enemy territory, was shot down by US Mustangs of 325th Fighter Group killing the pilot, Flying Officer J. Raynes, and his three passengers. When 3 RAAF Squadron's Mustangs, escorting the Lysander, turned to drive the attackers away, without shooting, the Americans thought they were under attack by Spitfires and took evasive action. Why they shot down a Lysander remains a mystery. How they mistook Mustangs for Spitfires is simply baffling.

The weather had been truly bad when, on 6 December, six of ten Mustang III and IVs of 5 SAAF Squadron were lost to bad weather over Yugoslavia. Three of the aircraft simply disappeared. The pilot of a fourth baled but was killed. A fifth bailed out safely but was made a prisoner of war. Only the sixth, Lieutenant A. E. Burnett, rescued by Yugoslav partisans after landing by parachute, made it back safely to the Squadron.

By Christmas, flying anywhere near the Gothic Line was downright dangerous, not because of enemy fire from the mountains but because of the weather. Ground operations, too, appeared to have ground to a halt. The Germans and the Italian National Republican Army seized the moment, making the last Axis offensive, with Operation *Wintergewitter* (Winter Thunderstorm). Launched at midnight on 26 December, this had the German 148th Infantry Division under the command of *Generalleutnant* Otto Fretter-Pico and the Italian Monterosa Mountain Division led by feather-capped General Mario Carloni attacking a chain of villages along mountain ridges centred on Sommocolonia in the Serchio Valley, on the west side of the Gothic Line, twenty-five miles north of Lucca.

The Axis force of 9,100 troops, of which 6,000 were Italian, faced the 18,000-strong US 92nd Infantry Division supported by 120 tanks and 140 artillery pieces. Despite incidents of heroic fighting, the 92nd was routed. When the weather cleared a little on 28 December, Thunderbolts were in action, as they were to be for the next two days, shooting up anything that might be associated with the enemy, including the hospital at Camporgiano, where wounded American soldiers were being treated side by side with German and Italian casualties. The Axis force beat a retreat as the 8th Indian Division, with Gurkhas in its ranks, reoccupied the villages and icy ridges with few shots fired.

For a day or two it had seemed as though, if backed by sufficient reinforcements, the Axis forces might just battle their way to Lucca, Pisa and Livorno, and in doing so, drive a wedge between Allied armies and the flanks of the Gothic Line. But with few resources behind it, Operation *Wintergewitter* proved to be more firecracker than thunderstorm. It was seen even then as the equivalent, if not in terms of numbers, as the Ardennes Offensive or 'Battle of the Bulge' fought in bitter winter conditions at the same time. A 410,000-strong German army attempted to split and then surround the Allies on the Western Front in a massive drive through the forests of the Ardennes between Belgium and Luxembourg. But the German numbers, on the ground and in the air, had not been enough. This last great battle in the West left the Germans fatally weakened. Even so, the very fact that the enemy had struck back rattled Allied commanders. The counter-attack in Italy suggested that the struggle to break out from the Gothic Line would be even harder than expected. 'Our strength was not enough to get across the final barrier to which the enemy clung,' noted General Clark. From now and until the spring of 1945, the Gothic Line barely wavered.

In the New Year, reconnaissance photographs – hundreds had been taken by high-flying, photo-reconnaissance RAF PR IX Spitfires over northern Italy from the autumn – revealed an uncomfortable, if long-suspected truth. DAF had made transalpine transport by road and railway to northern Italy all but impossible, its pilots even destroying vital targets as small (seen from the air at speed) as electricity transformers along the Brenner Pass railway, bringing trains to a sudden stop. And yet supplies for the German military and northern Italian industry were still arriving, if slowly, courtesy of ships revealed in these reconnaissance photographs sailing into Venice.

While the big new port built at Marghera on the mainland after the First World War, with its generous docks and oil refineries, had been viewed by the Allies as a legitimate Venetian target and bombed heavily, Stazione Marittima, located cheek by jowl with the historic fabric of the lagoon city, had been watched from the air, yet given the benefit of doubt. No longer. Venice, the one city that no one wanted to attack, was moving into the sights of Allied bombers. Until air reconnaissance had told a different story, Venice had seemed little more than a heavily brocaded and harmless sideshow. This had changed. The war was about to come to Venice, out of the air guns blazing.

What fun they were having. German soldiers taking a gondola trip on the Grand Canal, summer 1944.

NINE

VENICE *INTERMEZZO*

January 1945

It came as a blow. From January, a month of bad weather, the city's restaurants would close until official notice. In their place, state canteens would offer hot meals. Venice, though, had long been a city of survivors. That is, after all, how it had begun in the first quarter of the fifth century, a marshy refuge from the Ostrogoths and Lombards. 'You live like seabirds,' wrote Cassiodorus, a sixth-century Christian Roman states-man serving with Theodoric the Great at the Ostrogoth king's court in Ravenna, 'with your homes dispersed across the surface of the water.'

Now, though, as food supplies were increasingly cut off by Allied air strikes on roads, bridges, railway lines, goods yards and ports, and drinking water no longer a given in parts of the city, Venice was packed like never before. It became a safe haven – Allied air raids were directed principally at the

port of Marghera on the mainland side of the road and railway bridges, while high-flying DAF Spitfires flying
reconnaissance missions were nothing more dangerous than
vapour trails – and, tucked well behind Kesselring's seemingly
unbreachable Gothic Line, the city attracted an ever-increasing
number of people. By January 1945, its population was said
to be 200,000, a figure boosted by recuperating German and
Italian Fascist soldiers, freeloaders and those on furlough.
Germans in uniforms – of all ranks – had often been seen
the previous summer taking in the sights of old Venice from
the rocking seats of gondolas.

Venice was also the city where, soldiers aside, European
politicians, economists, bankers and civil servants met in a
mostly relaxed setting to discuss the Nazi German idea of a
continental European Commission, whereby nation states,
using a single currency, would be formed into an economic
and political union following the ultimate victory and, of
course, under German hegemony. If it seems odd that such
meetings could be held in all seriousness several months after
the German surrender at Stalingrad in January 1943 – the
turning point in the European war – then this is an indication of how deluded many Nazis and Fascists were. And
Venice was the perfect setting.

The restaurants may have been ordered to close, yet decent
meals could be had in veiled clubs and secret dining rooms
and also in the grander hotels which catered for high-ranking German soldiers, Nazi officials and Italian functionaries
of the puppet Salò Republic (*Repubblica Sociale Italiana*), of
which Mussolini was the nominal head. The puppet *meisters*
were Rudolf Rahn, a forty-four-year-old career diplomat

appointed German Plenipotentiary to the new Fascist republic by Hitler in September 1943, and SS-*Obergruppenführer* (General) Karl Wolff, an exact contemporary of Rahn's, whose brief included 'anti-partisan warfare'.

Rahn and Wolff were among the Germans, many in uniform, who when in Venice drank coffee and schnapps at the Gran Caffè Quadri in St Mark's Square. Opened in 1775, the café had long attracted an Austrian and German clientele. Effie Ruskin, too. Richard Wagner, who lived in Venice for many years, was a regular at Caffè Lavena, opposite Quadri. The composer observed that 'the Austrian officers... floated about publicly in Venice like oil on water'. At much the same time as Wagner arrived in Venice, William Dean Howells, the US Consul, recalled the 'glitter of uniforms, and then idling...carried on with a great noise of conversation in Austrian German'. Since September 1943, German conversation in St Mark's Square had been rather more guttural than it had been before, while the music played at Quadri, all too often by the Hermann Göring Regimental Band with its 'oompah' renditions of Bach and Liszt, had little or none of the lightness of touch of Strauss's 'Radetzky March'.

Venetians preferred Caffè Florian and its local, lighter band on the opposite side of the square. There were times when Venetian partisans sat there unrecognised and yet within sight of SS officers, Gestapo henchmen and even on occasion General Wolff himself. Partisan activity within the city had been growing, occasionally erupting and, when exposed, was put down brutally. From guerrilla raids on Gothic Line defences to sabotage missions throughout the Po Valley, and within Venice itself, the women and men of the partisans were among the bravest of the brave. On 17 June 1944, shortly after the German retreat from Rome, and uncharacteristically jittered, Field Marshal Kesselring had issued his infamous directive, 'New Measures for Combating Partisans', authorising reprisals of the 'utmost severity'.

The labyrinthine alleys and courtyards of Venice were good hiding places for the resistance. They had certainly helped many of the city's Jews to escape when the Germans arrived. Freed by Napoleon in 1797 from their infamous ghetto, established in 1516 by Doge Leonardo Loredan, and a part of Venetian life ever since, from September 1943 Venetian Jews faced annihilation. Some hid for the duration of the war. Others escaped, mostly to Switzerland or Allied-occupied southern Italy, leaving 246 unlucky souls to be deported to Auschwitz-Birkenau, of whom just eight survived. On the very day the Germans stomped into Venice, the Gestapo called on the distinguished Venetian physician, Professor Giuseppe Jona, since 1940 president of the Jewish community. He was given two days to list the names and whereabouts of all Venetian Jews. Destroying every possible incriminating document, Jona committed suicide before the Gestapo returned. His self-sacrifice saved the lives of 1,200 fellow Jewish citizens.

Venetians had not, as a rule, been anti-Semitic, nor especially had Italy. Jews had been free to join the *Partito Nazionale Fascista* (PNF). Some were even founder members (among them the Torinese banker Ettore Ovazza, a friend of Mussolini, who had taken part in the 1922 March on Rome), funded the PNF and, in 1934, had launched *La Nostra Bandiera* (*Our Flag*), an anti-Zionist Fascist newspaper.

Mussolini's biographer, mistress and one-time propaganda advisor, the art critic Margherita Sarfatti, was from a distinguished Venetian Jewish family. 'The Jewish problem does not exist in Italy,' declared the Duce. But that was in 1932, six years before the proclamation of Italy's race laws, designed to appease Hitler. It remains difficult to know the true extent of anti-Semitism in Venice.

The Nazi feature film *Jew Süss* was an anti-Semitic propaganda wrapped in the tissue of an outwardly engaging historical drama, with leading German actors in the key roles. It was in sharp contrast with the brutally crude documentary-style *Der ewige Jude* (*The Eternal Jew*, 1940) which Hitler preferred (being first screened in September 1940 at that year's Venice Film Festival). It received glowing reviews. The film's doomed Aryan heroine was played by Kristina Söderbaum, a favourite of Joseph Goebbels who was involved heavy-handedly in the film's scripting, casting and production. Curiously, the last film the Swedish actress appeared in was the bizarre *Night Train to Venice*, filmed in 1993, with Hugh Grant ('a stinker' said Grant in 2002 radio interview).

Italo Balbo, the dashing aviator, creator and Commander-in-Chief of the *Regia Aeronautica*, Governor General of Italian Libya and latterly Commander-in-Chief Italian North Africa, who had marched on Rome with Mussolini, he had been a key architect of the Fascist Party. He was also widely acknowledged to be the Duce's successor, and had been against the alliance with Nazi Germany, anti-Semitism and war. In Libya, he said he was pressed between the British in Egypt and French in Tunisia 'like a slice of ham in a sandwich'.

It was General Balbo who, in the summer of 1933, led the Atlantic Squadron or 'Italian Armada' of twenty-five beautiful *Regia Aeronautica* Savoia-Marchetti S.55 seaplanes from Ortobello to Lake Chicago, as a greeting from Italy to the Century of Progress International Exhibition, Chicago. The Italians were greeted with great enthusiasm. Balbo lunched with US President Roosevelt, was made 'Chief Flying Eagle' by the Sioux tribe, appeared on the cover of *Time* and for the most part was feted wherever he went. There were also protests by Chicagoans who knew of Balbo's leadership of gangs of Blackshirt thugs who broke strikes and beat up Italian communists, socialists and trade unionists before the March on Rome. If, though, he had chosen to stay in the United States, said Harry Stewart, the Chicago exhibition's commissioner, he could be the next President. A monument to celebrate Balbo's historic transatlantic flight stands today in a corner of Burnham Park overlooking Lake Chicago. It takes the form of a Corinthian column rising from a base bearing the inscription:

> This column
> Twenty centuries old
> Erected on the beach of Ostia
> Port of Imperial Rome
> To safeguard the fortunes and victories
> Of the Roman triremes
> Fascist Italy, by command of Benito Mussolini,
> Presents to Chicago
> Exaltation, symbol, memorial
> Of the Atlantic Squadron led by Balbo
> That with Roman daring flew across the ocean

In the 11th year
Of the Fascist era.

Mussolini had yet to invade Ethiopia, which he did in October 1935, with Balbo's air force using mustard gas in attacks on villages and Red Cross stations. Few Americans followed events in Ethiopia. The Italians remained popular.

On 28 June 1940, a tri-motor Savoia-Marchetti SM.79 light bomber was misidentified by Italian gunners defending Tobruk and shot down. General Balbo was on board, his body so badly burned that all there was left to identify him by were his teeth. Mussolini's reaction was to shrug his shoulders. Chance had rid the Duce of this turbulent pro-American, anti-war airman for whom anti-Semitism made no sense.

In a bid to keep in with Hitler, in May 1942 Mussolini sent Libyan and Italian Jews to a new concentration labour camp at Giado in Libya. There were smaller camps at Buq Buq and Sidi Azaz. Italian concentration camps were nothing new. Huge numbers of nomadic Libyan tribespeople died in the horrific camps that endured from the Italian invasion of Libya in 1911 until 1934, when Balbo was appointed Governor, and the camps were closed. Of the 2,600 Jews held at Giado, 562 died of starvation or typhus fever before the camp was liberated in January 1943 by British troops led by Brigadier Frederick Kisch DSO, himself a Jew, born in Darjeeling, educated in England and killed weeks later when he stepped on a landmine.

The British response to Balbo's death had been somewhat different to Mussolini's play of indifference. Air Chief Marshal

Arthur Longmore, Commander-in-Chief RAF Middle East Command, and a former fellow seaplane pilot, dispatched an aircraft to Tobruk to drop a wreath on the site of the wreckage. A personal note attached read, 'The British Royal Air Force expresses sympathy in the death of General Balbo, a great leader and gallant aviator, personally known to me, whom fate has placed on the other side.'

The following August, a blunt notice appeared on the door of Harry's Bar, until then a carefree haunt of glamorous and mostly wealthy visitors to Venice – Winston Churchill among them before the war – celebrated for its signature Bellini cocktail. A sign of the times, the new notice read 'No Jews Here'. This, it must be said, was not something Giuseppe Cipriani, the bar's creator and owner, wanted. When asked earlier by the Gestapo to point out Jews in the bar, he shrugged his shoulders and said, 'They're all Italians to me.'

In November 1943, however, Jews, now that the Germans were in charge, were officially declared 'enemy aliens' by the Italian Social Republic. In October, while trying to escape to Switzerland, Ettore Ovazza, together with his wife and children, were executed by order of the Austrian-born *Untersturmführer* Gottfried Meir of the 1st SS Panzer Division Leibstandarte SS Adolf Hitler. Their dismembered bodies were burned in the boiler room of Intra school on Lake Maggiore.

In March 1945, news seeped through to Venice's hidden Jews that the 5,500-strong Jewish Brigade, formed in late 1944 and seconded to the Eighth Army under the command of Brigadier Ernest Benjamin, had been fighting hard against *Generalleutnant* Heinrich Trettner's elite 4th Parachute

Division along the River Senio, key to Kesselring's defence of the Po Valley. In one memorable air-to-ground support mission during the offensive, SAAF Spitfires, several of whose pilots were Jews, flew over the brigade in a Star of David formation.

As for all those British visitors to the city who had been welcomed before the war, it seems unlikely that Venetians had ever truly despised them, although, with the Germans in control, it was wise to wear a mask of Anglophobia. In an editorial published in the May–July 1942 issue of *L'Ateneo Veneto*, the disappearance of the English from the Venetian life was said to have been no great loss. The journal referred to them as 'those angular wandering skeletons with their half-French hairdos and make-up and their vulgar horsey laughs from mouths much worked over with the gold of London dentists'. Good riddance to them, 'their Byron, Browning, Ruskin and their dogs!'

In January 1945, however, the far-from-effete English were fighting very hard indeed alongside their fellow British, Commonwealth, American and other allies drawn from around the globe ever closer to the Po Valley in the campaign to push the Germans from Italy. As for the Americans, one in ten US soldiers fighting in the war was from an Italian background. Why the heck was Italy fighting so many fellow Italians, many of whom had volunteered to cross the Atlantic and rough it in North Africa to do so? Italian-American women were in the picture, too, hard at work in factories manufacturing armaments and aircraft. The best known were Rose Bonavita and Jennie Florio, who worked at General Motors Eastern Aircraft Division in North

Tarrytown, New York. The fellow factory workers received a personal letter from US President Franklin Roosevelt congratulating them on drilling a record 900 holes and placing 3,300 rivets in an aircraft tail within six hours. Rosie was the inspiration for a Westinghouse Electric poster of 1943, little known during the war yet hugely popular when rediscovered in the 1980s, for the 'We Can Do It!' poster depicting a feisty young woman in a red bandana and bicep-revealing denim shirt.

Henry Wadsworth Longfellow had done much to popularise Venice for Americans since his visit to the city in 1828, when he was twenty-one. In later years, his works, among them the first American translation of Dante's *Divina Commedia* and reams of poems, became hugely popular. Here is 'Venice':

White swan of cities, slumbering in thy nest
    So wonderfully built among the reeds
    Of the lagoon, that fences thee and feeds,
    As sayeth thy old historian and thy guest!
White water-lily, cradled and caressed
    By ocean streams, and from the silt and weeds
    Lifting thy golden filaments and seeds,
    Thy sun-illumined spires, thy crown and crest!
White phantom city, whose untrodden streets
    Are rivers, and whose pavements are the shifting
    Shadows of palaces and strips of sky;
I wait to see thee vanish like the fleets
    Seen in mirage, or towers of cloud uplifting
    In air their unsubstantial masonry.

Americans had come to the white swan city, officially, in 1807 with the opening here of a US consulate, yet transatlantic visitors were rare. A 2001 article in *American Heritage* by the historian John Lukacs tells us, 'Emerson [Ralph Waldo Emerson, the American essayist, poet and philosopher] visited it in 1837. He did not like it. "It is a great oddity – a city for beavers – but to my thought a most disagreeable residence...any thing but comfort. I soon had enough of it."'

In 1861, twenty-four-year-old William Dean Howells was appointed consul in Venice at a time when the Venetians knew those few Americans they encountered as *inglesi*. Howells's books, *Venetian Life* (1866) and *Italian Journeys* (1867), sold well, encouraging well-heeled Americans to venture this way. In 1862, Howells married Elinor Mead, sister of the architect William Rutherford Mead, a partner of the great American firm McKim, Mead & White, who lived for many years in Rome, where he became president of the American Academy. He was dubbed Knight Commander of the Crown of Italy by King Victor Emmanuel for bringing Roman and Italian Renaissance design into American architecture. With the design of Penn Station (1910) and the General Post Office Building (1914), both on Manhattan's Eighth Avenue, McKim, Mead & White did this brilliantly, and on an epic scale.

The Howells lived in an apartment in Casa Falier overlooking the Grand Canal. In writing about it Howells helped set a tone for American journalists and novelists ever since. 'Our dear little balcony at Casa Falier! Over our heads dwelt a Dalmatian family; below our feet a Frenchwoman; at our right, upon the same floor, an English gentleman; under him a French family; and over him the family of a marquis in exile from Modena.' Surely there must have been a grand countess or a duchess fallen on hard times somewhere in that venerable building. The Howells moved on to a six-room apartment in Ca' Giustinian, by which time a palette of American artists, among them John Singer Sargent, James McNeill Whistler, William Merritt Chase, William S. Horton and Maurice Prendergast, had come to Venice to paint. 'But the most celebrated and most industrious American painter of Venice,' according to John Lukacs, 'was Thomas Moran, otherwise known as the pioneer landscape painter of the Rocky Mountains. In 1898, the publishers Brown & Bigelow printed an edition of 22 million of one of Moran's Venetian paintings, an extraordinary number considering that the population of the United States was then about 76 million.'

Americans came now to rent or even buy *palazzi* on the Grand Canal, while towns in the States were named after Venice. The city had become a passion. By the time Giuseppe Cipriani opened Harry's Bar, in 1931, with its promise of a perfect dry martini, Americans were flocking to Venice, even during the Depression years, in their many thousands. Which of them would ever wish to see it damaged?

Despite so much fighting, so much destruction up through Italy, Venice in fact still looked (swastikas on buildings aside and through rose-tinted binoculars) very much as it had before the war. Close up, it was suffering, or at least the city's poor were, of which there were very many. The main water supply was finally cut off following intensive bombing of the mainland industrial zones of Mestre and Marghera. Now there were daily queues to draw water from the city's old courtyard wells. These were filled by rainwater, as they had been for many hundreds of years. They had been no guarantee against cholera, though, which is why, finally, in 1884 an aqueduct set below the railway bridge was opened, fetching fresh water to the city from the Veneto. Intriguingly, the city-side pumping station was built within the walls of a former monastery destroyed by Napoleon, alongside the church of Sant'Andrea della Zirada, hidden today on the southwest corner of Piazzale Roma between a giant 1930s multi-storey car park and the elevated Austrian-built 'People Mover', opened in 2009, for the shuttle train connecting Piazzale Roma to the Stazione Marittima and the further car parks of Tronchetto island.

Here we need to ask, how on earth, or on water, did Venice find itself in this predicament? The answer, of course, was Fascist Italy's alliance with Nazi Germany. From La Serenissima's particular point of view, the misadventure began on 15 June 1934, when, at precisely 0945hrs, Hitler's personal Junkers Ju-52 tri-motor *Immelman II* flew from Munich to San Nicolo airfield. It was the German leader's first trip to Venice and his first official visit to a foreign country. The omens were not good. Stepping from his plane dressed in a drab belted brown gaberdine over a dark suit and tie, and clutching a fedora, Hitler, said Mussolini, looked 'like a plumber in a mackintosh'. The Duce himself, waiting to greet his German guest, sported the grey-green uniform of a Corporal of Honour of the Fascist Militia crowned with a black fez, adorned with red tassels and a dramatic eagle emblem.

Hitler had wanted a private meeting, which is why he was dressed in a suit, while Mussolini chose to make his visit a public occasion, complete with the press *en masse*, during which he made it ostentatiously clear that the German leader was the junior partner in what proved to be a never less than awkward affair. Hitler did not speak Italian. Mussolini spoke German, although he found Hitler's accent difficult to understand.

From the airport, the two dictators went by boat past St Mark's to the Grand Hotel on the Grand Canal. With guests either confined to their rooms or instructed to make themselves scarce for the morning, Hitler was shown to one of the esteemed hotel's palatial suites. The hotel occupied two historic buildings, the late fourteenth-century Palazzo Morosini Ferro and the larger seventeenth-century Palazzo Flangini Fini next door. The two buildings had been joined at the hip in the 1870s and turned into the opulent Grand Hotel. During the Second World War, German troops occupied the hotel. They were to be ousted in 1945 by their American counterparts. In a state of neglect, in 1972 the Grand Hotel was bought by the Veneto Regional Council. Renovated, it has been its headquarters ever since.

After a wash and brush-up at the Grand, Hitler was driven from the new Piazzale Roma, over the new Ponte Littorio and by fast roads, to the Villa Pisani at Stra, facing the Brenta Canal twenty miles west of Venice, for lunch and talks about the future of Austria. The Palladian-style house was an impressive setting for this first 'business' meeting between the two dictators. It had been commissioned in 1718 by Alvise Pisani, the 114th Doge. The original architect,

Gerolamo Frigimelica, died fourteen years later and the palatial house was completed in 1732 by Francesco Maria Preti. Sold to Napoleon Bonaparte in 1807, it had been in the hands of the Italian state for the past fifty years. D'Annunzio had set scenes of *Il Fuoco* here.

Lunch was an awkward affair, Hitler eating scrambled eggs and steamed vegetables and, of course, refusing even the smallest glass of wine. The Führer drank water. The Italians drank wine. For Mussolini, the afternoon meeting was trying. 'It is my will,' barked Hitler, 'and the indomitable will of the German people, that Austria become an integral part of the Reich.' Mussolini insisted that Austria would continue to be independent. The two men left in separate cars for Venice. While this might have been a sensible security measure, the divide between the two leaders was clear to those who had spent the afternoon with them at Villa Pisani.

A concert featuring the music of Verdi and Wagner followed that evening in the courtyard of the Doge's Palace. The next morning, Hitler and Mussolini met at the Giardini Pubblici – a gift of Napoleon once swathes of historic buildings here had been demolished – to visit the art biennale. The German Pavilion had yet to undergo its Nazi-style makeover by German architect Ernst Haiger. Hitler was not impressed by the 'decadent' modern art on show. For his part, Mussolini allowed any number of strands of art and architecture to flourish. Filippo Marinetti, the Futurist, had co-written the *Fascist Manifesto* (1919). Futurists, Classicists, Modernists, they all had their parts to play in the visual shaping of the new Fascist empire. British soldiers fighting through Libya were to be surprised by the ideal modern Italian settlers' villages they encountered there, so white, clean-cut, rational and modern, in complete contrast to traditional Arab settlements.

Hitler was also shown the newly renovated and extended Venetian docks – the Stazione Marittima – and, after an evening of parades and speeches in St Mark's Square, the fashionable delights of the Lido the next day. He was taken to lunch at the Circolo Golf Venezia (Venice Golf Club) recently built around Austrian fortifications and over the sand dunes at Alberoni on the southern tip of the island. Hitler had no interest in golf. The Golf Club and its nine-hole course had been laid out following Henry Ford's holiday jaunt to the Lido. Staying at the Excelsior Hotel, Ford had hoped to play a few rounds. His luggage included a set of clubs. Hitler much admired Ford, keeping a prominent photograph of the US car magnate on a wall in his Munich office. Ford's book *The International Jew, the World's Foremost Problem* had been published enthusiastically in Germany. Copies were displayed in the anteroom to Hitler's office in Munich. In 1931, he told *Detroit News*, 'I regard Henry Ford as my inspiration. In shall do my best to put his theories into practice in Germany.' But not to play golf, whether in Venice or anywhere else.

Ford's inspiration encouraged the Volkswagen, a low-cost car devised by Ferdinand Porsche in discussion with Hitler, designed like Ford's earlier Model T, to a put a nation on wheels.

Ford Germany went on to produce thousands of lorries for the German army used in the invasion of Poland in 1939.

General Motors made even more. Before it became illegal (after the US declaration of war with Germany in December 1941) for US motor companies to work with their German subsidiaries, Ford had been awarded the Grand Cross of the German Eagle, the highest state honour made to foreigners, for 'distinguished services to the Reich'. Soon enough, General Motors Blitz trucks would be seen working hard with the German army as it powered its way through Poland and then France, Belgium and the Netherlands. James D. Mooney, President of General Motors Overseas, who had met Hitler and *Reichsmarschall* Hermann Göring, was awarded the German Order of Merit of the Eagle Cross of the German Eagle.

While Ford was to renounce his public anti-Semitism – he was deeply troubled when, in 1945, he saw newsreels from the liberated Nazi concentration camps – he did his best to keep the US out of the war with Germany. When it came to it, Ford's contribution to the war effort was prodigious. Consolidated B-24 Liberator bombers, which did so much damage to Italian towns and cities, were produced in huge numbers along Ford's mile-long production line at its newly built Willow Run bomber plant in Michigan. Opened in 1941, this was the last of a thousand projects designed and overseen by the industrious architect Albert Kahn (1869–1942) for Ford. Curiously, Kahn was the son of a Prussian rabbi who, in 1880, had emigrated with his family to Detroit.

In 1937, the Duke of Windsor played golf at Alberoni. With his wife, Wallis Simpson, he visited Hitler later that same year, the Duke gamely returning the Führer's Nazi salute. After lunch at Alberoni, Hitler had a final meeting with Mussolini at the exotic Excelsior Hotel on the Lido beach before returning to San Niccolo, *Immelmann II* and Munich. 'A mad little clown', snorted Mussolini as the rain-coated Führer departed.

Venice had been a sideshow for both men. When Hitler returned to Italy in 1938, it was to Rome, the city both dictators worshipped. Mussolini had assigned guards for the occasion who, quite deliberately, loomed over the German leader. By now, however, Hitler was very much the senior partner, garbed for his visit not in a raincoat but in his fully fledged Führer uniform adorned with a single decoration, the Iron Cross First Class, a medal he won for bravery during the First World War. It had been recommended by his superior, Lieutenant Hugo Gutmann, a Jew. In 1938, Gutmann was arrested by the Gestapo, but released once his story was known. Leaving Belgium with his wife and children just before the German invasion of 1940, he settled in the United States, where, as Henry Grant, he worked as a typewriter salesman.

In Venice, meanwhile, new public works were executed on a Roman scale and in Roman style. There had been the straight-as-a-die dual-carriageway, Ponte Littorio, joining Mestre to the city, which Mussolini had declared open in April 1933 and over which Hitler had been driven in svelte Lancias to and from Villa Pisani. Built with impressive speed, the bridge touched down in a spacious new public square off which cars could be parked and where *vaporetti* and water taxis were on hand to take Venetians and visitors to all parts of the city, the Lido and outlying islands. The square might well have been named Piazzale Venezia, but Piazzale Roma it had to be, symbolising the centrality of Mussolini's Roman empire. The new works were designed and executed by Eugenio Miozzi, appointed Chief Engineer of the Technical Office of the Management of Venice (head of public works), in 1931. Miozzi also built the impressive single-span Istrian-stone Ponte degli Scalzi, arching over the Grand Canal between the Santa Lucia railway station and the Santa Croce *sestiere* (district), and a new canal – Rio Nova – establishing a shortcut between Piazzale Roma, Santa Lucia and St Mark's Square.

From 1937, it was possible to walk all the way from St Mark's Square to the Giardini Pubblici along the edge of the water without interruption or losing one's way. Mussolini and the city council approved, and Miozzi designed and built the generous Roman-style embankment, Riva dell'Impero, with its handsome paving stones edged in massive blocks of Istrian marble. Of course this meant tearing down old buildings, but this was how Venice found new ways of forcing itself into the twentieth century.

A competitive aesthetic relationship between the two dictatorships was one thing, Mussolini's political and personal kowtowing to Hitler quite another. Although playing his cards close to his chest and keeping the French, British and Americans guessing his intentions, Mussolini finally threw in Italy's military lot with Hitler on 10 June 1940, declaring war on France and Great Britain as the French government abandoned Paris. Of the Italians, Hitler said, 'First they were too cowardly to take part. Now they are in a hurry so that they can share in the spoils.' Italy's disastrous invasion of Greece in October 1940 prompted Hitler to intervene, successfully, on Mussolini's behalf, an action that delayed the German invasion of the Soviet Union by several weeks. In 1943, as we have seen, the Allies crossed from North Africa to Sicily and then on to the Italian mainland. Mussolini fell, was imprisoned and then was rescued by Hitler. The Germans took control of Italy. The SS moved in.

In Venice, the Germans set up seventeen command posts – an increasingly faded wartime direction sign to the *Platzkommandantur* in St Mark's Square can just be seen in Calle Renier off Piazza Margerita – while the Italian Fascist militia made its headquarters in the Hotel Bauer-Grünwald. German officers took quarters in the Grand Hotel des Bains on the Lido, flanking it with landmines. A fellow German, Thomas Mann, had stayed here in July 1911 with his Jewish-born wife and family and, subsequently, written *Death in Venice*, won the Nobel Prize for Literature, left Germany for the United States and made powerful broadcasts from there against Hitler and Nazism.

Sixty years after Thomas Mann's holiday on the Lido, the Italian film director Luchino Visconti's film *Death in Venice* was screened at the Palazzo del Cinema, a sculptural building designed by Luigi Quagliata and opened in August 1937 for the fifth Venice Film Festival. An avowed socialist, Quagliata was arrested later that month. Once released, he fled to the United States for the duration of the Second World War. During this time, Visconti joined the Italian Communist Party and the resistance. Forced into hiding in the Apennines, under the *nom de guerre* Alfredo Guidi, he helped escaping Allied soldiers while sheltering Italian partisans in his home in Rome. Caught and detained by the singularly vicious torture enthusiast Pietro Koch, Visconti was sentenced to death, saved at the last minute by the persuasive intervention of the glamorous Argentinian actress María Denis.

In Venice, the partisans did what they could to disrupt both the Germans and the Italian Fascists. Their scope for action was limited, as, although there were places to hide using the labyrinth of the city's alleys and, at the time, thirty *traghetti* ferry services criss-crossing the Grand Canal, it was hard to escape from or sneak into the city by road or rail. Given that there was only one way in and out of the city by train, bus or car – over the lagoon to and from mainland Mestre by the parallel railway and road bridges – it was not difficult for German and Italian Fascist patrols to check everyone arriving or departing from Santa Lucia station or Piazzale Roma, whether by passenger or goods train, private car or lorry.

The one way it was possible to disappear into early morning mists, dazzling summer sun or winter fogs was by boat. While motorboats were easily spotted, this was not always true of the small Venetian rowboats and sailboats that moved quietly and, whether surreptitiously or not, out into the Lagoon. The old Venetian saying '*Sottovento via!*' (Get under the wind and go) held true: move in a way that nobody notices. There were many types of small, flat-bottomed boats in the 1940s, among those familiar today, the *sàndalo* – rowed by one man or woman and used for general transport and, especially, for fishing – the *bragazzo*, a fishing barge, and the *topa* and *sanpierota*, small rowboats with collapsible sails. Only Venetians or strangers who knew the city intimately understood how to navigate the secret channels etched across the 212 square miles of the Lagoon and between its myriad islands, many free of human habitation. Some of these channels are no more than two feet deep, while what appear to be sea-like stretches of the Lagoon are six feet at most.

Out in those reaches of salt marshes and mud flats, of white egrets and silver herons, of ducks, ibis and geese, there were many places to meet and lie low. For those aiming to sail clear of the Lagoon, however, there were – and remain – just three inlets: Chioggia, Lido and Malamocco, all well-guarded, as were entrances to the Brenta Canal to the west of the city. What all this meant is that while Venice offered boltholes to partisans working in and around the city, it was not easy to get beyond the Lagoon, and the city was thus a difficult place, beyond the most clandestine attacks on the enemy, for partisans to operate in. Equally, Venetian partisans, no matter how much they hated their Italian and German enemies, had no particular desire to bomb or otherwise damage their wondrous city.

Because of this, most Venetian partisans, whether born in the city or on the Veneto mainland, fought mainly in the Dolomites to the north. On clear winter days, these mountain ranges appear as a fairy-tale backdrop to the city's skyline of domes and leaning campaniles, almost as if they were in walking distance. Up there in Bolzano on the winding road to the Brenner Pass and Austria was *Obergruppenführer* Wolff's headquarters.

Down by the water's edge on the Viale Giardini Pubblici, the Venetian monument to the Partisan Woman can now be found, a bronze of a young woman, her hands tied, bobbing in and out of the Lagoon water as the tide rises and falls like some distorted image of Malamocco's Madonna di Marina, seen as if through a glass darkly. The bronze is by Augusto Murer, who fought with the resistance in and around Belluno in the Dolomites. The irregular Istrian-stone base is the work of the Venetian architect Carlo Scarpa.

The monument, dedicated in 1969 and restored in 2020, is a reminder of the women who operated within and without the city and died often in the cruellest circumstances, fighting their cause whether or not with guns to hand. A frequently reproduced press photograph taken in May 1945, often captioned 'Laura D'Oriana and fellow women carrying rifles, Venice', but with no further information, captures something of the spirit of time.

Of those fighting in the Dolomites, Clorinda Menguzzato – Veglia was her *nom de guerre* – of the Gramsci Brigade, was beaten, raped, savaged by dogs and shot on 10 October 1944 after her capture at Castello Tesino on the orders of SS-*Hauptsturmführer* Karl Hegenbart after she refused to reveal names of her comrades. Clorinda was nineteen years old. Caught hiding in a pine tree after a fight, eighteen-year-old Ancilla 'Ora' Marighetto was brutally tortured and then shot by Hegenbart. Although sentenced *in absentia* to life imprisonment, Austria refused to extradite the former SS Captain, who lived there comfortably until his death in 1993.

Some of the young women partisans were only fifteen or sixteen years old. Among the 'older' women, Virginia 'Luisa' Tionelli, forty, a children's nurse in a Venice hospital and Communist Party member turned resistance courier, was burned alive in the crematorium of the Risiera di San Sabba concentration camp near Trieste. The gaunt five-storey brick former rice-husking factory was, from 1943 until 1945, used as a staging post from Italy to Auschwitz and a place of torture for captured partisans.

The curiously colourful abstract majolica sculpture by Leoncillo Leonardi, a former partisan active in Rome and Umbria, erected in 1957 in the Giardini Pubblici on a pedestal designed by Carlo Scarpa in memory of women partisans, was blown up by neo-Fascists four years later. The difference between the two works of art dedicated to partisan women seems significant. Leonardi's woman is a belligerent fighter, a decidedly modern action woman on the march. Murer's is more of a victim and martyr. Both memorials have been liked and disliked, yet their importance is that they have been in their different ways reminders of the bravery of the women of the Venetian resistance.

The first violent actions on the part of the partisans in Venice itself seem to have been in July 1944, when a group led by Aldo Varisco, later captured and brutally tortured, began assassinating Italian Fascist soldiers. On 26 July, 'Kim' Aracalli's group set off a bomb at Ca'Giustinian, a district headquarters for the *Guardia Nazionale Repubblicana* and home to German military offices. The building was wrecked. Thirteen people were killed. Two days later, thirteen partisans, arrested on previous charges – the youngest of them eighteen-year-old Francesco Biancotti – were executed in the palazzo ruins.

Reprisals tended to be immediate and dramatic. On the night of 2 August 1944, a German patrol boat sentry guarding a Kriegsmarine vessel moored alongside the Riva dell'Impero fell into the water and drowned. There had been a party on board the boat. As his body did not wash ashore for several days, the Germans assumed wrongly that he had been kidnapped or murdered by partisans. Streets and homes in the Castello district were searched by German soldiers. Unable to find the missing guard, the Germans dragged seven prisoners from Santa Maria Maggiore prison. They tied them to a rope strung between two lampposts on the Riva dell'Impero and then ordered a crowd of 500 local people – men, women and children – to attend the execution of the seven carried out by a twenty-four-strong firing squad at 7 a.m. as the prison chaplain, Don Marcello Dell'Andrea, held high a crucifix. Children were forced to swab the blood and guts from the pavement. A hundred and thirty-six men were taken hostage. The bodies of the executed men were left to rot for a week.

Those executed for a crime that was never committed were twenty-four-year-old Aliprando Armellin, a member of the Venetian resistance; the brothers Alfredo (twenty) and Luciano (nineteen) Gelmi, who had refused, along with Bruno De Gasperi (twenty), to join up with the RSI to fight the Allies; Girolamo Guasto (twenty-four), held on suspicion of helping the partisans; Gio Conti (forty-six), leader of the Cavarzerano resistance chapter; and Alfredo Vivian (thirty-six), military commander of the thirty-strong Venezia San Donà di Piave partisan group already under sentence of death for killing a German sailor in Piazzale Roma in December 1943. After the war, the Riva del'Impero was renamed Riva dei sette martiri (Shore of the Seven Martyrs).

The bravery of those who resisted Italian Fascist and Nazi German rule in Venice took many forms, including bombing, assassination, the distribution of leaflets, the running of weapons, hiding fellow members of the resistance and sabotage. A simple memorial set between platforms 8 and 9 of Santa Lucia station reminds passengers of the role of the Italian railway resistance. Bartolomeo Meloni, a forty-four-year-old Principal Inspector of Railways based in Venice, was arrested on 4 October 1943 and died in Dachau on 9 July 1944. Meloni used his senior position and expertise to distribute weapons by rail, to divert German and Italian military convoys by sending trains in wrong directions and to sabotage locomotives, wagons and stations. When arrested and subjected to horrific torture, he gave nothing away, no names, no details of operations. Dispatched to Dachau, he died from sickness and starvation.

One almost bizarre act of defiance, the legendary '*Beffa* [prank] *del Goldoni*' was organised by Giuseppe Turcato, Political Commissioner of the Biancotto brigade, during an evening performance on 12 March 1945 at Teatro Goldoni of Luigi Pirandello's popular comedy *Vestire gli ignudi* (*Dress the Naked*). The idea was, in part, to make the audience, packed with Italian Fascist and Nazi German officials and soldiers, laugh on the other sides of their faces. Bursting onto the stage during the First Act, Turcato's masked and armed performers called for insurrection throughout the city and announced the impending liberation of Venice:

Venetian people, the last quarter of an hour for Hitler and the fascist traitors is about to strike. Fight with us for the cause of national liberation and for the definitive crushing of Nazi-fascism. Liberation is near! Rally around the National Liberation Committee and the flags of the heroic partisans who are fighting for the freedom of Italy from the Nazi-fascist yoke. We are fighting to be able to guarantee, through progressive democracy and the unity of all anti-fascist parties, the future and reconstruction of our home-land. Death to fascism! Freedom to the peoples! Long live the Youth Front!

They vanished backstage while leaflets bearing the same message dropped, in the spirit of Marinetti and D'Annunzio, from the stage, and slipped out the theatre and into dark alleys before guards could apprehend them.

The Germans were getting quite twitchy at this late stage of the war. While Allied troops were held back at the Gothic Line, there was no telling for certain whether their air forces would attack Venice. While Mestre and Marghera were bombed heavily, Venice had seemed sacrosanct. The one air raid on the historic city to date, on 14 August 1944, had been a strange and disturbing affair. After hitting a ferry at Malamocco on the Lido as it plied between Venice and Chioggia and killing twenty-four people on board, three Allied aircraft (I have yet to identify them) headed towards the Bacino di San Marco where they bombed and strafed the German Red Cross ship *Freiburg,* built at Ancona in 1929. The 1,463-tonne vessel had been converted into a marine hospital at Marghera in 1943 and was moored between the Punta della Dogana and San Giorgio Maggiore, an island readily identifiable by its ineffably elegant landmark church with a tall belfry by Andrea Palladio. A passenger ship ploughing its way from Venice to Fusina on the mainland south of Marghera was also machine-gunned, killing fifteen and wounding fifty.

Crude concrete air raid shelters had been rushed up – one can still be seen, behind a fence on Campo Junghans on the Giudecca. As the Junghans factory made fuses for bombs, it was a potential target. Air raid shelters, however, could not be dug below ground. Venice all but floats on water, and any attempt to dig into its foundations of wooden piles would have endangered buildings and those living and working in them. Shelters were unlikely to have been effective. Bunkers and anti-landing defences, meanwhile, were constructed along the beaches of the Lido in case the Allies attempted an invasion of Venice by sea.

Furthermore, the port of Venice became increasingly busy with the arrival of armaments, fuel and materiel for Kesselring's defiant armies. Had the Allies really overlooked the role Venice played in helping to drag out the war in Italy?

A pilot of 450 Squadron RAAF inspects his armed Kittyhawk, Cervia airbase, March 1945.

TEN

PREPARATION

Cervia, 18 March 1945

From the beginning of the year, photo-reconnaissance PR IX Spitfires had been flying high over Venice, tiny speck-lets barely visible in the winter skies and, by this stage of the war, all but immune from attack. On 18 March, photo-graphs taken by one of the Spitfires of 318 'City of Gdańsk' Polish Fighter Reconnaissance Squadron revealed merchant vessels inside Stazione Marittima. Among the ships newly berthed at the dock was SS *Otto Leonhardt*, a 3,693-ton cargo ship built in 1911 by Robert Thompson & Sons at Southwick on the River Wear and owned since 1937 by Leonhardt & Blumberg, Hamburg. A pair of *Regia Marina* (Royal Italian Navy) *Spica*-class torpedo boats – fiercely armed and very fast, light destroyers with a record of shoot-ing down enemy aircraft – were berthed alongside the German freighter together with a coaster, a tanker and barges. Evidently, fuel and other vital supplies were getting through to Venice from Germany. And what else might be hidden in the docks? It was high time to unleash 'Operation Bowler'.

Now, the skills the Desert Air Force had acquired and honed campaigning from North Africa to northern Italy would be brought to bear on an exceptional and challenging target. A plan that had been brewing for some weeks was clear enough – a synchronised attack by DAF's 239 Wing and 79th Fighter Group 'to destroy by bombing, shipping and barge concentrations in the Venice lagoon'. Spitfire Mk VIIIs of 244 Wing would patrol the target area at 18,000 feet; DAF could not afford to be anything other than well prepared and vigilant. The 244 Wing Spitfires would be capable of seeing off attacks by ANR Bf109s and any other enemy aircraft still operating in the region. What remained of the Luftwaffe was based north of the Alps, although one could never be entirely sure what it might yet be capable of.

March had certainly thrown up surprises for DAF pilots. On 3 March, four Spitfire IXs of 4 Squadron SAAF, escorting eleven 12 Squadron SAAF B-26 Marauder IIIs on a bombing mission to the railway marshalling yards at Conegliano, thirty-five miles north of Venice, were attacked by a dozen ANR Bf 109s and Focke-Wulf 190s. Were the latter Luftwaffe? As far as anyone in DAF knew, the Italians had not been trained on Fw 190s. Fresh to combat, the keen young South African pilots saw off the attack, although the Marauders were attacked again during their bombing run. Quite how they all got back, five badly shot up, is anyone's guess. It had been a further reminder, if one was needed, that the Venice area was dangerous. And not everything that day had gone 4 Squadron's way. One of its Spitfires was shot down by an Fw 190 over Oderzo. Lieutenant Mervyn Reim bailed out at 16,000 feet. On landing by parachute, the twenty-four-year-old pilot was caught and killed by Italian Fascist militia.

The following day, 450 Squadron SAAF Kittyhawks were detailed to dive bomb a bridge in the Vittorio Veneto area, forty-five miles north of Venice. Lieutenant Barry Pyott was shot down, presumably by flak, and killed. He can be seen, on the far left of the back row, in a squadron photo taken at Fano the previous month with his fellow pilots from South Africa, New Zealand, Canada and Britain. Barry Pyott was twenty.

That same Sunday, the mighty Wright radial engine of 1st Lieutenant Donald Montgomery's 87th Fighter Squadron P-47D *Smartin Up* packed up. Forced to belly-land at Rovigo, just eight miles southwest of Venice, Lt Montgomery was taken prisoner of war. Hit by flak that morning over Nervesa, thirty-five miles north of Venice, 1st Lieutenant James Spraley ditched his P-47D at sea, and was picked up safely by a dependable 239 Squadron Walrus. The luck of the draw seemed to determine whether an Allied pilot fell into the hands of friends or foes and whether his foe might incarcerate or kill him.

Two more 87th Squadron Thunderbolts were shot down, over Yugoslavia and Austria, on 5 and 6 March. On 9 March, a pair of 250 Squadron Kittyhawks collided in the landing circuit at Cervia, killing Lieutenant D. B. Tattershall and

Lieutenant P. B. Somerset, both of whom, otherwise, would have taken part in Operation Bowler.

Flight Lieutenant Gary Blumer was lucky to be able to fly his Kittyhawk back to base on 10 March after being hit and wounded by flak as he dive bombed a dozen barges on the Adige thirty miles south of Venice. Gerry Teldon's 85th Fighter Squadron colleague 1st Lieutenant Clarence Paff was killed by flak on 18 March, the day before Operation Bowler. Squadron Leader G. L. Usher, 112 Squadron's CO, was shot down by flak while strafing a train near Kranj, Slovenia. Without ID, he was held by Yugoslav partisans for a month. That was the immediate background. Now everything over Venice would happen very quickly.

Surprise was all. From sea level, and supported by rocket-firing Mustangs, the 79th's Thunderbolts would aim to take out gun emplacements and flak positions sited at key points around the Lagoon. There were many of these, capable of concentrated and rapid fire. Kittyhawk and Mustang dive bombers would roar down on Stazione Marittima and the ships unloading there. Bombs were to be dropped on target areas marked precisely on pilots' maps 'in order to avoid damage to cultural monuments and civilian habitations'. As the combined target area measured 950 by 650 yards, about the size of eight football pitches, there would no room what-soever for error. The weather was predicted to be wet, cold and windy, with a few clear spells.

Air Vice Marshal Robert 'Pussy' Foster, Air Officer Commanding Desert Air Force, had been charged with planning the operation. He told Air Marshal Sir Guy Garrod, newly appointed RAF Commander-in-Chief, Mediterranean and Middle East, that the reason he chose the name Bowler for the operation was that if any part of Venice was damaged other than the docks, the Wing's pilots and he himself, of course, were likely to be given their bowler hats! Dismissed, that is, from service, incompetent cultural vandals shunted off to civvy street.

If anything went wrong – a single bomb going astray and demolishing a historic building – newspaper headlines around the world would suddenly wake up to what was happening on the 'Forgotten Front'. The Allied armies may have smashed their heavy-handed way up through Italy, destroying towns and villages and countless historic buildings, thankful in a way that the Italian campaign was lucky if it made the back pages of newspapers. Venice, though, was something different. Not only was there no city like it, it was also the stuff of picture books and fairy tales, and many soldiers on conflicting sides and of different nationalities knew it either first-hand, or else dreamed of being there. Who would want to see it bombed? Not even Hitler did.

As Wing Leader of 239 Wing, George Westlake would front the operation. Foster liked and trusted the good-humoured and seemingly unflappable Westlake, veteran to date of 300 operational sorties. In the thick of so much action, not once had George been shot down. He was indeed like a lucky charm. Foster himself, a charming and popular officer, had flown numerous sorties under intense enemy fire on the Western Front in 1917 and again in 1918. From the cockpits of Sopwith Pups and Sopwith Camels, he shot down or shared in the 'kill' of sixteen German aircraft. He was awarded the DFC in 1918. The citation reads, 'This officer has taken part in numerous combats and led his patrols brilliantly... On one occasion he attacked two biplanes single-handed; one he forced down and the other burst into flames and broke up in the air.'

Since late 1942, Foster's war service had mirrored George's. In November, he took command of 213 Group based in Lebanon. He was AOC (Air Officer Commanding) RAF Malta from March 1944 and later that year Head of the Air Commission in Italy and so CO of the Co-belligerent Italian Air Force. In December he was posted AOC Desert Air Force. The calmest of English gentlemen, Foster understood that Kesselring, who still held the Gothic Line, would continue to front a fierce resistance in northern Italy. He had to be hit hard somewhere, and his final supply lines urgently severed. That would trigger the end of the Gothic Line.

While Foster and his colleagues expected heavy flak at Venice, it was still hard to know if the Luftwaffe might yet be about. On 11 March, 112 Squadron's Mustangs encountered a dozen Focke-Wulf 190 fighters over Rieti, downing three. That same day, 3 Squadron Mustangs jostled with four Bf109s, an Italian SM.79 tri-motor bomber and a Ju 52 transport aircraft. On 20 March, 79th Fighter Group Thunderbolts strafed Campoformido airfield, Udine, eighty miles east of Venice. Its complement of Bf109s and Fw190s was a potential threat to the success of Operation Bowler. Destroying three aircraft on the ground, the American pilots reported concerning sightings of what they took to be the new 530mph Messerschmitt Me 262 fighter jet.

What they had actually seen from the cockpits of their speeding Thunderbolts was the futuristic-looking Arado Ar 234 light jet bomber. The face of aerial warfare was evidently changing. Allied pilots felt concerned. What wonder weapons did the Germans have up their military sleeves? There had certainly been a lot of talk about them in messes in Italy as elsewhere, although it was difficult to know if such weapons were real or simply a smokescreen put up to instil fear. Somehow, Shakespeare's King Lear's desperate lines – 'I will do such things / What they are, yet I know not: but they shall be / The terrors of the earth' – could, by March 1945, be Adolf Hitler's own.

While 239 Wing and the 79th Fighter Group would, of course, have to be very much on the alert as they dropped down from the Adriatic on Venice, they would also need to be focused acutely on their very particular targets. The Spitfires, it was assumed, would be capable of seeing off potential attacks by ANR Bf109s still operating in the region. While Luftwaffe fighters were possibly within reach of Venice, their priority, as they dwindled in numbers, was protecting the Fatherland from Allied bombers.

By March 1945, it was difficult for RAF and other air force officers to gauge just how close the end of the war in Italy or Europe was, especially with the Fifth and Eighth Armies still held up at the Gothic Line. Gerry Teldon's Group Commander, Major Beck, though, had already led the 79th on an aerial cavalry charge to Hitler's alpine retreat, as if signalling the end. The rumour had gone around, from army camp to air base, that Hitler was planning a last defiant stand in the Alps. The 79th crossed the mountains and bombed

and strafed Berchtesgaden, the Bavarian town where Hitler
had built the Berghof, said Alpine retreat. Rather rather
Hitler's holiday home, Thunderbolt pilots wrecked trains.
They had, though, left their mark and made a point.

Throughout the five days before the operation, the
79th Fighter Group flew numerous intense missions at
minimum altitude through heavy German fire to help
pierce the enemy line held on the Santerno River, the
border between Ravenna and Bologna north of the
Gothic Line. If only the Allied armies could break through
and storm across the Po Valley. With German supply lines
in the north cut, the Italian war must surely end. George
Westlake could have had no better comrades and allies.
The decision as to which American squadrons and pilots
would fly the mission was, though, to be made only at the
last minute. There were so many enemy targets for the
fervid 79th to hit. For the American pilots, Venice was
just one of them.

George Westlake flew into Cervia on 18 March. The
previous months he had been busy scoring direct hits dive
bombing railway stations and lines in and around Padua,
familiarising himself with the P51-D Mustang and flying
liaison missions between various headquarters and squadron
bases at the helm of a single-engine, high-wing, four-seater
Fairchild Argus. This must have reminded him of his pre-war
days flying for Reg Salmon's Fox Photos.

Operation Bowler force was pretty much ready when
George arrived. A few days earlier, AVM Foster had flown in
to Forli with Generals Władysław Anders (Polish II Corps),
'Dick' McCreery (C-in-C Eighth Army), John Cannon (Air

C-in-C, Allied Air Forces, Mediterranean), Sir Archibald Nye (Vice Chief Imperial General Staff) and Sir Bernard Freyberg (C-in-C New Zealand Expeditionary Force), among other top brass. They wanted to watch 239 Wing and the 79th Fighter Group put on a precision rocket and dive-bombing display by the very aircraft that would fly Operation Bowler.

When the smoke faded, the results were clear. Complete destruction of the targets contained within a tight circle. Impressive stuff. It was late in the day in terms of the war's progress, yet DAF's 239 Wing Mustangs and 79th Fighter Group's P-47Ds were now capable of reaching enemy targets pretty much anywhere in Italy, and targets beyond in Yugoslavia and Austria, and hitting them hard. This reduced the need for heavy day bombers. If they could hit the docks at Venice as accurately and effectively as they did in this demonstration at Forli, there was the promise of being able to attack key targets in and around towns and cities with the minimum loss of life. Of historic buildings and monuments, too. If only the Allies had been able to fly and fight like this from the beginning of the Italian campaign, rather than raining bombs down indiscriminately on villages, towns, cities and Monte Cassino from 15–20,000 feet, from which height eight football patches of land appeared no bigger than a postage stamp.

And that was flying in broad daylight. RAF Bomber Command flew mostly by night. In August 1941, an official report analysing 633 target photographs taken over the industrial cities of the Ruhr showed that half of all bombs dropped fell into open countryside. While the report encouraged the formation of Pathfinder squadrons with advanced patrol aircraft leading the bombers to their intended targets, this lack of accuracy was an encouragement to those like Air Chief Marshal Arthur Harris, Commander-in-Chief Bomber Command, who believed in carpet bombing enemy cites. Harris's contention was supported by the Lindemann Report of March 1942, written by Winston Churchill's Chief Scientific Advisor Frederick Lindemann (Viscount Cherwell), suggesting that Bomber Command concentrate its raids on working-class districts of industrial cities and, by doing so, undermining German and Italian manufacturing capabilities.

This was certainly not DAF's role. The big and immediate question now was whether or not Westlake could replicate the level of accuracy displayed in front of senior staff at Forli when the pilots of Kittyhawks, Mustangs and Thunderbolts under his command dived towards Venice and into what they assumed would be murderous flak. That would take a steady nerve even with the experience DAF pilots – those not lost or killed – had built up over many months of intense combat. Meanwhile, there was also new weaponry to master just a day before the mission, with Mustangs of 260 Squadron employing 60lb rockets for first time on 20 March on a raid on a factory at Copparo to the south of the Po. In service from 1943, the RP-3 rocket flew at 500mph and had a range of a mile, a distance it could span in seven seconds. Although unguided, in the hands of resolute pilots it was a formidable weapon.

Assembled and ready to scramble at short notice, DAF pilots waited for a break in the weather at three separate

Adriatic airbases: Cervia, eighty miles south of Venice (where 239 Wing had moved in February), Bellaria, twelve miles south of Cervia (244 Wing – the Spitfires) and Fano, fifty miles south of Cervia (79th Fighter Group). Coordination was going to be critical. George drew up the order of take-off from Cervia. Twelve P51-D Mustangs of 5 Squadron SAAF led by Major Hendrik 'Tank' Odendaal DFC would be first into the air. Odendaal had flown P-40 Kittyhawks in ground support sorties at Monte Cassino.

The twelve Mustangs of RAF 112 Squadron would follow with Flight Lieutenant Paul Forster in command. Joining the Royal Air Force Volunteer Reserve in November 1940, Forster had flown Spitfires with 603 Squadron in Malta and Hurricanes and Typhoons with 186 and 245 Squadrons. By the time of Operation Bowler, he had flown 175 Kittyhawk and Mustang sorties with RAF 112.

George's 250 Squadron – a dozen Kittyhawks – would be chased into the attack by the twelve Kittyhawks of 450 RAAF Squadron led by Acting Flight Lieutenant Edward 'Ted' Strom. Strom and his fellow pilots had a special hatred for the Germans. Two of their former colleagues, Squadron Leader John 'Willy' Williams, a champion surfer and fighter ace, and Flight Lieutenant Reginald 'Rusty' Kierath, a fellow Australian who had attended the same school as Williams, were among the fifty British and Commonwealth officers murdered by the Gestapo after their 'Great Escape' from Stalag Luft III at Sagan, Lower Silesia, on the night of 24/5 March 1944.

Next off would be the anti-flak Mustangs of 3 Squadron SAAF under Flight Lieutenant Kenneth Richards DFC, an

Australian who had risen from the ranks and flown in North Africa and the Syria–Lebanon campaign. A ground attack by 3 Squadron on German positions at Mezzouna, Tunisia, on 3 April 1943, had seriously wounded the German officer Claus von Stauffenberg, who, the following July, attempted to assassinate Hitler with a bomb at the Wolf's Lair in the hope of prompting the overthrow of the Nazi regime.

Led by Captain Roy Rogers DFC, an SAAF pilot on secondment to the RAF, four rocket-equipped Mustangs of 260 Squadron would complete the flight of sixty-four fighter-bombers. They would meet up with twenty-four Thunderbolts of two of the 79th Fighter Group squadrons armed with rockets and fragmentation bombs. Escorted by high-flying Mk VIII Spitfires of 244 Wing, these eighty-eight warplanes would race north together to Venice. A PR Spitfire would fly above Venice to record the effects of the raid. An air-sea rescue Catalina and a Walrus, guarded by Spitfires, would patrol as close to the Lagoon as they could to pick up stricken pilots parachuting over or ditching into the sea.

On the morning of 20 March, 92 Squadron, commanded by Captain Ronald 'Hank' Jacobs SAAF, had been directed to attack fuel barges making their slow way to Milan and Turin along the Po. As the Spitfires turned to the dive, the sky appeared to ignite – 88mm flak. Lower down, a screen of 37mm and 20mm gunfire covered the river. Some pilots were able to release 500lb bombs, to questionable effect. Jacobs ordered the Squadron to turn towards Venice to get clear of the murderous ground fire. As they neared the fabled city, the flak only became more intense. 'Get out of it, and head over the coast, out to sea,' called Jacobs, his own plane hit. Jacobs bailed out over the Adriatic and was picked up, uninjured, by an air-sea rescue Catalina. That afternoon he was playing football with the Squadron, but it had been a close-run thing. Venice would be no milk run.

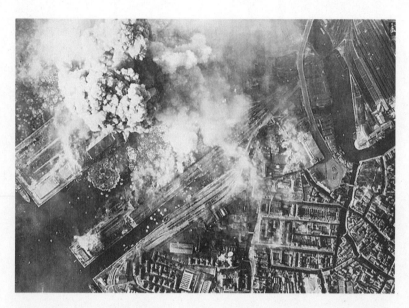

Operation Bowler direct hits caught by photo-reconnaissance Spitfire.
Santa Marta housing district bottom left. Piazzale Roma, centre.

ELEVEN

THE ATTACK

21 March 1945, 1430hr

George Westlake fired up his Kittyhawk. The six squadrons of sixty-four fighters and dive bombers of 239 Wing committed to Operation Bowler flamed and crackled into life, nosed their way onto steel mesh strips and thundered, one after the other, up into the Adriatic sky. Sixty-four war machines – 768 cylinders, 88,800 horsepower, with 54,000 pounds of bombs, thirty-two 60lb air-to-ground rockets and 384 0.5-inch Browning machine guns – joined up over Ravenna, minutes away, at 12,000 feet with twenty-four USAAF Thunderbolts of 79th Fighter Group from Fano, fifty miles to the south.

Overhead, twelve Spitfire Mk VIIIs – the best of the Spitfire marks from the pilot's point of view, according to Jeffrey Quill, Supermarine's chief test pilot – from RAF 244 Wing met this aerial armada, darting and weaving above it, on high alert for enemy aircraft. Flying higher still, a solitary

PR Spitfire was primed to photograph the action. Over the Adriatic, Mk V and IX Spitfires of 7 (SAAF) Wing escorted the Walrus and Catalina air-sea rescue aircraft as they nosed towards the Venetian Lagoon. They were to stay on guard to protect them from possible enemy attack.

It was good to be up in the air. The morning had been long drawn out, a little tense, as pilots and ground crew watched the sky waiting for veils of mist and mournful low rain clouds to disperse, although there had been no guarantee of this, as what had been a wretched Italian winter made way begrudgingly to an uncertain spring. While they waited, George had pepped his team. What gave him confidence in today's unprecedented mission, despite the dangers ahead, was 239 Wing's ability to strike challenging targets with increasing precision.

A few months before he took command – 5 May 1944 to be precise – 239 had been directed to attack the 371ft concrete, iron and steel dam across the River Pescara, twenty miles southwest of the Adriatic town of Pescara. Completed in 1931, the dam fed a new hydroelectric power station, its power lines stretching to Rome. If the dam could be breached, Rome – still in German hands in May 1944 – would suffer a significant loss of power while German troop movements and supply lines on the eastern edge of the Gothic Line would be seriously affected. The Pescara dam lay behind German lines.

The RAF had scored a famous victory, albeit with the loss of many aircrews' lives, with Operation Chastise on the night of 16–17 May 1943, when nineteen four-engine Lancasters of 617 Squadron led by twenty-four-year-old Wing Commander

Guy Gibson breached the Möhne and Eder dam with the ingenious 'bouncing bombs' invented by the Vickers engineer Barnes Wallis. Both massive structures were linked to hydroelectric power stations. The damage inflicted on them by 617 Squadron caused significant damage to German industry in the Ruhr, together with a great loss of life among civilians and slave labourers unable to escape the torrent of flood water cascading in 40ft-high waves from the Möhne dam.

Operation Chastise had been flown at night with the big Avro bombers flying through flak at sixty feet above the water towards the dams. Each Lancaster carried a single bomb weighing more than an air-ready Kittyhawk. The bombs were designed to explode deep under water in contact with the dam walls. The German dams were huge, dense structures, and only very powerful bombs could have damaged or destroyed them.

The story had certainly done the rounds. Everyone serving with 239 Wing knew it. Guy Gibson himself had written about it, while temporarily 'flying a desk' in Whitehall, in a series of articles published in the *Daily Express* in December 1944. One of Gibson's ghostwriters was none other than Roald Dahl, who George had flown with in the Middle East. As for Wing Commander Gibson, he had been killed in September 1944 when, back in action, his Mosquito was shot down and crashed near Steenbergen in the Netherlands flying home from a mission to Mönchengladbach. News of his death had been made public in January 1945.

If it had taken nineteen Lancasters, of which eight were lost, carrying purpose-built 9,250lb bombs to breach the German dams, how could 239 Wing's single-engine

Kittyhawks and Mustangs, carrying conventional 1,000lb bombs, pull off the same stunt in Italy? The answers were thorough planning, practice, concentrated bombing and sheer guts on the part of the pilots flying in broad daylight into anti-aircraft fire. Preparation for the mission had included the making of scale models of the dam and its surrounding landscape as well as close attention to aerial reconnaissance photographs shot from high-flying Spitfires.

Flying from Cutella, 239 Wing was led by Lieutenant Colonel Laurie Wilmot DFC, a veteran of the Desert War. In action over Eritrea in 1940 with 1 Squadron SAAF, he was shot down and held prisoner of war before being freed and returning to 1 Squadron to fight in Egypt the following year. The attack on the Pescara dam was made in three determined waves. The new Mustangs of 260 Squadron powered in first, with Flight Sergeant Alexander Duguid making a direct hit on the dam's iron sluice gates. As the Mustangs climbed to 5,000 feet and circled to observe the effect of their bombing, 3 Squadron RAAF dived down into flak, its Kittyhawks carrying a 2,000lb bomb load for the first time. Flight Lieutenant Ken Richards scored a direct hit, compounding Duguid's work. The Kittyhawks of 5 Squadron SAAF followed. With accurate bombing confined to a small, vulnerable target area, the sluice gates gave way. Water poured down and across the valley. The power station was put out of action, the land occupied by German troops flooded and the streets of Pescara inundated under four feet of water.

The raid on the dam had been a triumph of planning, practice, skilled flying and forensic bombing. All three squadrons returned safely to base. Duguid was awarded the DFM (Distinguished Flying Medal, a 'DFC' that is for non-commissioned officers) and Wilmot the DSO. The story was taken up by newspapers around the globe. Wired from Italy by war correspondent A. C. Sedgwick, it made the front page of the *New York Times*. 'Waters Rush Onto Pescara, Imperiling German Defense. Allied Dive-Bombing of Great Dam Sends Great Wave Powering Toward the Adriatic Hinge of the Enemy's Line'.

Today – 21 March 1945 – 239 wing needed to be as precise again with the attack on Venice. The one big difference aside from the greater number of enemy guns protecting the city – identified by aerial reconnaissance – was that, while the Pescara dam stood in open countryside, the Venice docks were part of an exquisite historic city alive with thousands of civilians, including partisans fighting on the side of the Allies.

The Wing was perfectly aware of the effect of inaccurate low-level and wayward high-level bombing. Pescara itself, birthplace of leaflet-dropping Gabriele D'Annunzio and home to key railway marshalling yards, had been bombed heavily nine times by the USAAF between 31 August 1943 and 14 May 1944. The first raid made on the railway yards by forty-five B-24 Liberator bombers on 31 August missed its target completely. Rather than on tracks and sidings, bombs fell on streets and squares, killing 1,900 civilians. By the ninth high-level, four-engine US bomber raid, thousands of people had been killed, including those aboard passenger trains trying to escape the city, and 80 percent of the city centre's buildings had been destroyed. 'No one likes mass slaughter,'

Guy Gibson had written in 1944, 'and we did not like being the authors of it.'

The weather broke. At 1530hrs, the Wing's Kittyhawks, Mustangs and Thunderbolts were racing in from over the sea and across Venice from the east at 7,000 feet, and George asked the Thunderbolts to take out the eight heavy and twenty light guns aligned along Litorale di Lido at Malamocco, where, until remarkably recently, Venetians had come to sunbathe and swim. In the 1920s, Schneider Trophy racing planes in pursuit of national triumphs and world air speed records had crackled over and along the beaches here, the mighty R-type engines of the triumphant British Supermarine aircraft inspiring the development of the twenty-seven-litre Rolls-Royce V12 Merlins powering the Spitfires guarding 239 Wing today. The Mustangs were fitted with a US variant of the Merlin built mostly by Packard in Detroit, with some by Continental at Muskegon on Lake Michigan.

As the Thunderbolts, under the command of Colonel Gladwyn E. Pinkston, a young Californian mining engineer turned fighter pilot, struck, eight Mustangs of 3 Squadron RAAF strafed and dive bombed the anti-aircraft guns on Punta Sabbioni guarding the main sea entrance to the Lagoon. Rebuilt by the Germans in 1944, the Gothic Line-style concrete fortifications at Punta Sabbioni bristled with 100mm Italian flak guns.

Three of the Squadron's Mustangs silenced the four heavy guns on the island of Sant'Erasmo, known for its venerable Renaissance and Napoleonic fortifications, and before the war its market gardens and much-prized artichokes. A pair of

Mustangs of 260 Squadron made rocket attacks on the forti-fied islet of Trezze close by Stazione Marittima, and, as they did and with at least some of the flak suppressed, George led 250 Squadron into the dive on the dock itself, his Kittyhawk plummeting full throttle from 7,000 feet at an angle of sixty degrees towards its target. No one seemed to know just how fast a Kittyhawk could be in a dive. The recommended offi-cial maximum was 480mph, although much higher speeds had been attained on test. The Kittyhawk carried a single 1,000lb bomb. There was to be no 'going around' for a second attempt. It took a very cool nerve and a level head to fly at such breakneck speed, the Kittyhawk fishtailing slightly, and into flak without flinching before releasing the bomb from 1,500 feet and pulling up hard and away, engine scream-ing, without blacking out.

Diving behind George, Lieutenant Senior's P-40 was hit by flak. Turning instinctively out to sea, Senior bailed out ten miles to the east of Choggia. As Spitfires of 7 Squadron circled overhead, a twin-engine air-sea rescue Vickers Warwick, a Supermarine Walrus and a Consolidated PBY Catalina flying boat shelled by shore batteries were all quickly on the scene. A Catalina crewmember dived into the water to help the pilot now in difficulties in the intensely cold water. Helped aboard the Catalina, Lietenant Senior was flown to safety while under fire from German-manned Venetian gun batteries.

After 250 came 450 Squadron RAAF, its pilots firing their 0.5-inch machine guns all the way down, before releasing their bombs and twisting up through the flak. RAF (112) and SAAF (5) Mustang squadrons were quick to pursue the attack as the Kittyhawks headed seawards. And then, *whoomph*, a great sulphurous column of dust and debris rising from below. One or more of the dive bombers had hit an unexpected store of sea mines. The massive explosion blew a crater into the dock, the shock waves so great that they caused the PR Spitfire, recording the raid at 22,000 feet, to bounce in the reverberant sky.

Executed in twenty thunderous minutes, Operation Bowler had involved the dropping of ninety-three 1,000lb bombs, thirty-one 260lb semi-armour-piercing bombs, the firing of 114 air-to-surface 60lb rockets and the countless release of armour-piercing bullets from 0.50-calibre machine guns. The 3,682-ton *Otto Leonhardt* was severely damaged and seen, by PR Spitfires, submerged two days later.

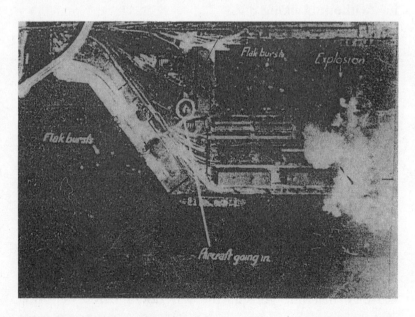

Operation Bowler; 239 Wing coming in to attack viewed from 22,000 feet by photo-reconnaissance Spitfire, 21 March 1945.

Two German-crewed Italian torpedo boats (some sources say one), one small freighter and two lighters were sunk, and dock-side installations, rolling stock and railway track were severely damaged. The sea mine store was wholly destroyed and, along with it, a training school for submariners.

Venetians themselves were witnesses to the sound, fury, spectacle, efficacy and accuracy of the raid. Those on balconies and *altane* rooftop terraces, aware that this was an Allied attack, gawped and cheered. 'Bravo!' yelled thirteen-year-old Tudy Sammartini, the future art historian who first alerted me to the story of Operation Bowler.

For the loss of a single aircraft – Lieutenant Senior's Kittyhawk IV – and flak damage to two of the Mustangs, no casualties, and everyone safely home, George and his fellow pilots had put Stazione Marittima out of action, boosted Allied morale and foreshortened the war in Italy. As far as the pilots could tell, every bomb had fallen within the target area. As they raced back south along the Adriatic, it was good to know that no one would have to wear a bowler hat.

American soldiers enjoying a gondola ride through liberated Venice, 5 May 1945.

TWELVE

CODA

April–May 1945

Buried beneath the avalanche of fast-rolling war news, Operation Bowler had been an astounding success. George Westlake and his colleagues had severed a crucial German supply line for no losses to the pilots of 239 Wing and 79th Fighter Group under his command, and with the least possible damage to Venice itself. The only immediate casualties – twelve, it was thought – were those manning the port, and crewing ships berthed there.

In his logbook, Westlake noted 'Attack Venice Harbour. Whole Wing show with twenty-four P47s of 79th A/Flak [anti-flak]. Whole show successful.' Operation Bowler had helped determine not just the fate of Italy, but also the timing of the end of the war in Europe. Air Vice Marshal 'Pussy' Foster messaged his DAF wings, groups and squadrons. 'The results are excellent, and the maximum damage has been done by a comparatively small force. Bombing was most accurate, and no apparent damage has been done to any of the cultural monuments in close proximity to the target. My best congratulations to all those who took part in this neatly executed operation.' 'A very neat little operation,' echoed Air Marshal Sir Guy Garrod, the newly appointed Commander-in-Chief Mediterranean and Middle East, who was to fly over Venice on 4 May to observe the results of the action. 'It was interesting to see with what precision the raid had been carried out,' he wrote.

The sheer ferocity of the attack, however, meant that there had been unforeseen civilian casualties. A house in the working-class district of Santa Marta close to the Stazione Marittima collapsed in the wake of the raid. Twenty-five people are said to have died. Aside from a weather-worn stone tablet near the long-abandoned church of Santa Marta, there is no obvious public record of the event. The desire for the war to end and the shadowy years that followed while Italy recovered socially and politically before blossoming in the 1950s – the years of the country's 'economic miracle' – meant, perhaps, that such memories were edited from Venetian minds. When, on 21 March 2015, I mentioned Operation Bowler and the dramatic events of 21 March 1945 to Venetians of different generations living in several different parts of the city, it drew a repeated blank. Incidentally, in Italian, a bowler hat just happens to be a *bombetta* (a little bomb).

What is remarkable is that so few people were killed on 21 March 1945, and that there was little or no damage to the city or its peerless architectural and art-historical heritage, save for that one elusive house that collapsed somewhere in Santa Marta. If any of Westlake's pilots had mistimed their attacks, the results might have been very different. To stand in front of the deconsecrated church of Santa Marta, it seems remarkable that no bomb or rocket hit it or desecrated it further than the French had already done in 1811, when the church's monastic buildings had been razed to the ground and its fourteenth-century nave was turned into a store for animal fodder. The city itself demolished Santa Marta's campanile in 1910. How lovely it looks in eighteenth-century paintings by Guardi and Canaletto. By 1945, the church was a railway warehouse, itself a possible target.

This forlorn church stands on the fringe of the Santa Marta housing district, its regular rows of 1920s apartment blocks designed, successfully, in a nominally Venetian style by the public housing architect Paolo Bertanza for the families of workers employed by the vast *Cotonoficio* – the Venice Cotton Mill (1883–1960) – housing the city's university architecture school and its student accommodation today. The explosions of bombs raining down on the docks on 21 March 1945 would have resounded and reverberated through the streets of Santa Marta, and yet no bomb fell here.

The slightest imprecision in attack might well have destroyed Sant'Andrea della Ziarada, a fourteenth-century abbey church to the immediate south of Piazzale Roma, rebuilt in 1475, that had forfeited its monastic buildings when the anti-clerical French, led by Napoleon, ravaged Venice. Wayward bombs could easily have hit Piazzale Roma – so close by – and the Santa Lucia railway terminus. The venerable church of San Nicolò dei Mendicoli, its thirteenth-century structure resting on seventh-century foundations, and the glorious Chiesa dell'Angelo Raffaele, its sixth-century foundations supporting twin campaniles and an early seventeenth-century Greek cross superstructure, added to in later decades by Francesco Contino, were both too close to the docks for comfort.

Given the proximity of the Stazione Marittima to Stazione Santa Lucia, its depots and sidings, a few bombs and rockets directed at these railway targets would have been a further guarantee by DAF of staunching supplies to the German armies. From January 1944, direct railway lines between Italy and Germany had been heavily bombed and made largely impassable. All lines, that is, save for the railway that snakes up from Trieste to the Austrian border at Villach. Set in deep, narrow ravines in mountainous country, bridges including those at Dogna and Muro proved to be impervious to aerial attack.

A raid on the docks made by four-engine bombers releasing their deadly cargo from as high as 20,000 feet would have caused enormous damage to Venice and a great loss of life. Who wished to repeat the damning experience of Monte Cassino, or anything resembling that heart-rending raid? We should be grateful that Venice was not considered to be a legitimate military target until late into the Italian campaign.

By now, DAF had formed itself, over those long months fighting at first in North Africa, then in Sicily and slowly up the spine of Italy and over and around the Gothic Line, into a highly effective, heavily armed, well-coordinated and hard-hitting international tactical war machine. It says much that, for the American pilots of the 79th Fighter Group,

Operation Bowler was just another of the missions they executed on their furious, gun-blazing way north and east up into Yugoslavia and Austria. The 79th's pilots were either dealt the Venice card at the last minute, or not. Any of these young men were deemed capable of taking part in Operation Bowler.

Gerry Teldon missed the action. Just. Following several days of particularly intense combat, he had finally been sent on much-needed leave, to Capri:

> We stayed at the Quisinana Hotel, the most prestigious on the island, and stayed drunk most of the time. There I was, 21 years old and still alive to tell the tale. I had in a very few years crossed from a kid out of school to manhood, from egg to adult without the benefit of a chrysalis... I returned (from leave) expecting to be sent home – I had flown 62 missions, and the war seemed to be over – when orders came transferring the Group to an airfield, Hörsching, outside of Linz, Austria, to await and stem the advancing Russians. Yes, those in charge were certain that would happen.

Until 8 May, Hörsching airfield had been home to *Jagdeschwader* 52, the Bf109 fighter wing that had shot down more than 10,000 enemy aircraft in the past five years. Among its pilots were the three highest scoring fighter aces of all time: Erich Hartmann (352 victories), Gerhard Barkhorn (301) and Günther Rall (275). All three were to retrain as combat pilots in the US, returning to democratic West Germany to become senior commanders of the new

Luftwaffe, formed on 1 January 1956 following pressure from Washington concerned with the Soviet Union and Eastern Bloc's ambitions for Europe. None of these formidable aces had fought in Italy. They were needed on the Eastern Front and then in Germany itself as the Red Army closed in.

The DAF fought on with relentless determination in the weeks following Operation Bowler, George Westlake's logbook recording several raids flying P-47s and P-51B Mustangs in early April in support of Allied ground troops, which finally broke through the Gothic Line after much heavy fighting and as the horrific winter finally ceded to a patchy spring towards the end of the month.

The all-out push into the Po Valley was well thought through, as it should have been given that its planning had been in the making for several months. The winter had been a long waiting game. Now, with German supply lines severed, not least thanks to Operation Bowler, the Allies finally opened up with concentrated artillery and aerial bombardments on 9 April, with advancing infantry making a pincer movement around the Gothic Line. Up through the mountains, American and Brazilian infantry fought a truly heroic path across the most daunting terrain. The specialist US 10th Mountain Division, newly arrived at Naples from Virginia in January 1945, enabled the 85th Infantry Division to take Monte Belvedere (3,740 feet), which, as the keystone of a line of mountain defences, had allowed German guns to intimidate and command vast swathes of territory below. The surmounting of Monte Belvedere, swept of the enemy, was a key moment in the breaking of the Gothic Line.

George Westlake and 239 Wing were involved in the great April assault. They were also on the lookout for new dangers that might be lurking somewhere in the clouds above. George's logbook for 7 April records an 'Anti-Jet Patrol (No luck)'. There were sightings of the new Arado Ar234 jet bomber on reconnaissance missions, and rumours concerning the very real danger of the Me 262 jets now being flown as potent fighters, but as yet north of the Alps. Among their most successful pilots was *Generalmajor* Adolf Galland (104 victories), who claimed six kills with the Me 262 in April.

In 1935, Galland had been one of the first of Göring's Luftwaffe pilots. He flew in combat from the Battles of France and Britain until surrender to the Americans was the only option left to his *Jagdverband 44* jet fighter unit. His *Jagdverband 44* colleague *Oberstleutnant* Johannes Steinhoff (176 victories), who had fought in North Africa and Italy in 1943 and 1944 before being posted to the Eastern Front and completing at least a thousand combat missions, went on to play a leading role in the formation of the West German Luftwaffe and its integration into NATO.

Continuing pilot casualties in the aftermath of Operation Bowler, meanwhile, reflected DAF's wholesale transformation into a multinational air force, a precursor of NATO operations. On 24 March, Flying Officer F. D. Devlin, a twenty-six-year-old American from New Jersey of 250 Squadron, was killed when the American engine of his Kittyhawk cut out while dive bombing a bridge at San Giorgio di Nagaro north of Venice. Imagine trying to pull open the canopy in a dive and to climb out from the cockpit as the ground rushed towards you. The slipstream would have been overwhelming. Devlin's parachute caught on the aircraft's tailplane. He went down with it.

On 1 April, Lieutenant K. O. Embling's 7 Squadron SAAF Spitfire IX exploded in mid-air while dive bombing barges on the Po northwest of Ferrara. On 11 April, a 3 Squadron RAAF Mustang III flown by Flight Lieutenant James Edmonds, a British officer on a temporary posting with the RAAF, crashed while failing to pull out of a dive after an attack on a building near Imola between Bologna and Ravenna. This was on one of the five daily missions DAF flew throughout April in support of the Eighth Army.

At the same time, squadrons fought to the east of Venice. On 5 April, Pilot Officer Brian Brown's 450 RAAF Squadron Kittyhawk IV burst into flames in a dive-bombing attack near Palmanova after an earlier attack on rail targets in the Udine-Grado area. Palmanova itself is a fortified geometric town laid out in the pattern of a nine-pointed star in 1593 by the Republic of Venice. From the air, Palmanova (like Venice, now a UNESCO World Heritage site) looks like the gun sight of a Second World War bomber, a perfect target if there ever was one. Physically, it appears to have escaped the war unscathed, although as a base for Fascist militias, it might have been attacked.

With the Allied armies finally breaking out from the Gothic Line on 9 April, DAF was busier than ever before, clearing every possible obstruction in the way of victory. By 17 April, DAF was flying a thousand sorties a day. Major Hillary 'Nobby' Clarke, CO 5 Squadron SAAF, brought his badly hit Mustang III down to land at base. It was the twenty-first time Clarke had been hit by flak. 'They tell me the first

twenty are the worst,' he quipped. Two weeks later, the twenty-six-year-old Major from Springs, Transvaal, was shot
down after an anti-shipping strike between Trieste and
Grado, his stricken Mustang, its wing shot off by flak, ploughing into the sea. He was the last South African and, I think,
the last Commonwealth pilot killed in the war.

DAF pilots continued to fly a knife edge balance between
life and death with the end of the Italian war now just days
away. On 19 April, 450 RAAF Squadron's Flying Officer
P. D. Allen failed to pull out of dive, his Kittyhawk smashing
into the ground at Imola. At much the same time, Lieutenant
P. Muir of 5 SAAF Squadron crashed twenty miles southwest
of Venice while recovering from a dive on a ferry terminal
on the Po. Warrant Officer of 3 RAAF Squadron was hit by
flak on 28 April, crash-landing his Mustang on a beach near
Venice. He returned back safely. On 30 April, 260 Squadron's
Lieutenant R. H. Veitch was hit by flak over Udine, ditching
his Mustang III in the sea. It was his third drenching in a
month. He was rescued by an RAF High Speed Launch.
These magnificent thirty-five-knot machines with a range
of 500 miles and equipped by 1941 with a sick bay below
deck, aircraft-style machine-gun turrets and a 20mm
Oerlikon cannon, had been designed by Hubert Scott-Paine,
who had bought Supermarine in 1916 and employed
Reginald Mitchell of future Spitfire fame, with the expert
help of Aircraftman T. E. Shaw, better known as Colonel T. E.
Lawrence. By May 1945, RAF High Speed Launches had
saved the lives of some 13,000 British airmen. Pilots of the
Desert Air Force had every reason to be grateful to Lawrence
of Arabia.

At the beginning of May, George Westlake was awarded the DSO. 'This officer,' the citation reads,

> has displayed skill, courage and devotion to duty of a high order. He has participated in a large number of sorties, and his achievements have won the greatest praise. In March 1945, Wing Commander Westlake led a large formation of aircraft in an attack on the docks and shipping in the port of Venice. Harbour installations and stores were extensively damaged, whilst a medium sized merchantman, a naval vessel and a small coaster were destroyed. In April 1945, Wing Commander Westlake took part in an air attack against forward enemy positions in support of an assault by our ground forces. The attack was pressed home with results which greatly facilitated the task of the infantry in their subsequent successful attack. By his excellent leadership, great tactical ability and exceptional determination, Wing Commander Westlake played a good part in the success achieved. In air fighting this officer has been responsible for the destruction of eleven enemy aircraft.

And although severely hampered by a lack of supplies and with the Allied armies storming up across the Po Valley, still the Germans fought on doggedly, although what appeared to be a united German front was anything but. Field Marshal Kesselring had left Italy days before Operation Bowler to take command of the Western Front, replacing the veteran Field Marshal Gerd von Rundstedt, dismissed by Hitler two days earlier after the Americans crossed the Rhine.

In his memoirs, Kesselring admitted to feeling 'utterly at sea'. Having fought a tenacious defensive war in Italy, where he had been more or less in control of events, now he was faced with an entire front collapsing as the Allies closed in on Germany and with the Red Army storming from the east towards Berlin. 'I felt like a concert pianist who is asked to play a Beethoven sonata before a large audience on an ancient, rickety and out of tune instrument. In many respects I found conditions which contradicted all my principles, but events were moving too swiftly for me to have time to influence them much. My post was too important and my rank too high for me to shirk the responsibility.'

In Italy, General Heinrich von Vietinghoff had been appointed supreme German commander in Kesselring's place with, of course, SS General Karl Wolff at his side. While no one could doubt von Vietinghoff's skill as a general, he, too, was faced with an impossible situation. Following Operation Bowler and the Fifth and Eighth Armies finally breaking through the Gothic Line, just how long could the German army in Italy defend itself?

Others, including Wolff, had been asking the same question for some while. A few days before Operation Bowler, Wolff attended secret meetings in Switzerland organised by Allen Dulles, the US lawyer and head of the Office of Strategic Services (OSS), Bern. The meetings were held in Ascona fronting Lake Maggiore during a spring festival, when the pretty Swiss resort bustled with cheerful life. Also in attendance among twenty officials and bodyguards were Major General Lyman L. Lemnintzer from General Eisenhower's staff representing the United States and, batting for Britain, Major General Terence Airey, Assistant Chief of Staff to General Alexander. Airey and Lemnitzer, who flew to Switzerland together, posed as Irish businessmen. They stayed at the Villa Roccolo, a house owned by Edmund Stinnes, a German-American industrialist and anti-Nazi activist. Stinnes's brother-in-law, the German economist Gero von Schulze-Gaevernitz, a naturalised US citizen, led the negotiations on the American side.

The meetings were held on the lake front in Villa Margiana, attendees dressed in civilian garb as if the war had never happened. To compound this sense of detachment from the reality of conflict, Major General Airey, posing as Mr MacNeilly, had told immigration officials and anyone else who cared to ask that he had been on his way to Ascona to buy a German dachshund. If this contrivance seemed a touch absurd, the entangled story of the German surrender in Italy comes across like the plot of some convoluted Baroque Venetian opera.

The Germans had, in fact, been working towards tentative negotiations with the Allies behind the scenes for a separate surrender in Italy for several months, as early perhaps as the previous summer. On 3 March 1945, SS *Hauptsturmführer* Guido Zimmer, *Obersturmbannführer* Eugen Dollmann and Baron Luigi Parrilli, the Italian Nazi sympathiser with, nevertheless, good contacts in the resistance and who before the war had distributed American Nash cars and Kelvinator refrigerators in Italy, met with the OSS's Paul Blum in Lugano. This led to an initial meeting ahead of Ascona between Dulles and Wolff in a Zurich apartment on 8 March. Dulles had agreed to the meeting on condition that Wolff release Ferruccio Parri, a high-profile member of the Italian resistance, from prison, which the SS general did immediately. Parri was to become the first post-war Italian Prime Minister.

Dulles was aware that Wolff had previously negotiated with Pope Pius XII to ensure a peaceful German exit from Rome and that he had helped move works of art from the Uffizi Gallery, Florence, to safety. These were points that counted in his favour with the Americans. What he didn't know was that a second prisoner, a certain Captain Hall, whom Dulles wanted released as a sign of good faith on Wolff's part, had been tortured and killed at the Bolzano concentration camp. Hall had not, as Wolff later claimed, hanged himself in his cell.

The exact history of what the Americans knew or didn't know or who was pulling the wool or Wolff over the others' eyes during Operation Sunrise remains as byzantine as it is hazy. What is particularly interesting, though, especially from the point of view of how Italy's art-historical heritage might be saved, is the way Wolff listened to Eugen Dollmann, one of the more enigmatic SS officers operating in Italy. Born into an aristocratic Bavarian-Austrian family in 1900, Dollmann had come to Rome to take up post-doctoral studies in art and ecclesiastical history. Living in Piazza di Spagna, he spent much time researching in the Vatican Library.

A remarkably well-connected socialite fluent in Italian and invited to all the smartest parties, Dollmann was introduced to Heinrich Himmler when the *Reichsführer* was on a visit to Rome and in need of a trustworthy translator.

Himmler introduced Dollmann to Wolff, his personal adjutant. In 1935, Dollmann was appointed chief of the Italian NSDAP Press Office. Two years later he was commissioned SS-*Oberststurmbannführer* (Lieutenant Colonel) and was soon, courtesy of Wolff, translating at international meetings at the highest level, including those between Hitler and Mussolini.

An unlikely SS officer, the dapper Dollmann took great pleasure in mocking what he considered to be the awkward petit-bourgeois manners, mannerisms and speech of Hitler, Himmler and other leading Nazis. He made fun of his Italian superiors, too. An aesthete perhaps above all else, he sailed with help of his many useful contacts through the darkest days of the war and its aftermath.

The British government assumed that Kesselring was aware of the meetings and that Wolff spoke for him. 'The first indications,' noted Harold Macmillan, 'that some of Kesselring's officers wished to treat for terms had reached us on 8th March.' It is difficult to know quite who knew what exactly or what their personal motives were. Kesselring may have been sounding out the possibility of Swiss citizenship, although he must have given up this idea, whether realistic or not, once he was given command of the Western Front and publicly declared his undying allegiance to the Führer. Nevertheless, Wolff visited Kesselring on 23 March hoping to persuade him to allow von Vietinghoff to surrender. While, it seems, Kesselring approved of what Wolff was up to with Dulles in Switzerland, he told the SS general that nothing could be done while the Führer was alive.

In Berlin, Hitler had got wind of the affair through the ever-suspicious Heinrich Himmler. Summoned to Berlin twice, Wolff was able to persuade the Führer that the discussions with Dulles were merely a device to divide the Allies and to delay their advance. The Russians had not been invited to the Ascona table. Stalin, who was told of the situation by Churchill, is known to have been angry, complaining vociferously to both the British Prime Minister and the US President Franklin Delano Roosevelt. Roosevelt died on 12 April. Vice-President Harry S. Truman, an implacable foe of communism and the Soviet Union, took his place at the White House.

For Truman, talk of deals with the Germans went against the grain of the Casablanca Declaration made by Roosevelt and Churchill at the end of the Casablanca Conference held in January 1943. In no uncertain words, the Declaration called for the *unconditional surrender* of Axis forces. Truman insisted on a Soviet military presence at the signing of the surrender document at Caserta. For now, at least, Stalin needed to be kept sweet, as if such a thing were possible. The Soviet dictator had yet to agree to join the Allies in the fight against the Japanese. Atom bombs had yet to be dropped on Hiroshima and Nagasaki to bring the war with Japan to a sudden halt.

Truman must surely have been aware of Churchill's attitude towards the Soviets at this late stage in the war. In May, British chiefs of staff working closely with the Prime Minister drew up plans for Operation Unthinkable, one strand of which was for British and American divisions stationed in Germany to make a sudden, overwhelming attack on the Red Army. This would, ideally, curtail Stalin's plans for Germany and Poland, too, the country that Britain had ostensibly gone to war for in September 1939. It would have been General Wolff's dream come true. The operation remained a flight of fantasy. The Red Army greatly outnumbered Allied ground forces and a total war with the Soviet Union would have been madness.

Hitler, meanwhile, ordered Wolff back to Italy on the condition that he was no longer to visit Switzerland. General von Vietinghoff wished the war to end, too, but only if there was a guarantee that his troops would be treated honourably. An officer of the old school, he hoped to see his soldiers marching back in good order to Germany and not held as prisoners of war in unknown conditions.

Ultimately, there was no good order in the surrender negotiations. Convolution piled upon convolution until finally, on 28 April, *Oberstleutnant* Victor von Schweinitz, von Vietinghoff's Chief of Staff, and *Sturmbannführer* Eugen Wenner, representing Wolff, arrived by plane at Caserta. They were joined by Gero von Schulze-Gaevernitz, Major General Airey (without dachshund), Major General Lemnitzer and Lieutenant General William Morgan, Field Marshal Alexander's Chief of Staff.

The document the Germans signed the following afternoon in the presence of a Russian observer – Major General Aleksey Pavlovich Kislenko, Soviet delegate to the Allied Control Commission in Rome – was, after so many feints and ploys on either side, for an unconditional surrender. There were to be no concessions to Wolff or von Vietinghoff. To give time for the word to reach frontline troops, many fighting in remote locations, hostilities were scheduled to end at midday GMT on 2 May.

To add one further twist to a knotty tale, confirmation of. the surrender from von Vietinghoff was received by 15th Army Group (US Fifth and British Eighth Armies under the overall command of General Clark) only on the morning of 2 May. As Commander-in-Chief West, Kesselring had dismissed von Vietinghoff for, effectively, going against Hitler's orders to fight on, replacing him with General Friedrich Schulz, commander of Army Group G. When Kesselring received news of the Führer's death on 30 April, von Vietinghoff was reinstated and the surrender put into effect.

By this late date, so much else had happened. Many Italian towns and cities, Venice included, were already liberated, whether by the Allies, the partisans or the two working in tandem. The large number of Italian-American troops in Italy, especially those fighting hard in the brutal conditions experienced across and in the winter shadows of the Gothic Line, had helped in the establishing of good and effective relationships between the Americans and the partisans, although mistakes were made. Infamously, two aborted attempts made by OSS (Office of Strategic Services) in February to blow up a strategic railway tunnel on the Ligurian coast between Framura and Bonassola south of Genoa – well behind enemy lines – led to the capture and summary execution of the fifteen Italian-American soldiers involved in the second mission. While those led by First Lieutenants Vincent Rosso and Paul Trafficante were able to hide in a 'safe house' barn, they were given away to Fascist militia by a fisherman who had seen their rubber dinghies.

The delay in bringing the Italian war to a conclusion led to many unnecessary deaths and continuing suffering for soldiers on both sides and, of course, civilians. In his book *The Decisive Campaigns of the Desert Air Force, 1942–45*, Bryn Evans cites the evidence of Flight Sergeant Stan Watt of RAAF 450 Squadron – which took part in Operation Bowler – who, having completed his tour of operations in March was to return home, but only after a spell as CO of a Mobile Operations Room Unit in April when the Allied ground offensive north of the Gothic Line finally burst into action:

> They reported at least a thousand German trucks, self-propelled guns and tanks milling around the south-side of the Po with no bridge left for them to make a crossing. I called up every available aircraft in the Cab-rank. Within fifteen minutes the dive bombers had begun their deadly work. It was a massacre. For the rest of the day successive squadrons each spent ten minutes raking the vehicles with machine-gun fire and dropping their bombs. When their bomb racks and magazines were empty, they returned to base, re-armed and flew back into the fray. The attack was finally called off when night fell, and the planes were unable to see their targets.

Note 'the planes', as if the machines alone were responsible for the carnage. It was, of course, rare for a combat pilot to witness the effects of ground attacks. The following morning, Flight Sergeant Watt drove through drizzle to where the Germans had been pinned down by DAF. 'Bodies [between 800 and 1,000] were hanging out of vehicles or splayed like rag dolls across the ground. Wisps of smoke still drifted lazily from burnt-out trucks. Flies were already buzzing, disturbing what would otherwise have been an unearthly silence. One soldier appeared to have taken a fighter's cannon shot in his stomach, causing it to burst like a watermelon.'

With DAF covering the skies above and blasting everyone and everything that stood in the path of the Allied armies, Bologna was taken on 22 April, Ferrara and Modena on 23 April, Mantua on 25 April, Genoa on 27 April, Padua on 29 April and Turin the following day. The Allies gained Milan, Trieste and Venice on 2 May.

DAF's dominance ensured the final collapse of the German military in the Po Valley. In April alone, it had flown 21,000 sorties, 3,020 of them made by 79th Fighter Group's relentless Thunderbolts. The accuracy of DAF's attacks had improved, with 73 Squadron's (324 Wing) Spitfire Mk IXs led by Captain Thomas Taylor DFC flying 670 sorties and scoring 25 percent direct hits.

As General von Senger recalled, 'We could still move when required at night, but we could not move at all in the daytime due to the air attacks. It was the bombing of the River Po crossings that finished us... owing to the destruction of the ferries and the river crossings we lost all our equipment. North of the river we were no longer an Army.' General von Vietinghoff echoed his tank commander. Of DAF's Kittyhawks, Thunderbolts and Mustangs, he said, 'They hindered practically all essential movement at the local points. Even tanks could not move during the day because of the employment of fighter-bombers. The effectiveness of fighter-bombers lay in that their presence alone over the battlefield paralysed every moment.'

'DAF,' wrote Lieutenant General Sir Richard McCreery, Commander-in-Chief Eighth Army, 'has achieved a degree of efficiency in close support of ground forces that has never been equalled in any other partnership.'

Two momentous events had occurred at the end of April before German, and, indeed, DAF's, guns could be silenced. On 28 April, partisans executed Mussolini and his mistress Claretta Petacci, along with their company of Fascist leaders and officials caught the previous day near Dongo on the northwest shore of Lake Como. Their motor convoy had been hoping to cross the Swiss border over the Brenner Pass. Mussolini and Petacci were gunned down at the entrance to Villa Belmonte in the village of Giulino di Mezzegra. Walter Audisio, a communist partisan, was by most accounts the executioner, although because this was a political act, others, notably Sandro Pertini, future President of Italy, were credited with the kill.

The corpses were driven to Milan's Piazzale Loreto close to the Brobdingnagian central railway station designed by Ulisse Stacchini and opened in the presence of Galeazzo Ciano, the Italian foreign minister and Mussolini's son-in-law. The station featured a special waiting room with a swastika floor for Hitler's use and a secret platform, Binario 21, from which 1,200 Italian Jews were dispatched to extermination camps. Ciano had voted in favour of the Duce's removal from power, yet there was no escaping Mussolini's vengeful clutches. Tied to a chair, he was executed by firing squad in January 1944.

After a savage beating by a frenzied crowd in Piazzale Loreto, not far from Milano Centrale – Mussolini's face was kicked to pulp, as gruesome US press photos have revealed – the deposed leader and his mistress were strung upside down from a steel girder of a half-completed Esso petrol station.

News of Mussolini's humiliating and gruesome demise reached Hitler in Berlin. The German leader had already decided to take his own life as the Red Army blasted its way ever closer towards the Reich Chancellery and the concrete bunker madhouse beneath it. The Führer shot himself on 30 April. While the German commanders in Italy had made their own arrangements to end the war, for a brief and disturbing moment it seemed as if they might yet be foiled. Hitler's chosen successor was Grand Admiral Karl Dönitz. The Admiral knew the war was lost, yet nevertheless he initially ordered the fight to continue, especially against Russia. He was aiming, mostly, to gain time to allow tens of thousands of German soldiers to escape the clutches of the Red Army. He ordered the war in Italy to continue. Kesselring, obedient to the last, went so far as to order the arrest of von Vietinghoff and his senior generals and spent two hours on a heated phone call to Wolff, as if he could somehow stop events in Italy. While this was largely bluster on Kesselring's part – the European war ended on 8 May – it confused the situation, allowing fighting to continue.

On 4 May, *General der Panzertruppe* Fridolin von Senger, representing von Vietinghoff, reported in Florence to US General Mark Clark, since December 1944 Commander of the 15th Army Group (US Fifth and British Eighth Armies). The German general's journey had been imperilled on and off along the arduous way by partisans. Senger told Clark that it was hard for German troops to simply stop fighting in territories where partisans were active. Given that the most aggressive armed partisan groups were communists, or communist led, Clark was also keen to prevent German weapons and supply depots from falling into their vengeful hands. American troops would need to move quickly and deftly into these areas. This was easier said than done, as Clark had only recently encouraged partisan units to fight the Germans hard on and beyond the Gothic Line. With great reluctance on the part of many of their number, partisans were only finally to lay down their arms publicly on 15 June.

Meeting face to face was an emotional experience for both Clark and von Senger, although neither man would have shown it at the time. They had been rivals for several months as they fought up and around the Gustav Line and in the attack on and defence of Monte Cassino in the winter and spring of 1943. The German general was a seasoned and fine commander with a long record of successes in France and Russia. An intellectual Roman Catholic aristocrat from a long line of soldiers, he had been a Rhodes Scholar at Oxford – one of two Germans and six Americans in 1911 – spoke English and French fluently and, an Italophile, treasured Italian Baroque art, architecture and music. By 1944, he spoke Italian well. In discussions with Kesselring, he had helped ensure that the reach of the Gothic Line excluded Bologna, Florence, Lucca and Pisa, four cities brimming with art-historical and architectural riches. Any closer to Kesselring's defences and these cherished cities may have been bombed heavily by the Allies.

For his part, General Clark was to be haunted by his failure to tackle von Vietinghoff's 10th Army, which included von Senger's XIV Panzer Corps, when he made his dash to Rome and the Germans escaped north from Monte Cassino to fight again and again over all too many arduous months ahead. Clark was well aware of many of his own Catholic troops' abhorrence of the destruction of Monte Cassino. But this was May 1945; now a few more punches and the war would surely be over.

Partisans were a cause for concern at this late stage for the British, too. Quite how the war would pan out to the east of Venice was still unknown. On 1 May, the Eighth Army finally encountered Marshal Josip Tito's Yugoslav partisans at Montfalcone, twenty miles northwest of Trieste, 80 miles east of Venice. The partisans had beaten the Allies to Trieste, the port city that had bounced between Venetian and Habsburg rule over the centuries. A part of Italy since 1918, it had been occupied by the Germans from Mussolini's fall in September 1943. In an uncomfortable stand-off between the British and Yugoslav forces, Trieste remained in Tito's iron grip until 12 June, during which time anti-communist Italians and Slovenes were arrested and disappeared.

During the same weeks, what has been called the 'last battle of the Second World War in Europe' was fought on 14–15 May at Poljana (Croatia) between the Yugoslav army and a 30,000-strong division of retreating Germans heading west to the Austrian border. The division included Chetniks, Croatians, Serbs and Montenegrins loyal to Nazi Germany, together with the XV Waffen SS Cossack Cavalry Corps. The day- and night-long fight involving intense artillery exchanges ended only when some twenty British tanks arrived.

The British refused to accept the surrender of the Germans and their allied troops. They were handed over to the Yugoslav army and promptly massacred. The Cossacks, as a matter of British policy, were placed in the tender hands of the Red Army. Most were killed in a mass execution near Lienz, Austria. There was to be no happy ending of the war on the Eastern Front.

At first, the liberation of Venice was also a violent event. On the night of 27 April, an uprising led to fierce gun battles between partisans, armed civilians, political prisoners newly freed from the Santa Maria Maggiore prison and the Italian Fascists and German occupiers. The fight spread the following morning across Piazzale Roma and Stazione Marittima. Two days later, the Germans abandoned Venice as Allied Forces under Lieutenant General Freyberg entered the city. As an opening gambit, Freyberg ordered two tanks across the Ponte Littorio. 'They raced each other down the causeway neck and neck,' according to James (later Jan) Morris in *Venice* (1960), 'and one New Zealander reported that as his vehicle clattered pell-mell over a flyover near Mestre, he looked down and saw the Germans racing helter-skelter in the opposite direction underneath.' Those soldiers of the 2nd New Zealand Expeditionary Force were billeted in the opulent, if crowded, Hotel Danieli. If only George Westlake could have been with them. He would have been amused to find, along with Blanchailles au citron, Poulet en casserole and Asperge hollandaise, Bombe with fraise á la crème on the menu.

Fine dining and flowing champagne were everyday occur-
rences in Bolzano, the Italian city set high in the South Tyrol,
one hundred and twenty miles north of Venice, that had
been home to General Wolff's headquarters since September
1943. This predominantly German-speaking gateway to the
Brenner Pass seemed, unlike Venice, ungrateful to be liberated. There were no cheering crowds as the Americans drove
into town. In his essay 'In the Shadow of Sunrise: The Secret
Surrender of Italy' (2008) for Welfare History Network,
Dennis Whitehead quotes Ted Ryan of the OSS Caserta
station arriving in Bolzano on 9 May with Allen Dulles and
Gero Gaevernitz for post-surrender talks there with Wolff
and von Vietinghoff:

> It was a peaceful scene, rather like lunchtime at the MGM
> Studios... A bronzed lad in khaki Afrika Korps shorts,
> balanced on the handlebars of his bicycle a smiling girl in a
> red-and-white striped dirndl. Austrian types in black
> Homburgs and velvet jackets moved casually through the
> streets. In a field at the roadside lolled some hundreds of
> Wehrmacht troops only mildly interested in the American
> staff car which rolled by them. The first traffic control we
> encountered was, indeed, not an American MP but a square,
> very correct German soldier with an automatic weapon
> slung over his shoulder.

General Wolff played host at his headquarters at the palace of
the Duke of Pistoia, 'a monumental red brick building
enclosed in a compound the size of a good New York City
block'. Here, Prussian formalities were observed with

heel-clicking, and toasts with schnapps, four-course meals with champagne and wine and *faux*-modest apologies from the host for the fare.

For American soldiers, Bolzano was their world turned upside down. The 87th Division records note, 'After the memory of the seared browns of the Apennines and the recent dust of battle, the May colors in the foothills of the Alps seemed unbelievably fresh and vivid. The towns were pastel-colored and more picturesque in architecture than the Italy of farther south. Every view seemed like a children's book illustration.' As Whitehead notes, 'Wermacht [*sic*] soldiers sped around in convertibles with their girlfriends, inhabited restaurants and cafes, and lived in houses and hotels while GIs slept in tents...' A member of the US 86th Mountain Infantry was heard to remark, 'We fought the war and they're celebrating the end of it.' It needed a Fellini or even a Pasolini to do justice to the surreally sybaritic scenes unfolding before GIs' eyes.

Here in the centre of Bolzano was a great Fascist-style Victory Arch and the Casa del Fascio, a monumental party headquarters building completed in 1942. Designed by the architects Guido Pelizzari, Francesco Rossi and Luis Plattner, it boasted an ambitious bas-relief the width of the façade depicting *The Triumph of Fascism* with the Duce on horseback and incorporating his slogan *Credere, Obbedire, Combattere* (Believe, Obey, Fight) by the Austrian artist Hans Piffrader who, settled in Bolzano in 1931, became a member of the Fascist Party in 1940. Since 2017, an illuminated LED sign, created by Italian artists Michele Bernardi and Arnold Holzknecht, reads 'No one has the right to obey', a line written in 1960 by the German-American political theorist Hannah Arendt, reporting on the trial in Jerusalem of the former SS-*Obersturmbannführer* and Holocaust administrator Adolf Eichmann for the *New Yorker*. Eichmann's defence was that he was, of course, only obeying orders.

In 1945, however, it looked to the GIs – bemused or flabbergasted – as if the Fascists were still obeying orders and were in the ascendant. The Casa del Fascio dominated what was then named Piazza Arnaldo Mussolini in homage to the Duce's younger brother, a newspaper editor, environmentalist and Fascist political advisor who died in 1942. The lead architect of the building was Guido Pelizzari, who trained in Venice and first worked for Le Corbusier in Paris. During the war, Le Corbusier worked for the Vichy regime. Architects, whatever the true nature of their politics, if any, want to see projects built.

Pelizzari had been a member of the Fascist Party since 1927 yet carried on in Bolzano after the war as if little or nothing much had changed. He added a vertiginous 'Venetian' tower to his church of Christ the King, consecrated in 1940, and as late as 1958 completed the Rationalist-style (for which read Fascist) Court House, these two buildings forming with the Casa del Fascio a monumental centrepiece in the heart of the city designed as the most visible symbol of Mussolini's pre-war strategy to 'Italianise' Germanic Bolzano.

On Sunday, 13 May, the tables were finally turned on Fascists and Nazis alike. Wolff's lunchtime forty-fifth birthday party at the Ducal Palace was interrupted by the arrival in the courtyard of a pair of 2½-ton trucks. Champagne corks had only just been popped, yet the SS general in crisp white dress uniform, his wife, children and a number of guests, members of both the SS and von Vietinghoff's staff, were ordered into the trucks by US military police and driven away as prisoners of war to a spartan camp. The springtime weather in the mountains was glorious.

The palace Wolff left behind was a reflection of both the fragility of hubristic politics and the enduring order of architecture. The Wolffs had lived here for just under three years. The Nazi regime they served prevailed for twelve years, 988 years short of its leader's promise. The Fascist Italian empire endured for twenty-one years. Although built as recently as 1932, the Ducal Palace echoed a style of elemental classical architecture dating back 2,000 years. Its architect was Fernando Forlati, the longstanding Superintendent of Monuments, Venice. During the First World War, it was Forlati who had supervised the removal of the horses of St Mark's for safekeeping to Rome. And, it was Forlati who provided anti-aircraft protection to Venetian buildings and monuments during the Second World War. It is to Forlati's ingenuity that we owe the survival of the sublime fifteenth-century Venetian church of San Giovanni e Paolo ('Zanipolo'), its voluminous red-brick structure harnessed from 1920 in an ingenious concealed cage of iron and reinforced concrete.

Before discovering what happened to the key characters and charismatic places caught up in the maelstrom of the Italian war – focused as it drew to its end through the lens of Operation Bowler – we should take stock of the human loss involved. Published figures vary, yet the twenty months of the Italian campaign had caused at least 330,000 Allied casualties: US, British Dominions (Commonwealth), Free French, Polish and Brazilian. German soldiers known to be killed, wounded or missing numbered as many as 430,000. Something like 67,000 Italian troops were killed, while partisan casualties added up to 66,000. More than 150,000 civilians were killed in bombing raids and in German reprisals. A further 9,000 were deported to Nazi Germany, many through Bolzano and its murderous transit concentration camp. Infantry casualties in the Italian war are said to have been proportionally higher than they were on the Western Front during the First World War.

One of DAF's final operations in the Italian campaign took place after the surrender on 2 May. Twin-engine Boston light bombers of 13 Squadron flew out to the mountainous area between Tolmezzo and Pontebba, where Waffen SS units were holding out, because either they were unaware of the surrender, or they intended to carry on the fight. Flying Officer Rankin's Boston dropped not bombs but leaflets.

A week later a DAF Communications Anson XII was shot down over Graz, Austria, by marauding Soviet La-7 fighters, killing its three-man crew. The Soviet pilots claimed they had mistaken the Anson for a Junker Ju-52 despite the fact that the two aircraft types look nothing like one another. The war was over, yet the icicles of the Cold War were already forming.

Armed women partisans, Venice, May 1945.

THIRTEEN

FINAL CURTAIN

On 28 May, Air Vice Marshal Foster staged a Desert Air Force commemorative flypast over Udine-Campoformido airfield. Foster took to the dais with Sir Guy Garrod, C-in-C Mediterranean and Middle East, and Brigadier General Thomas D'Arcy USAAF, in charge of the 79th Fighter Group.

With the Kittyhawks of 250 Squadron led by Major Felix Weingartz, who had scored one of the direct hits on the ships in the Stazione Marittima on 21 March, out in front, five hundred aircraft from forty-two squadrons roared overhead. They flew in an orderly yet rousing fashion, each squadron opting for a stylised formation of its own. The Mustangs of 3 RAAF Squadron (Squadron Leader Murray Nash) flew in line abreast, 5 SAAF Squadron's Mustangs (Major 'Tank' Odenhaal) in four 'vics' of three forming a giant V for Victory symbol, and the Thunderbolts of the 79th Group's 85th, 86th and 87th Squadrons commanded by Lieutenant Colonel Roger Files, Captain Alfred Fetters and Major Benjamin Cassidy in a thrilling '79' sign in the sky.

There was much to celebrate. Victory in Italy. Victory in Europe. DAF's emergence as a dynamic, cohesive and highly effective tactical air force working closely with ground troops and otherwise seen, to spectacular and optimum effect, in Operation Bowler. The melding of pilots, air crews and ground crews from so many different countries. The working together of the USAAF and RAF. The dominance of Italian airspace when the Germans had still been anchored in the Apennines behind the once impenetrable Gothic Lines. The development of new battle-ground techniques like Rover David. Of how so much had been learned cumulatively from the fighting in North Africa and on across the Mediterranean through, first, Sicily and then Italy itself.

There would also be much to mull over in years to come. Of how a war might be fought in future with as little damage to the fabric of villages, towns and cities as possible and minimum loss of life. A fine hope, of course, yet Operation Bowler – among DAF's finest hours – demonstrated how there had been no need to carpet bomb Palermo and Naples, to erase Monte Cassino, to hit Pompeii even if by mistake, to reduce mountain towns to rubble, to ravage the heritage of people who, while they might or might not be on your side at the time, may well be your allies and even your close friends in the near future. At Monte Cassino, Lieutenant General Freyburg had nearly got it right. Get 239 Wing to punch holes in the walls of the abbey to allow Allied troops to enter the abbey before, mistakenly, the four-engine bombers could be called on to obliterate fourteen hundred years of learning, art, architecture and prayer.

It must have been odd to think, as DAF came back down to land and drinks were served, that just weeks before Campoformido had been buzzing with German airmen, technicians and engineers busily extending this Veneto airfield for a new generation of jet bombers and fighter. There was something curious too in the bittersweet choice of Campoformido, although perhaps no one might have thought this at the time. The village is where, in 1797, Napoleon Bonaparte and representatives of the Habsburgs signed the Treaty of Campoformio through which France made the Veneto over to Austria in return for Habsburg territories in the Netherlands. The fate of the Republic of Venice was sealed. The deed was done in the handsome house belonging to Bertrando del Torre, a local merchant, in the town centre. In 2025, it's home to the Trattoria al Trattato, adorned inside with Napoleonic memorabilia.

As for AVM Foster, a Wykehamist who had graduated from Sandhurst as a Gentleman Cadet and seen extensive air force experience in India and Iraq before the Second World War, he rose to the rank of Air Chief Marshal, holding postwar commands in Austria, Italy and Germany, as well as back home in England. He retired of his own accord in 1954 to make way, he said, for younger officers. Deputy Lord Lieutenant of Suffolk, he lived with his wife and family in Great Glemham, as peaceful a spot as any in East Suffolk, although happily still flown over on occasion by Spitfires, Mustangs and other historic 'warbirds'.

George Westlake also remained with the RAF, specialising in fighter operations in Germany, Indonesia and Scotland, with a spell at HQ Air Defence Command, Colorado Springs with the USAF, until his retirement with the rank of Group Captain in 1969. He was an aviation consultant in Kuwait before retiring a second time and living at first in Cyprus, where he had flown in combat with 213 Squadron, and then Stratford-upon-Avon.

A keen fly-fisherman, he enjoyed drawing and painting. He particularly liked sketching buildings. A man on a mission in his mid-eighties, George strafed the streets of Stratford-upon-Avon with his electric tricycle as if, local people said, he were still at the controls of his Second World War fighter. 'We all stepped back when we heard him coming.' Feisty, funny and never less than determined, Group Captain Westlake DFC DSO was known to have been a wartime ace, and yet it was not until two years after his death in 2006, when his medals were put up for auction in London, that the story of Operation Bowler flickered for a day or two in several national newspapers.

By the end of the war, George's brother, Lieutenant Commander 'Pluto' Westlake DSC, was based in Sydney commanding submarines. He went on to serve with the Marine Police in Singapore, the Ugandan Police and the Marine Police in North Borneo and, like George, was involved with the Indonesian confrontation (1963–6). The allure of the East was hard, it seems, for 'Pluto' to resist. If only there had been a posting to Rangoon.

Shot down by flak over Celje having destroyed an anti-aircraft train at Dravograd station, Yugoslavia, on 3 April

1945, Major 'Tank' Odenhaal made it back to 5 SAAF Squadron on 12 May, in good time to take part in Foster's flypast. In the weeks he was missing, he had joined Yugoslav partisans led by Josip Tito and fought in a battle to liberate the pretty town of Litija to the east of Ljubljana from German occupation.

Odenhaal served with SAAF in the Korean War and was awarded a US DFC in 1954. Charged with choosing a new SAAF jet trainer, he opted for the Italian Aermacchi MB326B, known as the Impala in South Africa, where most of those flown by the air force were built under licence. Under Odenhaal's command, Impalas, operating at times from makeshift airfields, flew missions between 1975 and 1989 against FAPLA (People's Armed Force for the Liberation of Angola) and Cuban expeditionary troops in Angola. DAF-style, Brigadier General Odenhaal's pilots flew these light attack jets at speeds of over 400mph at just fifty feet above ground.

Field Marshal Kesselring surrendered to the Americans on 9 May at Saalfelden, Austria. Well treated at first, he was put up in a hotel in Berchtesgaden by Major General Maxwell D. Taylor, CO of the US 101st Airborne Division. Taylor had been the first Allied general to land in France on D-Day, dropping by parachute with the rest of his men. For a moment, Kesselring may have thought there was the chance to put himself forward as a proactive peacemaker. Thousands of well-disciplined German soldiers could be made available for work in post-war reconstruction. He also thought, as did Wolff and many other German generals, that the Allies would be keen to have him on their side ready to fight Stalin together. His captors thought differently. Taken into custody, in March 1946 Kesselring was a witness at the Nuremberg trials conducted that year, where he was cross-examined by Justice Robert H. Jackson, the US Chief Prosecutor:

MR. JUSTICE JACKSON: You testified that you took vigorous steps to protect the art treasures of Italy.

KESSELRING: Insofar as I was informed of art treasures, yes.

MR. JUSTICE JACKSON: What steps did you take, and against who did you take them?

KESSELRING: Primarily they were preventive measures: First, by excluding places of art and culture from the field of battle; secondly, by having these places cleared if they were liable to air raids by the enemy; and thirdly, by co-operating with General Wolff and having these cultural and art treasures removed to secure places. I make mention of the art treasures of Cassino and Florence.

MR. JUSTICE JACKSON: Did you know that any art treasure was removed from Mount Cassino, for instance, and taken to Berlin?

KESSELRING: Much later... I heard about that. At the time all I could recollect was that they were handed over to the Vatican in Rome.

MR. JUSTICE JACKSON: Oh. Did you know that art treasures were taken and delivered to Goering from Mount Cassino? Did you ever hear that?

KESSELRING: I once heard something about some statue of a saint, but I cannot really give you any more details.

MR. JUSTICE JACKSON: And if Goering received such a thing from Mount Cassino, was it a violation of your orders? KESSELRING: The Hermann Goering Division was stationed in that sector. It was commanded by the former adjutant of Hermann Goering, and it is clear that there was a certain connection here, but to what extent I cannot tell you.

So far, so good for Kesselring. He had certainly done more to protect Italy's art treasures and historic architecture – even entire cities like Florence and Rome – than the Allies had. The following year, however, as a defendant in a British military court in Venice, he faced charges for war crimes. His life was in the balance. Held for questioning in London beforehand, he may have charmed his captors, and was even taken on a sightseeing trip there, but German brutality in Italy was something he was unable to shake off. Those orders he had given for how partisans should be dealt with came back to haunt him.

SIR DAVID MAXWELL-FYFE (British prosecuting counsel):... let me remind you what was done at Civitella – that was on the 18th of June, one day after your order.

'Two German soldiers were killed and a third wounded in a fight with partisans in the village of Civitella. Fearing reprisals, the inhabitants evacuated the village, but when the Germans discovered this, punitive action was postponed. On June 29' – that, you will remember, Witness, was nine days after your proclamation to reinforce your order – 'when the local inhabitants were returned and when feeling secure once more, the Germans carried out a well-organised reprisal, combing the neighbourhood. Innocent inhabitants were often shot on sight.

'During that day 212 men, women, and children in the immediate district were killed. Some of the dead women were found completely naked. In the course of investigations, a nominal roll of the dead has been compiled and is complete with the exception of a few names whose bodies could not be identified. Ages of the dead ranged from one year to 84 years. Approximately one hundred houses were destroyed by fire. Some of the victims were burned alive in their homes.' That is the report of the United Nations War Crimes Commission on the incident. Now, Witness, do you really think that military necessity commands the killing of babies and people?

KESSELRING: No.

Kesselring's trial lasted the best part of three months. Finally, he was charged with 'being concerned in the killing as a reprisal of some 335 Italian nationals' in the Ardeatine Caves, and with 'inciting and commanding...forces...under his command to kill Italian civilians as reprisals in consequence of which a number of Italian civilians were killed'.

Found guilty, Kesselring was sentenced to death by firing squad. That, at least, would have been a soldier's death rather than being hanged like a common criminal. Churchill and Field Marshal Alexander, now Governor-General of Canada, thought it wrong he should be executed. Churchill, now the Leader of the Opposition following the Labour Party's victory in the July 1945 general election, represented those on either side of the Atlantic keen to have Germany on board now that the Iron Curtain had fallen across Europe. Germany would need to be re-armed. It was time to put the Second World War in its box. Alexander took the commonly held view of British soldiers engaged in the Italian Campaign that Kesselring had conducted a clean war. They were thinking mostly of engagements fought between soldiers, of the generally fair treatment of POWs on either side, and not of the lot of civilians caught up in the fighting, nor of the savagery of Fascist militia and SS alike. And little of the physical havoc, the destruction of entire villages caught in the path of advancing armies. Alexander had no complaints.

One popular view was expressed by a US military historian, Brigadier General Samuel 'Slam' Marshall. Writing in May 1947, Marshall argued, 'The verdict would appear to be that Kesselring, in taking reprisal, overstepped the bounds. But what are the bounds? I believe that Kesselring was the victim of unavoidable circumstance, and that any competent commander put in the same position would have found it impossible to come through with clean hands.' Even the Pope was on Kesselring's side. In prison, he attended Mass every Sunday.

Kesselring lived, his death sentence commuted in May 1947. He now faced a twenty-one-year prison sentence. Calls for his release grew. For Konrad Adenauer, a Christian Democrat politician and, from 1949, the first Chancellor of the new Federal Republic, the freeing of what he considered to be political prisoners was a key issue. Finally, after hospital treatment for throat cancer, on 22 October 1952 Kesselring was granted a pardon by Queen Elizabeth. His bestselling memoir, *Soldat bis zum letzen Tag* (*A Soldier to the Last Day*), written for the most part when in prison, was published the following year. While there were those who had hoped to see Kesselring as German Chancellor, 'Smiling Albert', while never a member of the Nazi Party, never really changed his tune. He thought Germany and democracy did not mix. A darling of many politically unreconstructed German veterans, he died in 1960.

Karl Wolff, the SS-*Obergruppenführer*, outlived Kesselring by a quarter-century. What saved him from the hangman's noose was the role he had played trying to bring the war in Italy to an end in those meetings in Switzerland with Allen Dulles. With the help of Dulles, who was appointed Director of the CIA in 1953, Wolff walked out the Nuremberg courtroom, dressed in a decent suit, and into Allied custody for four years before he resumed civilian and business life, successfully, in advertising. He was arrested, however, in Germany after the Adolf Eichmann trial led to the uncovering of documents implicating him in the transportation of 300,000 Polish Jews to the Belzec and Treblinka death camps. Italian Jews, too, during his years in Italy. He was sentenced to fifteen years in prison, serving nine.

For some viewers at least, it was extraordinary to see him popping up on the small screen as an interviewee in Jeremy Isaac's magisterial *The World at War*, a twenty-six-episode series made in 1973–4 for Thames TV. Wolff, smartly turned out as always, appeared in Episode 20, 'Genocide'. He died in 1984, by now professing the Muslim faith to which he was introduced by his daughter Fatima (formerly Helga). The headstone on his grave at Prien am Chiemsee, Bavaria, is inscribed 'General, retired'.

If Wolff got off lightly, SS-*Sturmbannführer* Eugen Wenner, who represented him at the signing of the German surrender in Italy at Caserta, escaped any form of punishment or censure. Through, presumably, Allen Dulles, he was spirited to South America, where he worked for the CIA.

General von Vietinghoff was held in captivity like other senior German commanders, among them Field Marshal von Runstedt, at Special Camp 11, at Bridgend Island Farm in South Wales. Here, just weeks before the end of the war, between seventy German POWs had tunnelled their way out, some reaching Southampton, others Birmingham, before being caught. After his release, von Vietinghoff's principal post-war work concerned the matter of German re-armament. In October 1950, with other former wartime Wehrmacht officers, he was ensconced at Himmerod Abbey, in the Eifel close to the French border, writing the Himmerod Memorandum for Adenauer's government. This was a key document in the process that led to the reestablishment of the German armed forces in 1955. By all accounts, Heinrich von Vietinghoff was never anything other than a professional soldier.

As was General Fridolin von Senger und Etterlin. As much academic as frontline general, von Senger was at Himmerod Abbey in October 1950 with von Vietinghoff. He was a regular contributor to the annual Königswinter Conference held at the spa of that name near Bonn from 1950, aimed at fostering British–German relations, where he advised politicians, diplomats, academics and journalists. He was one of the interviewees grilled, in 1960, by John Freeman in the BBC series *Face to Face* (1959–62). Freeman, who was in turn an advertising copywriter, soldier, Labour politician and minister, television interviewer, editor of *New Statesman*, diplomat, TV executive and professor of international relations, had served during the war in the Middle East, North Africa, Italy and Germany, rising to the rank of Major. He was, said Field Marshal Montgomery, 'my best brigade major'. Freeman bristled condescendingly throughout his interview with von Senger, who seemed more a polite and conscientious German professor than a battle-hardened soldier who had experienced some of the fiercest fighting in Italy.

Naturally, former Italian partisans were all for the execution of Kesselring and disappointed when the Field Marshal was spared the firing squad. Most partisans, however, whatever their feelings, eased back into civilian life in Venice as elsewhere. Some pursued politics, Sandro Pertini serving as President of Italy from 1978 to 1985. I met him in Rome in 1984 while working as Assistant Editor of the *Architectural Review*. By extraordinary chance his friends included Tudy Sammartini, the *Architectural Review*'s Venice correspondent who witnessed Operation Bowler, and Elizabeth Ashford-Russell, the magazine's Editorial Secretary.

When in her early twenties, Elizabeth had served as an SIS agent in Italy, based first in Bari, under Brian Ashford-Russell, who, wounded while serving with 7 Commando in the North African desert and made a prisoner of war, had, quite remarkably, persuaded a German medical board to repatriate him under the terms of the Geneva Convention. Back in

London in 1943 he was recruited by the SIS and dispatched to Italy. With Ashford-Russell – they married in 1946 – Elizabeth helped recruit, train and land agents, of whom she became one, by submarine or Lysander up and across Italy. Sandro Pertini was among the SIS recruits.

After the war, Italian women partisans were instrumental in helping to shape the country's new constitution, adopted in December 1947, that gave women equal rights, pay and opportunities. When the new national parliament met in May 1948, it comprised 801 MPs, of whom forty-one were women. More than half had served as partisans.

Venice – 'La Serenissima' – had long been thought of as a female city. In one of the panels of the great gilded ceiling of the Sala del Collegio in the Doge's Palace, painted by Paolo Veronese, Venice sits enthroned in splendour. Garbed in white and gold cloth overlain with a fur-lined mantle, this youthful embodiment of the Serene Republic is attended by Justice and Peace, both women, and, at her feet, the winged lion of St Mark.

There was work to do on the face of post-war Venice before it might be said to be serene once more. The Stazione Marittima was rebuilt. Pulled from the water, SS *Otto Leonhardt* was re-floated and recommissioned. In 1947, this English-built cargo ship returned to service as the *Albatros* with the *Navigazione Libera Veneziana*.

Bombed, damaged European cities were rebuilt for the most part in the bombastic modern style that the Futurists and influential modern architects, notably the Swiss-French iconoclast Le Corbusier, had campaigned for from the early 1920s. In the spirit of the Futurists, Le Corbusier had posited

303

the idea of demolishing and rebuilding huge swathes of old cities in a rational modern style. In his book *Aircraft* (1935), he used aerial photographs to look down on the serpentine streets of old cities. His battle cry in the books was *L'avion accuse* (the aircraft indicts), as if imagining dive bombers pounding these putrid abominations into rubble.

How strange that the foundations of this alienating idea should have been forged, by Marinetti, in Venice of all cities. And stranger still, how Allied dive bombers screaming down on Venice in March 1945 worked to safeguard the very city the Futurists and Le Corbusier would have willingly sacrificed, or so they claimed in strident tracts, in the name of modernity. Le Corbusier himself, however, moved on. Not long after the publication of *Aircraft*, he began to see Venice in a new light. In the years immediately before his death in 1965, he was busy with the design of a new hospital to the north of the Stazione Marittima. It would have been a meeting of old Venice and new thinking about how the city might go forward without destroying the very character that has drawn so many people to it since the early nineteenth century.

The occasion, perhaps, that re-enthroned Venice post-war, restoring her status as one of the world's most beautiful, enchanting and enigmatic cities, was Le Bal Oriental (a dazzling, high society ball) given in September 1951 by Don Carlos 'Charlie' de Beistegui at Palazzo Labia on the Grand Canal. In 1945, a munitions boat had exploded here, damaging the structure and décor of this ambitious seventeenth–eighteenth-century *palazzo* commissioned by the Labia family, Catalan *arrivistes* who, in 1646, paid their way – a fee was required – into the Venetian nobility. The frescoed ball-room painted by Giambattista Tiepolo and Girolamo Mengozzi Colonna had fallen in pieces to the floor.

In 1948, Palazzo Labia was bought by de Beistegui, a wealthy French-born Basque Etonian. In the early 1930s he had Le Corbusier design him a Parisian penthouse apartment overlooking the Champs-Élysées and sporting a roof terrace by Salvador Dalí. An enthusiastic interior decorator, he lavished attention on his new Venetian home. When complete, he designed his spectacular masquerade ball. The count greeted guests dressed as a generously bewigged seventeenth-century Venetian judge. His long red robe concealed sixteen-inch platform boots that allowed him to stand head and shoulders above the well-heeled, if less artificially elevated, and otherwise fashionable throng. Winston Churchill was invited but was unable to attend. The British parliament was dissolved that month in the lead-up to the general election Churchill was to win in October. The roll call of guests didn't disappoint de Beistegui. Stepping out from a fleet of gondolas and attended by seventy liveried footmen were the likes of Lady Diana Cooper, Orson Welles, the Aga Khan, the Duchess of Devonshire and a rich confection of European aristocrats with ineffably and entertainingly complicated names.

The evening was the making of Pierre Cardin, who designed costumes for thirty fellow guests including Salvador Dalí who, in turn, designed Cardin's. Cecil Beaton was there to photograph the revellers, among them twenty-year-old Tudy Sammartini. Now it truly seemed hard to believe that the city had once been targeted and bombed from the air.

Or that, beyond the explosive confines of the Second World War, anyone – least of all artists, architects and poets – had, within living memory, called for its destruction.

Filippo Marinetti was not at Le Bal Oriental. In the summer and autumn of 1942, at the age of sixty-five, the Futurist mouthpiece, co-author of the *Fascist Manifesto* and bane of old Venice, had fought on the frontline on the Eastern Front. He died, suddenly, in December 1944 at Bellagio on Lake Como while editing his poems in praise of the ultra-Fascist *Decima Flottiglia* MAS (Motoscafo Armato Silurante, torpedo-armed motorboat), a special force that first set out on daring missions to sink Allied shipping, which it did successfully, and later fielded notoriously vicious anti-partisan units on land after the 1943 Armistice, when, with *Capitano di Fregata* Don Junio Borghese in command, it fought a nasty war alongside the Germans.

Perhaps the worst of the atrocities committed by Borghese was at Crocetta del Montello, a small town in the Veneto, thirty miles northwest of Venice. When Borghese was brought to trial for collaborating with the Nazis, Adriano Calabretto, an eyewitness, told the court how the partisans captured there,

> naked to the waist, one at a time, were placed with their backs on a small stool and their bodies thrown backwards, until their heads touched the ground and until they assumed a balance position. Then these, still bare-chested, were whipped with a whip and then cans of petrol were brought to subject them to the torture of fire. The interrogations began at eight o'clock in the evening and continued

uninterrupted until three in the morning and I heard the screams of those who were being interrogated, combined with gunshots.

Borghese's sentence of twelve years' imprisonment was reduced by three years because, other 'glorious expeditions' aside, in 1945 he had built a line of defence on the Tagliamento River to hold back Marshal Josip Tito's Communist Yugoslav partisans, who believed the British had given them the go-ahead to occupy the Veneto east of Venice.

Borghese served four years. After his release from prison, he pursued neo-Fascist politics, founding the *Fronte Nazionale* in 1967 and attempting a coup on 8 December 1970. It failed and Borghese fled to Fascist Spain. Hero to some, villain to most, accomplished soldier and savage torturer, Borghese was a member of the famous Sienese family that had produced contentious cardinals and a Pope, and that had built the opulent sixteenth-century Palazzo Borghese in Rome. Junio Borghese died, possibly poisoned, in Cádiz in 1974. He is buried in the papal Basilica of Santa Maria Maggiore in Rome, a church consecrated in 434 and retaining much of its fifth-century classical structure. The traces of the war in Italy are often as strange as they are disturbing.

As for Operation Bowler, it is hard to find a trace of this audacious and brilliantly executed mission today either in Venice or in the guise of who fought with DAF that day. My one living connection is Gerry Teldon, and he was sent on leave the day before the operation was flown. For the three squadrons of the 79th Fighter Group, the Venice raid had been just another made that month in a relentless sequence of missions fought at a breathless pace and into wing-shredding flak over northern Italy.

Due to some official oversight, Lieutenant Teldon never received the decorations he should have been awarded. In July 2022, on a visit from his home in San Miguel de Allende, Mexico – like Venice, a UNESCO World Heritage Site – to San Antonio, Texas, for his great-grandson's bar mitzvah at the Chabad Center for Jewish Life and Learning, Gerry, then ninety-seven, was presented by Lieutenant Colonel Andrew Stein, 502nd Operations Support Squadron Commander, with a long-overdue Air Medal with oak leaf cluster.

The five other medals for the American Campaign, the European-African-Middle Eastern Campaign, the World War Two Victory medal, National Defense Service medal and the Distinguished Unit Ribbon were pinned on Gerry's jacket by his five grandchildren.

In an interview with Texas Public Radio, Teldon said, 'I was a fighter pilot, and as a fighter pilot, you never see the action that resulted from what you did. And now when I received these medals and they announced what the reasons for the medals were, I was absolutely amazed that I was involved in that. I call myself "Mr Lucky". I mean, to live through sixty-two missions and live to be ninety-seven, you got to have a lot of luck for that.' In August 2024, Gerry celebrated his hundredth birthday.

George Westlake had lived through more than 300 missions and lived to be eighty-seven. He had also been lucky. Venice, now 1,500 years old and, to date, still above water, had been lucky, too.

Gerry Teldon receives overdue war medals, Texas, July 2022, his grandson performing the honours.

ACKNOWLEDGEMENTS

This book was inspired by the story my friend Tudy Sammartini (1931–2016) told me years ago of a heavy bombing raid on Venice she witnessed in spring 1945. At the time I had no idea that Venice had been bombed and certainly not by the Allies. When I lived in Venice, the story came back to haunt me. What role did Venice play in the Second World War? Why would anyone on any side wish to assault this city as work of art?

My thanks to Richard Westlake, who filled in details of his remarkable father's life and sent me copies of Wing Commander George Westlake's wartime logbooks; to Jenny Whybrow, George Westlake's daughter; to Peter Summerton and the Royal British Legion, Stratford-upon-Avon, who put me in touch with Jenny Whybrow and thus Richard Westlake; to Air Commodore Graham Pitchfork, David Erskine-Hill, Johnny Warrender, Robert Hewison and Mark Joyce, manager of the 79th Fighter Group website. Thanks especially to Gerry Teldon, who flew and fought up and over Italy with the 79th; to Rowland White for encouragement; to Sam Carter of Oneworld, who gallantly commissioned and edited the book; to Oneworld's Hannah

Haseloff, Rida Vaquas and Paul Nash, and to Neil Burkey for copy-editing. And thanks, of course, to Jessica Bullock and Sarah Chalfant at the Wylie Agency.

SELECTED FURTHER READING

Barzini, Luigi, *The Italians* (Hamish Hamilton, 1964).

Bosworth, R. J. B., *Italian Venice: A History* (Yale University Press, 2014).

Brown, Eric, *Wings On My Sleeve* (Weidenfeld & Nicholson, 2006).

Duncan Smith, W. G. G., *Spitfire into Battle* (John Murray, 1981).

Englund, Peter, *November 1942: An Intimate History of the Turning Point of World War II* (Alfred A Knopf, 2023).

Evans, Gwyn, *The Decisive Campaigns of the Desert Air Force 1942–1945* (Pen & Sword, 2020).

Fielden, Lionel, *The Natural Bent* (Andre Deutsch, 1960).

Flintham, Vic, *Close Call: RAF Close Air Support in the Mediterranean. Volume II, Sicily to Victory in Italy: 1943–1945* (Crécy Publishing, 2022).

Hewison, Robert, *Ruskin on Venice* (Yale University Press, 2010).

Holland, James, *The Savage Storm: The Battle for Italy 1943* (Bantam, 2023).

Huxley, Aldous, *Along the Road: Notes and Essays of a Tourist* (Chatto & Windus, 1925).

Kesselring, Albert, *The Memoirs of Field-Marshal Kesselring* (The History Press, 2015).

Malaparte, Curzio, *The Skin* (New York Review of Books, 2013; first published in Italian as *La pelle*, 1949).

Moorehead, Caroline, *A House in the Mountains: The Women who Liberated Italy from Fascism* (Chatto & Windus, 2019).

Morris, James (Jan), *Venice* (Faber & Faber, 1960).

Morton, H.V., *A Traveller in Italy* (Methuen, 1964).

Neer, Robert M., *Napalm: An American Biography* (Harvard University Press, 1966).

Newby, Eric, *Love and War in the Apennines* (Hodder & Stoughton, 1971).

Platt, Margaret, *Venice, Fragile City: 1797–1997* (Yale University Press, 2002).

Rainey, Lawrence, et al. (ed), *Futurism: An Anthology* (Yale University Press, 2009).

Ruskin, John, *Praeterita: Outlines of Scenes and Thoughts Perhaps Worthy of Memory in my Past Life* (George Allen, 1900).

Shores, Christopher, Giovanni Massimello, et al., *A History of the Mediterranean Air War 1940–1945. Volume Five: From the Fall of Rome to the End of the War 1944–1945* (Grub Street, 2021).

OTHER SOURCES

Baldoli, Claudia, 'Fascist Italy's Aerial Defenses in the Second World War', *Global War Studies*, Vol 15, 2018.

Commonwealth War Graves Commission: www.cwgc.org.

Sangster, Andrew, *Field-Marshal Albert Kesselring in Context* (PhD Thesis, University of East Anglia History School, 2014).

Westlake, G. W., *Pilot's Logbooks* (Richard Westlake, private collection).

ILLUSTRATION LIST

INDEX

INDEX

INDEX